BARRY McGUIGAN

BARRY McGUIGAN
THE UNTOLD STORY

BARRY McGUIGAN
with **GERRY CALLAN**
and **HARRY MULLAN**

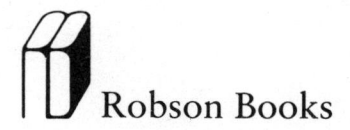

Robson Books

First published in Great Britain in 1991 by
Robson Books Ltd, Bolsover House, 5–6
Clipstone Street, London W1P 7EB

Copyright © 1991 Barry McGuigan, Gerry
Callan, Harry Mullan
The right of Barry McGuigan, Gerry Callan and
Harry Mullan to be identified as authors of this
work has been asserted by them in accordance
with the Copyright, Designs and Patents Act
1988

British Library Cataloguing in Publication Data
McGuigan, Barry *1961–*
   Barry McGuigan: the untold story.
   1. Boxing – Biographies
   I. Title II. Callan, Gerry III. Mullan, Harry
   796.83092

ISBN 0 86051 698 9

All rights reserved. No part of this publication
may be reproduced, stored in a retrieval system,
or transmitted in any form or by any means,
electronic, mechanical, photocopying,
recording or otherwise, without the prior
permission in writing of the publishers.

Typeset in Times and printed in Great Britain by
Butler & Tanner Ltd, Frome and London

For our fathers
RIP

ACKNOWLEDGEMENTS

A great many people helped in one way or another with the telling of this story. Some have asked that their contribution remain unacknowledged; in particular, the true identity of the character referred to in the book as 'Fight Fan' must remain a secret.

We particularly thank Brian Hitchen, editor of the *Daily Star*, who generously allowed us to reproduce a selection from his newspaper's extensive photo files on Barry. Katie and Dermot McGuigan, Leo Rooney, Ross Mealiff, Stephen McElroy of Lasertype, Sean McGivern, Father Brian D'Arcy, Frank Warren, Michael Deeny, Michael McGeary, Bob Arum, Dan Duva, Mogens Palle, *Boxing News* publisher David Kaye and Mickey Duddy were all unfailingly helpful.

John Rodgers of Sport & General Agency and Chris Smith of the *Sunday Times* gave us some splendid action photos, while Gerry Callan is indebted to his sister Mary, who patiently transcribed over forty hours of taped interviews.

Harry Mullan is especially grateful to his *Boxing News* colleagues, Daniel Herbert, Claude Abrams, Bob Mee and Mike Gillender, and Callan and Mullan owe a debt to Terry and David of Canterbury Computer Centre, whose electronic wizardry salvaged the project from the kind of problems which never afflicted authors in the days before word processors.

Finally, the book could never have been completed without the patience, tolerance and back-up provided by Sandra McGuigan, Sue Callan and Jessie Mullan.

Barry McGuigan
Gerry Callan
Harry Mullan

PROLOGUE

Over 27,000 people came to watch me win the featherweight championship of the world, and my fans stopped the traffic in Belfast and Dublin to welcome me home with the title. Great times, great memories ...

I've had plenty of approaches to tell my story since then, but I was determined to wait until I felt the time was right. I'm close enough to my boxing days for them still to be fresh, and for me to see them with a fighter's eye, but it's long enough ago to enable me to stand back and look at my career fairly dispassionately. I've stayed involved in the fight game and I still train, so I know what the fighters go through. I'm young enough to understand, but I'm that much more adult in my outlook. I have matured a lot through the tough times I've experienced.

It is impossible to tell the story of my career without discussing my relationship with Barney Eastwood, who managed and promoted me up to the time I lost the championship in Las Vegas in June 1986. We had a bitter parting, and so far nobody has heard my version of what happened between us. This is my chance to give my side of the story.

But I don't just want to talk about Eastwood, I want to tell people what it was like to be a fighter, what I went through in the build-up to a fight, what it was like an hour before getting in the ring, what I felt and thought while the punches were flying. The fans can go and buy their tickets and cheer their heads off, and then go home and forget about it, but I had to live with the possibilities that winning or losing could bring. Those experiences made me what I am, for better or worse.

All in all my career was a fabulous, roller-coaster ride, and I loved the good times and learned from the rest. This is my story, so far.

Barry McGuigan

CHAPTER ONE

'I have a feeling, young man, you are going to go a long way.'
Felix Jones, President of the Irish Amateur Boxing
Association (IABA), presenting Barry McGuigan with the
Best Boxer award at the Irish Juvenile Championships,
1977

Leo Strong, Liam Flanagan, Rex Flanagan, my elder brother Dermot and myself were the MacCurtain Street Hotspurs; MacCurtain Street led up to the Diamond in Clones.

At that time there was a big old mill down by a meadow – there's new houses built there now – owned by a fellow called Dan McPhillips. We would go down there and play all kinds of games. On our way there one day we were going past this broken-down old building, down beside Frank MacAughey's shop on Analore Street, and we took a look in it.

The house had been derelict for years, but we found an old pair of boxing gloves in it, and we took one each and started thumping one another for a bit of crack. After a while the others dropped out one by one, until there was only me and Liam Flanagan left. He was bigger than me – I was about eleven – and a southpaw. I had the right glove, he had the left, and we thumped the living daylights out of one another. I was delighted when one of the boys said, 'Ah, that's enough – call it a draw.'

We put the gloves back in a drawer, but when we went back the next day they were gone. I never saw another pair for six months. Johnny McCarthy, a bandsman in Clones who used to supply all the wind instruments and band equipment, had an actual set of four red gloves. He brought them into the house and loaned them to my father. The loan was supposed to be for a fortnight, but it lasted the rest of my life – he never got them back.

Dermot was always more skilful than me, but I'd batter the head off him after a while. From a very early age I was naturally strong.

When I was six stone I could knock guys spark out with one punch. I was never aggressive, though, but it was great to know that I could look after myself. I loved to hear the boys at school say to one another, 'Don't aggravate him – he can handle himself.' That's probably why I started boxing. From the time I was very young, I could handle nearly all the boys in the class. There were a couple who were bigger than me and I didn't mess with them, but I never bullied anybody either. The boys had a bit of respect for me, which was all that I wanted anyway.

The first time I went to the Wattlebridge amateur club was on a late summer evening. My father drove us there. Most of the guys who ran the club were farmers. There was Tom Conlan, Padraig McCafferty and Paddy Fitzsimmons, an old Irish Army guy who trained them. Down the hill from Wattlebridge there was a sawmill at the crossroads. It was about 7 o'clock, and Paddy brought us out there. Most of the boys at the club would work at the farm as long as there was light in the day, so you'd never know if they would turn up for training or not. The season hadn't really started, although we didn't know that; we thought you boxed all the year round. This was around late August, and the boys probably only worked out once a week. There wasn't a lot of discipline in the club at that time.

We sat there for an hour and nobody turned up, so we drove to Redhills and played football on the Green. After about an hour we decided we'd go back, and on the way we saw this guy carrying a punchbag up the hill. It was Michael Lyttle, a bantam who lived down in Redhills. We went up to the club with him.

It was the first time I'd been in a gym, and I thought it was the greatest thing I'd ever seen in my life. It was in an old primary school. There was a roped-off ring with a wooden floor. The walls were blue, and there were lots of cobwebs. There was a beam going across the room that they'd put in themselves, an overhead ball, a spring ball, floor to ceiling, and a light canvas bag that wasn't in great shape. A number of old gloves were hanging over the ropes, and there was a fireplace up against the wall as you went in the door. The club colours were green and black, and I used those all the time in the amateurs, even when I was with Smithboro, whose colours were green and white.

I came back the next night with Noel McGovern, who was a good fighter. Noel and I cycled out to the club most nights, and sometimes Tony Coyle would drive us there. After a couple of months, when I was twelve, I had my first fight for them, in Clones. My father wasn't going to let me fight because I'd done something wrong at home. I begged him until finally he said OK.

I hadn't as much as a tingle of nerves that night. I wanted to get in there so badly. The whole town was there, and I wanted to put on a show. It never occurred to me that I might get beaten; if they'd put me on with somebody a stone heavier, I couldn't have cared less. Tom Conlan had warned me that I mightn't get a fight, which was a real downer. I thought I would automatically have a fight, once I'd been picked to box on the show. As soon as I walked in, the matchmaker said, 'Come over here – will you box him?' He pointed to a dark-haired guy, called Ronan McManus. He could have had thirty fights, but I didn't care. In fact, he had had a couple of fights, but was nothing great. They just measured me up against him – there were no weigh-ins or comparing records or anything like that. We were stood against one another, and somebody said, 'That'll do.'

I couldn't wait to get on. We were gloved-up – no bandages in those days. We were the first contest on that night. Albert Uprichard was the referee and my Uncle Dennis was doing the timekeeping. I had no kit at all: canvas shorts I got from my brother, an old pair of dirty-looking guttees [plimsolls] with holes in them and ankle socks. We went to the centre of the ring, and Uprichard put his hands on our shoulders and gave us the usual instructions. When he took his hands away, I thought that meant we could start, so I gave your man a wallop and he hit back, and the crowd were going clean mad, laughing.

Uprichard gave me a severe telling-off. 'You're supposed to go back to your corner first,' he said, so I said, 'Oh, sorry, I didn't know that.' I had no gumshield or anything. McManus was much better equipped. He had satin shorts, in the blue colours of Enniskillen, with a light-blue stripe down the side. He had proper boxing boots and a gumshield. I just overwhelmed him, didn't stop throwing punches at him for three rounds. I didn't even know *how* to punch; at that stage nobody had actually said, 'Look, you're supposed to throw punches like this.' I just went round-house at him, but I beat him by a mile.

When it was over they gave me a trophy, and I've still got it. I thought this trophy was brilliant and I asked the man on the door,

'Will you let me back in the hall if I go home and show it to my mother?' It was the greatest feeling, as if I'd won the world title. I went up to show my mother, who was working in the shop. 'Well done,' she says, 'that's great.' I jumped with joy down the street, showing it to everybody I met. I never let go of it all night. That trophy was the only thing that survived the fire in my mother's house the night I won the world title. Everything else went; all my Irish medals were welded together.

The next tournament was in Kinally, and I boxed the same guy again. They thought he could beat me this time, but I stopped him in the third round. That whole morning long in school, I wasn't listening to a word the teacher said, I was so nervous. I took the afternoon off. It was so important, this simple little contest – three one-and-a-half-minute rounds. My stomach was churning, and I said to myself, 'If you're so worried, it's not worth it', and I got so worked up that I was going to give it up. That's the way it nearly always was: I'd go to the fight, hit the guy; bingo! down he'd go, the fight would be over and I'd say, 'Why were you nervous? What were you so worried about?'

After a while the teacher would accept the fact that I had a boxing match on and know that my guts were churning up inside me. The school was great to me; they knew that boxing meant everything to me.

Myself and McGovern used to cycle to the gym on the unapproved roads around the border. It was easy cycling, about forty minutes on my big Triumph bike. We would do a workout – not that I knew what a workout was at that time; I'd just belt away at the bag until I was knackered.

As we were coming home one night we saw the blue flashing lights, and as we cycled past they were lifting two bodies out of the hedge. Two guys had been pitchforked to death. It later transpired that a couple of drunken British soldiers were responsible, not that we knew that at the time. The RUC said, 'What are you doing on this road? Get away on home as quick as you can.' When we got home my mother had heard about it on a news bulletin, and she told me I was not going to Wattlebridge again. My father, who was encouraging me, told me to find an alternative club.

Wattlebridge closed down not long after then. They had had a few good fighters there, though. Padraig McCafferty was an absolutely dynamite middleweight who could knock guys out. I used to love watching him – a wicked puncher. But every time he went in the Junior Championships he failed in the finals. It was a shame, because he was very dedicated and could have been really good. Paul Connolly was the most successful boxer Wattlebridge had, an Irish champion who represented the country a few times.

Around this time Smithboro club had been revived, and had opened again on new premises. It started off with Frank Mulligan, Brendan Trainor, Sean Tierney and a few others, and they got a very good trainer, Danny McEntee. McEntee had all the technique and Mulligan the enthusiasm, and between them they were a brilliant combination. Danny died while I was actually working on this book, and this is as good a time as any to put on record how much I owe him.

Frank had boxed himself, and was the assistant trainer, and as soon as I went there Mulligan took a liking to me. He was very keen, and for the first time there were other kids in there who could work with me and spar with me. Frank spent hours with me in the gym. He even used to live with me, to make the work at home easier so that we'd be able to train together.

I started winning things and becoming successful. I boxed four times in two days to win my first Mid-Ulsters, at Downpatrick, and lost in the Ulster final to Gary Spiers, who won the All-Ireland that year. The next year we didn't enter for the Ulsters because the Troubles were so bad, and we didn't fancy travelling to tournaments and coming home at night on lonely roads. The officials at the club were afraid of the mothers complaining, so we asked permission from the Ulster Council to take part in the Leinster championships. We got clearance from the Leinster Council to take part in the Golden Shamrock tournament, which included the other three provinces, bar Ulster. I won the Shamrocks, beating four good fighters. I knocked out Jimmy Coughlan, a four-times Irish champion, in the final. They couldn't believe it; he'd been expected to lick me. He was a tall guy, fragile, but a brilliant boxer. But I knocked him spark out.

I entered the Leinsters the same year, but I couldn't make the six-stone weight that I'd done for the Shamrocks. I was fourteen at the time, and it was just too much of a struggle. I entered at six stone seven, and Coughlan, the guy I had knocked out, was the only entrant who didn't complain. The others all lodged a protest, and when I went to get on the scales I was not allowed to take part in the championships. The Ulsters had already been held, so I'd missed them too. Coughlan went on to win the All-Ireland again, so we were bitterly disappointed.

Next year I won the Mid-Ulsters, the Ulsters and then the All-Ireland. It was tough work: I must have had about ten fights altogether. I got the award as the Best Boxer of the Championships. Felix Jones, the President of the Irish ABA, presented it to me, and I'll never forget what he said. 'I have a feeling, young man, you are going to go a long way.'

Chapter Two

'Other boys could sting an opponent... but I would flatten them.'
Barry McGuigan, explaining what distinguished him from his contemporaries in juvenile boxing

Right from the very start, I trained really hard. There was a guy called Barney McBride, a middleweight, who must have sparred hundreds of rounds with me. I was only six and half stone, so he would take it easy. He was great for me, but when I got to be a senior flyweight and bantam, I was too good for him. He reached the All-Ireland Junior final as a light-middleweight, but never got any further than that. Barney was a brilliant help to me. He runs a milk float now, just outside Clones.

I was so keen that when I boxed in my first Mid-Ulsters I kept dumbbells in the car. Between contests I'd sit in the car, lifting these dumbbells and telling myself, 'I'll make myself so strong that when I hit him, I'll break him in two.' This would be half an hour before I was due in the ring. That's how determined I was. I was boxing a local boy from Downpatrick in the final, a long-haired fellow in a light-blue singlet and navy shorts. He was a very sharp boxer, very quick.

I'd met a guy from Dublin, called Sweeney; I think he was an ex-pro. He told me, 'The first thing you do after you've touched gloves is to hit him as hard as you can. You'll put the fear of God into him, and after that you'll have the fight won. It doesn't matter if it's only a jab – just put everything you have into it, so that you'll make him think, "My God, what has this guy got in his gloves?"'

So as soon as the referee said 'Box', I came over the top with a right hand, and I could see his eyes spin. He went on his bike for the three rounds, and I won the fight, although he came back strongly, boxed well and gave me a good fight. In the Ulster quarter-finals I boxed a guy called Hawkins from Holy Trinity, Belfast. He was a relation of Gerry Hawkins, who boxed on Irish teams with me later on, and he was very experienced. I was three ounces overweight at the weigh-in, so I had a pee and tried again. This time, after taking my underpants off, I just made the weight.

The ring had a slight tilt to it, and Danny McEntee – what a shrewd coach – spotted it. 'Always attack him when he's on the lower side, because with the gravity you'll have a bit more power and impetus.' I outpointed Hawkins soundly, and then beat another Belfast boy, a big skinhead who looked half a stone heavier than me. In the Ulster final I boxed Gary Spiers, from White City. By this stage it was getting tough to make the weight, but I did it this time. The finals were held in the old Queen Elizabeth Hall, down at the back of the City Hall. It's gone now.

Brendan Trainor drove me up from Clones, and all the way there we kept seeing magpies – one at a time. Trainor said, 'I don't like this – you know the old rhyme, "One for sorrow, two for joy"?' He was right, too, and every time I see a magpie now I think back to that night, and I spit for luck.

Spiers was too good for me. I was coming forward throwing punches, but I wasn't experienced enough and he outboxed me. He won on a majority decision. My first defeat; I was absolutely devastated.

But already, I was beginning to believe that I had a special talent. The awareness grew on me gradually, from my early juvenile days when I started knocking guys over regularly. When I boxed in local tournaments, they would always keep my fight until the later stages of the show. I was a knock-out puncher, and none of the other kids could do it. That made me an attraction. Other boys could sting an opponent and make the referee give him a count, but I would flatten them. I realized that I had something here, but I knew too that I had to keep working at it. I always had the idea that the better I got, the more of a target I would be for the boys coming up, so that every time I got a stage further I had to keep working and working to get better, to stay ahead. It was everything to me; I was sleeping, living, breathing, eating boxing. Nothing else mattered to me.

*

The impetus and the inspiration for McGuigan's boxing came from his father, Pat. The elder McGuigan loved the sport, though as an observer rather than as a participant. His family had moved south from Tyrone to work on the railway, which was the living heart of Clones, and Pat followed his father to work there himself as a stoker. When the railway died in the mid-1950s, the town virtually died with it, and a large percentage of the local workforce found themselves unemployed. McGuigan was luckier than most: he was a semi-professional singer, and after a spell as a bus conductor in Glasgow he returned to Ireland and a full-time career in show business.

By the mid-1960s he had his own four-man band, Pat McGeegan and the Big Four. ('McGeegan' was reckoned to be easier to remember and pronounce than McGuigan: British boxing writers and commentators would later have the same problems with his son's surname.) The high point of his career came in 1967, when he was placed third in the Eurovision Song Contest with a number entitled, appropriately, 'Chance of a Lifetime'.

The demands of a show-business life can play havoc with domestic tranquillity, but his wife, Katie, provided a solid family base for their eight children in the grocer's shop she took over in the Diamond, Clones.

*

My father used to go to as many of my fights as he could, and if he couldn't be there – usually because he was on the road with the band – he would ring to find out how I'd got on. All those little contests that meant nothing to anybody else meant a lot to him. He'd watch me train at home, and try to hold the pads for me. But he wasn't very good at it, so he'd put his shoulder up for me to hit instead and many a time I left him with bruised and black arms. He'd often be out working and travelling all night, but however tired he was when he got home, he always came to watch me train. He even taught me how to skip.

I used to do stacks of gym work but I didn't like running, so he did his best to encourage me to go out on the road. Often he'd get in the car and pace me, driving round the roads with the hazard lights on at all hours of the night.

He got me all the boxing magazines and books, and when he went to America he always brought me back bits of equipment, bandages and the like. Rudy Greco, a New York lawyer who represents quite a few of the fighters over there, was a good friend of my father's and took him around the gyms and the shows at Madison Square Garden or the Felt Forum.

I remember one day I was trying to make six stone seven for the Golden Shamrocks. I was fourteen at the time. I'd trained myself so hard, battling to get the weight down, and this was the third time I'd worked out that day, trying to break sweat in that cold room at the back of the house. I'd got myself so run down and so weak, hitting this canvas bag in a cold old shed, that I was nearly crying with annoyance and frustration.

He was holding the bag for me, saying, 'Come on! Come on!' and it was so cold that every time he spoke you'd see the breath coming out of him like steam. And then I burst out crying, and he knew that I'd given it everything and still couldn't get the weight down. He put his arm round me and said, 'Don't be killing yourself, son. Let yourself develop fully, and then you can start paring your weight down. You shouldn't hold your weight down while you're growing.'

It was good advice, but I didn't take it. I made the weight eventually, but I've often thought since that if I'd let myself grow properly I would have been certainly a light-welter. Even now, although I'm still working out, I walk around at about ten stone four. Everybody in the family is bigger than me, even my sisters, and I have no doubt that all the training I did stunted my frame. If I hadn't been such a fanatic about paring myself down to the limit every time, I'm sure I'd have been a much bigger man.

I doubt if my father missed more than half a dozen of my pro fights. He always came up to the gym to see me before I left for the fights, and on the night he'd come in the dressing-room and tap me on the head with a rolled-up programme and say, 'All the best, son', but he'd never linger.

My mother didn't like me boxing, ever, but she never created any obstacle for me. She only saw me fight once, against Kenny Bruce from Enniskillen in the 1979 Ulster Seniors after I won the Commonwealth Games. We cracked heads and I got the first cut I'd ever had – it needed seven stitches – and my mother ran out of the hall to the toilet.

Anyway, in 1976, we didn't enter the Ulsters, but the following year, 1977, I knocked out everybody in the Mid-Ulsters. I was seven stone seven, and I walked through the lot of them. I beat Danny McAllister in the Ulster finals, at the Holy Family gym – had him down twice. Danny later became a good pro, fighting as Young Patsy Quinn. He fought like a pro even then, but I was very strong and put him down twice. I got through to the All-Ireland finals, where I stopped my first opponent in the first round, won my semi-final easily, and then fought Martin Brereton in the final at Limerick in May. I had Martin down, and won it on a unanimous decision. I was voted the Best Boxer of the tournament. Martin and I later became good friends, and we were on the 1980 Olympic team together; he was a light-welterweight by then.

Boxing News reported the finals, and described me as 'a 16-year-old with a big future'. It was the first time I'd been mentioned in the trade paper.

It was at those championships that I got friendly with Gerry Mitchell, who'd boxed me twice before. The first time was in his home place, Wilkinstown, outside Navan. Gerry's father trained him, and asked Ollie Nesbitt from Kingscourt to find a boy who could give Gerry a good test.

I had known Ollie for a long time. He had a boy in his gym called Paddy Reilly, and I have no doubts that if Paddy had been 'discovered' he would have been one of the world's best professionals. He was a southpaw, but he could wallop. He was half a stone lighter than me, but he wiped out everybody he fought. Eventually he and I had to fight each other, although our clubs had tried to keep us apart. He hit me harder in the first round that I'd ever been hit before, and when I came back to the corner Danny McEntee said, 'You'd better get out there and do something about this fellow.' I dropped him twice in the next round, and stopped him. So Ollie knew that I was good, and he told Mitchell Senior that I could give Gerry a go.

Mitchell was tough, and half a stone bigger than me. He was really fit, and a lovely boxer. I could feel his punches, but I hit him even harder and put him down at the end of the first round. He came back well, but I won a fairly close decision. They thought he should have got it, so we boxed again in Drogheda. This time I won it even more clearly than the first. We boxed again at Edenderry, and I knocked him out really badly. He was out for three minutes. I'd knocked guys out before, but never for that length of time. He was in a bad way, and the priest even got in the ring to him. But he recovered, and went on to box his way through to the All-Ireland finals. Gerry later studied for three years for the priesthood, but left it and he's now in social work. He and I are great friends. His father, Pat, died in April 1990. He was a lovely man, and a good help to me.

Winning the All-Irelands was the start of my association with the Irish ABA, and they were great to me. I have nothing but respect for them all. Everywhere I went, I had nothing but the best treatment from the IABA. I captained the European junior team in Rimini, and the IABA people were fantastic: they sent out steaks for us, gave us expenses money, sent us to training camps. There is a lot of bitterness and rivalries in amateur boxing, but I never encountered any of it.

Chapter Three

'This guy's going to knock you out.'
Noel Reynolds, a semi-final victim of the sixteen-year-old
McGuigan in the Ulster Championships, to Barry's final
opponent, Sean Russell

I had made seven-seven all the way through the All-Irelands, but as soon as the championships were over I allowed my weight to increase again. I boxed Phil Sutcliffe on a tournament in Edenderry when I was barely sixteen. He was nineteen at the time, had just won the Irish junior title, and took the senior title a couple of weeks later, but I beat him on points. He hit me with quite a few punches, but mine were harder. The fight was over two-twos and a three, and I went at him slam-bang. He was very fit – he always was – and he was resilient. I hit him with shots that would have knocked most guys down, but he stayed with me and I knew then that I was stepping up a grade.

I won it well, but Sutcliffe's people complained that he had done enough. The crowd were with me, but when the final bell went I knew that I had been in a hell of a fight. He went on to win quite a few Irish senior titles, and bronze in the European championships in 1977 and 79. That was the only time Phil and I fought, but I went down to the Stadium in Dublin to help him get ready for the Europeans.

I was picked to box for Ireland in a youth international match in Wales – there were always a couple of youth matches as a curtain-raiser to the full senior match. I boxed Nigel Page, who later turned pro in Belgium after being refused a licence in Britain because of a problem on his brain scan. It was the first time I'd been away with the senior team. I thought they were going to give me an Irish vest, but you were expected to wear your own in youth contests. Gussie Farrell, the Enniscorthy bantamweight on the senior team, let me use his gear, which was good of him.

I had high black leather boots on, and they were slipping all over the place. Page was a lovely mover, a good boxer, who kept out of the way. But I stayed on top of him and won, though it was close enough. After that experience I always boxed in the short Adidas boots, which were much better.

I had outgrown the juveniles by this stage, so I entered the Ulster Juniors at bantamweight and stopped Danny McAllister in the final. In the All-Ireland semi-finals in Dublin in January 1978 I met Mick Holmes, and I boxed like a prat – absolutely terrible. I was mauling, clawing, holding on, and I lost. It was very disappointing.

Danny McEntee was involved in a bad accident and was partially paralysed. He couldn't get in and out of a car, and only came to the gym occasionally, so Frank Mulligan took over the training. Frank entered me for the Ulster Seniors, which everybody thought was silly because I'd lost in the Irish Juniors. He had been in two minds about entering me, so he rang Pat McCrory, who was the Ulster secretary. Pat had worked with me as a juvenile and had watched me training, and he told Mulligan to go ahead. McCrory believed in me and saw there was potential there.

It was my first senior fight, but I was very confident. I boxed a boy called Noel Reynolds, who had been in Ulster and All-Ireland senior finals before but lost to Sean Russell from Belfast. Russell's younger brother, Hugh, won British titles at flyweight and bantam and boxed on a lot of my bills.

I completely changed my approach. It wasn't the normal, get-stuck-in style; I boxed the head off Noel Reynolds and put him down twice. Frank had done a good job on me.

Sean Russell came in the dressing-room afterwards to congratulate me – he had drawn the bye to meet the winner in the final. I had never known an opponent to shake hands with me before we went out to fight, and I wanted to know what he was at. Reynolds saw him, and told him, 'This guy's going to knock you out.' Russell laughed, and said, 'He's just a wee kid – he's not going to knock me out.'

The finals were in the Ulster Hall and were televised. Albert Uprichard, a lovely man who'd refereed my very first fight, came to see me in the dressing-room. 'You're going to win this, you know,' he said. I looked at him, because everybody else thought I was going to get hammered.

Danny McEntee was back in my corner with Frank Mulligan. I

told myself, 'It's just like another sparring match; don't worry about it.' Sean Russell came dancing out towards me, with a very confident-looking style. He was good, but towards the end of the round I hit him with the right and I could see his eyes go, and his legs wobbled. I had him down twice in the second. The crowd were mainly Russell supporters, and they were stunned when they saw him go down. He saved face by not coming out for the third.

It was the second time I had gone three-minute rounds, and I really felt that this was what I needed. I couldn't do the job properly in two minutes, maybe because I wasn't able to get the amount or the quality of sparring I needed at home. That evening we drove home like bats out of hell, trying to get back in time to watch the fight on TV. We weren't going to make it to Clones, so we drove into the Four Seasons Hotel in Monaghan and watched it in their TV room. I'd never seen myself on TV before, and I was proud as punch. The headlines next day were great. I remember Jack Magowan in the *Belfast Telegraph* and Michael McGeary in the *Irish News* were particularly impressed. I was sixteen, the youngest-ever Ulster Senior champion. (Jack likes to say that he has written over a million words about me.)

A month later, on 6 March, I had my first representative match. East Germany had fought a full international in Dublin, and then they came north to meet an Ulster selection. I boxed Torsten Koch, a tall, slim bantamweight who'd battered Gussie Farrell in Dublin. Koch was nearly six feet, with a lovely pair of shoulders. I don't know how he ever made bantamweight. We boxed in the Working Men's Club on the Shankill Road, and got a great reception there. Pat McCrory and Gerry Storey were in the corner, and they told me to work to his body. I was very nervous, because East Germans at that time were considered the best in the world. For nine minutes, I never left him alone and I won it easily. The Germans gave me a special award, because I was so young and they were so impressed with me.

The European Junior Championships were being held in Dublin that year, and I set my heart on winning a gold medal there. The last time an Irishman had won a European gold was also in Dublin, when Ger Ó Colmain won the heavyweight title in 1947, and that was my goal. Besides, Mick Holmes was my rival for the team place and I wanted to pay him back for making me look so bad the night he beat me in the Championships. Four of us entered for the Irish

Under-Nineteens: myself, Holmes, Danny McAllister and Brendan Scullion. I boxed McAllister in the semi-finals and completely overwhelmed him. I was going through a phase at the time where, when I hit guys, they would really go. If he hadn't been as strong as a horse, he couldn't have lasted the distance.

Holmes beat Scullion, knocked him out with a left hook. We watched Holmes fight, and I was really impressed. He had the Davitts in his corner, Tony, P J and Tommy, and I always thought that Tony Davitt was a great trainer, really professional. But Danny assured me I would beat him, and sure enough I outboxed him completely in the first round. In the second, I had him all over the place with a left hook, and then put him down with another. He was gone, and Tony Davitt was shouting to the referee, 'That's enough,' but the referee counted him and then said, 'Box on,' so I went in and finished him off.

The Irish Senior finals were next, and once again I beat Holmes in the final, which meant I'd beaten him two out of three. I was enjoying the squad training for the European Juniors, in camps at Drogheda and Dublin. We'd go away for a week, and come home for a weekend. I'd come home to watch the boys from the club box in a tournament at the Starlight Ballroom in Clones, and while I was waiting to go to the show, I picked up the *Sunday Independent* and read that Holmes had been picked instead of me. The rules were that only boxers born in 1959 or 1960 were eligible, and I'd been born in February 1961.

I went down, tears tripping me, to see Mulligan, but he had already seen the paper and was furious. He contacted the selectors and had a row, but there was no point; it was done. They said that they had sent us a letter, but the papers had got the news before the letter arrived. Anyway, I wasn't picked. Holmes had been in training camp too, but I thought he was only there for sparring for me. What made it worse was that Holmes went on to win four contests and reach the final, where he lost a 3–2 split decision to a Russian, Samson Khachatrian.

He would have won it too, only the first round ran for four minutes fifteen seconds and poor Mick punched himself out. He had the Russian in trouble but just couldn't put him away, and that's why the timekeeper got so excited. Somebody said to him, 'This seems a long round.' He looked at his watch and said, 'Oh, Christ!' and rang the bell quick. The Russian was strong and fit, and kept going at the same steady pace. But Holmes was knackered. He'd had four fights, and there was nothing left.

As the Europeans ended I got word that I'd been picked for the Northern Ireland Commonwealth Games team in Canada. That took away a bit of the disappointment, but I knew I could have beaten Khachatrian and won the gold medal at home. That would have been fabulous.

We trained for the Games at Newcastle, County Down, and sparred at Downpatrick gym. I remember the team well. Jimmy Carson was light-fly, Hugh Russell the flyweight, I was bantam, Kenny Webb featherweight, Gerry Hamill lightweight, Ken Beattie welterweight, and Tony McAvoy was the heaviest at light-middle-weight. We ran on the beach in the mornings and did circuits. Storey made us do loads of sprints in the mornings, weights in the late morning and gym sessions in the evening. Sometimes we'd have four sessions a day. It was tough work. We'd jog and sprint alternately, going round and round until Storey said enough. And then we'd finish with ten 120-metre sprints, with ten seconds' rest in between. It was the first time I had experienced peaking in fitness. I had trained hard before, but not like this.

Going to Edmonton was a big event for me – the only time I'd been away before was when I boxed in Wales. A guy called Dennis Boulauire, a friend of Gerry Storey and Jack Monaghan from the Irish team, was great to us. He had a big ranch outside Edmonton and we all went out there.

I never saw any of the Games, only when the other boys on the team were boxing. We all went along to support each other. I beat George Lowe from Scotland on a disqualification in my first contest, and then beat Michael Anthony from Guyana, who won a bronze medal in the 1980 Olympic Games. I outpointed him on a unanimous decision. Then in the semi-finals I stopped Bill Ranelli from Canada, a big, handsome guy, well built and solid. I hit him with so many punches. It was the first time I started putting combinations together properly; Storey helped me a lot. In the third round, I must have hit him fifteen punches before he crumpled in a corner and the referee stopped it.

The final was against Tumat Sogolik from Papua New Guinea, and he gave me a hell of a fight. He was the biggest bantamweight I've ever seen. He was huge – thick arms and shoulders. Thinking back on it, I was too courageous. I should have been smarter, and not tried to fight with him so much. He caught me twice, put me down once and made me take one standing count. It was an iffy decision. I was lucky – one of the few times I had the luck with me.

Gerry Hamill won the lightweight gold medal in style, but the fact that I was so young – one of the youngest winners ever – seemed to catch the public's imagination. When we landed at the airport in Belfast, I said to Gerry Storey, 'I wonder if my father will be here to meet me?' and Gerry said, 'You needn't worry about people meeting you – there'll be plenty.' I didn't realize how much the medal meant to other people; I knew that it meant everything to me, but I was amazed at the crowd there was to welcome us. I was busy signing autographs (nobody had ever asked me before) in a big, slow scrawl – it took me about four hours to sign half a dozen autographs. They paraded me round the town in Monaghan, and there was a big party at the house. I loved it all; the taste of things to come.

*

The perception of McGuigan as a hero with an appeal separate and distinct from his actual boxing took root with the TV images, beamed around the world, of the handsome teenager weeping on his winner's rostrum in Edmonton. The moment had enormous emotional impact, enhanced by the grace and dignity Tumat Sogolik showed in accepting a defeat which few impartial observers believed he deserved. It was an echo of a time when sport was cleaner, before cash dictated decisions and behaviour, when winners were not ashamed to shed a tear and thank their Mum, and when losers could shrug off disappointment with a smile and a handshake. It was the moment when the McGuigan legend was born, and the game's money men began to pay close attention to the progress of the young Irishman.

Chapter Four

'I can count on one hand the number of fighters I have written to ... But you are one of the most promising fighters I've seen.'
Mickey Duff, writing to Barry McGuigan in 1978

After the Commonwealth Games, I was picked to box for Ireland in a multi-nations tournament in October 1978, in Rotterdam. I had to struggle to make the weight, sometimes doing forty rounds a day in the gym. I would skip and shadow-box in a sweat-bag, with the training gear on top of that. I could get the weight down, but it was weakening me to hold it there.

I won the tournament, stopping a Czech in three rounds in my first fight, beating David Rose of England in the semis and Russell Jones of Wales in the final. Rose and Jones should both have been pulled out by their corners, I felt, but they left them in there. Herol Graham and I shared the Best Boxer of the Tournament award.

At the end of the year I moved up to featherweight, and fought my first full international against Neil Anderson of Scotland at the National Stadium in Dublin. We had a great team that night: myself, Mick Holmes, Gerry Hamill, Phil Sutcliffe, Mel and Terry Christle. The place was jammed. The crowd actually broke the doors down, and an extra thousand people crammed in. I beat Anderson on a unanimous decision, and put him down in the third.

I boxed in the Ulster Seniors in February 1979 – the only time my mother saw me fight – and Kenny Bruce cut me. It was a bad one, and I was out for a couple of months. The referee stopped the fight, but under Irish rules it went to a points decision and I got it. I was out of action until I went to East Germany, to fight Torsten Koch, whom I'd already outpointed in Dublin. I was badly sick before the fight – never been so sick in my life. I had the runs and the doctor gave me a tablet to stop them. It made me retch, to dry me out, and I felt awful. I was supposed to be a featherweight, but

I almost made bantam. I beat Koch on points, but was very much under the weather.

The German bantamweight Mario Behrendt had hammered Ritchie Foster in that match. He was an unbeaten southpaw whose father Wolfgang had beaten Freddie Gilroy in the semi-final of the 1956 Olympics. I was down to eight-eight, but was feeling a bit better by this stage, so when they suggested that I box him in the second match I agreed. He was a brilliant counterpuncher, and he could really whack. I found it hard to get to him in the first round, but I closed the distance down on him in the second and battered him the rest of the way. They only gave it to me on a majority, but the Germans couldn't believe that their boy had been beaten. He went downhill after that, and never amounted to much.

After that I was picked for a multi-nations event in Romania. We were the only Western team in the tournament, and I won the gold medal. I beat the junior, senior and military champions of Romania, in three good contests – hard guys, all of them. Once again, I got the Best Boxer award.

The soldier I fought in the final winded me for the one and only time in my career. In the second round I went back against the ropes, and the referee moved in. I thought he was coming in to break us up, so I relaxed – and my opponent buried his fist in my stomach up to the elbow. He knocked all the wind out of my lungs, and must have paralysed them somehow. I couldn't get a breath for what seemed like thirty seconds, and I needed the whole minute's interval to get back to normal again.

I was a regular international now, and boxed against Wales, Canada and Hungary. But already I was having trouble with my hands, and at the start of the next season I nearly destroyed them altogether. It was an Ulster *vs.* Dublin match, and I was supposed to fight Mick Holmes. Four days before it, Holmes was pulled out and Ritchie Foster substituted. They may have thought I wouldn't box Foster, but I'd never backed away from anybody in my life.

The guy who was putting the gloves on us at the ringside complained about the bandaging I'd put on my hands. It was all legal, but I'd also put crisscross strips on the back to hold the bones together. It wasn't over the knuckles or anything, but strictly speaking it wasn't allowed. He said, 'Get that off you.' I was tense anyway, and I blew up at him. 'Look,' I said, 'I've come down here to box as a favour to you people, and I've filled the house for you.'

But he wouldn't budge, so in a fit of temper I ripped all the bandages off and went in the ring with the gloves on my bare hands – and broke them both. I knocked Foster down four times, which nowadays would have been enough for a stoppage. I won by a mile, but it cost me a metacarpal fracture in the left hand and a fractured support bone and dislocated knuckle in the other. I ended up missing the Ulster Seniors, but boxed Damien Fryers in the Irish semis and broke my hand again.

As a consolation for missing the Irish finals I got picked for the European Juniors in Rimini in May 1979. Dave McAuley was there. He fought Janos Varadi of Hungary, and lost on points in a real up-and-downer. At that time Dave smoked like a train and liked his vodka too, but it never seemed to do him any harm. I'd been friends with McAuley for years, since we were in the juveniles together at Limerick. He was stopped that year in the semi-final by Ritchie Foster.

At least we had a lot of laughs together in Rimini. Gerry Hawkins – 'Diddler' – was the light-fly, and the funniest little fellow I've ever seen. McAuley was the flyweight, Foster the bantam, I was feather. David Irving went out as a lightweight and finished up boxing at welterweight, and Martin Brereton was the light-welterweight. I won a bronze, and so did Martin, but that was all.

We used to fly about Rimini on these little automatic motorbikes. I couldn't handle them at all, but Brereton was expert. You rented the bikes by the day and had to leave your passport as security. You weren't supposed to take them off the road, but we used them as dirt-bikes in the park. Diddler Hawkins rode up alongside Foster, gave him a push, and sent him smack into a tree. The bike was a write-off and when Ritchie came round he was wanting to kill Diddler, who was busting himself laughing. A couple of the boys were cute enough to ride on and return their bikes early, so they could get their passports back, but four of us went with Ritchie and his wreck of a bike.

The guy who rented out the bikes was livid, and wouldn't give Ritchie his passport until he'd been paid for the damage. So we all had to have a whip-round, and we just about raised enough. I had to put in £35, which was near enough every penny I had, so it was a dear laugh.

I beat Dragon Kohovalov of Yugoslavia in the first series of the European Juniors, but got robbed against Juri Gladychev of Russia in the semi-final. The judges gave it to him 3–2. Felix Jones protested on my behalf, but got nowhere. Gladychev went on to win the gold.

Losing in the European Juniors was a great disappointment, especially having captained the team, and to make it worse I was just pipped for the Best Boxer of the competition award by Nick Wilshire of England. But there wasn't time for brooding about it; the Olympics were closing in on us. I had been away from home for six weeks, but when I came back from Italy I kept my training up to pace. I always murdered myself training, and never allowed myself to go down and then come back up again. I found it hard to peak – I never knew what it was like to peak. As far as I was concerned, I was always peaking.

Frank Mulligan and I trained together morning, noon and night. His whole world revolved around getting me ready for the Olympic Games. I know that he was very disappointed not to go to the Games with me, because he felt that he would be able to control me mentally, but the politics of Irish amateur boxing kept him away. The people who run the sport there think he's a bit of an eccentric, and being out in the sticks doesn't help, so all he's had off them is the odd trip to England, or maybe working with bits and pieces of an Ulster team. He lives, eats and sleeps boxing; he's a boxing nutcase. Mulligan arranged for some businessmen to give me a few quid every week for training expenses. I was getting forty quid a week, and in 1980 that was a lot of money to me. It enabled me to give my mother a few pounds for my keep.

I hadn't been home for more than a couple of weeks before I went back into camp for the Olympics, down in Drogheda with Gerry Storey and Phil Sutcliffe, Sean Doyle, P J Davitt and Martin Brereton. Eddie Thompson was the team manager, and Storey the national coach. I found it very hard; we were doing recovery training, with lots of sprints. In the early part of training I hurt my left hand, which had been giving me trouble all the time – separation of two knuckles – and so I couldn't spar at all. I left it until five weeks before we were actually due to box, when I sparred two rounds each with Sutcliffe, Damien Fryers and Tommy Davitt, P J's brother, who was a good pro lightweight. Tommy was wearing small gloves, and near the end of the fifth round he nailed me with a body punch that cracked a rib. So that was the end of sparring again, and I was back to punching bags and pads. I was bored stiff, training every day but only hitting the punchbag.

By the time we got to Moscow I was stale, mentally as well as physically. I fought Isaac Mabushi of Tanzania first, and stopped him in the third. It should have been much sooner, but because I was slow and sluggish it took me a few rounds. On BBC TV, Harry Carpenter was saying, 'And now it looks as if McGuigan's hand problems are over, and he's through to the next round.' Yet at that very moment, as I walked back to my corner, I was saying to Storey, 'The hand's gone again.'

Two nights later I had to box again, a big, tough, durable Zambian called Wilfred Kabunda. You were allowed to have a local anaesthetic, so I went to the doctor to have my hand frozen. But in the ring, it was the same story: I was stale as hell and my timing was so bad. He was a long, gangly guy who kept jumping around and in and out – just the hardest fight I could have had. I hit him a couple of good shots, but he never looked like he was going.

The judges gave it to him 4–1, which I thought was a bit harsh. I knew it was close, but I still thought I had done enough. But if I had got through that one, I have no doubt at all in my mind that I would have won the gold medal. Kabunda got his just reward in the next round; he met Rudi Fink of East Germany, and according to Dermot and all the reporters that were there, he boxed the head off him but they gave Fink the decision, and he went on to win the gold medal.

I felt gutted for all the people who'd helped me get to the Games. They knew that I had the ability to win the gold medal, and it was a great disappointment when I didn't make it. Amateur decisions, by that stage, had got the better of me. I'd had two defeats, one in the European Juniors, which was vitally important, and another in the Olympics, which also mattered a lot to me. Back in 1976 I made a board in the woodwork class in school, a T-square on a deal frame, and I wrote on it, 'Please God, let me win the gold medal in 1980', and I used to take the board out and stare at it. Winning that gold medal meant everything to me. I dreamed of standing on the rostrum listening to the National Anthem, the medal round my neck.

Anyway, it didn't happen in Moscow, but I thought there'd be one more chance. The ABA were having a multi-nations at Wembley to celebrate their centenary, and I was entered along with Peter Hanlon, Ian McLeod and Renard Ashton – whose brother John later became a very good friend, who helped me a lot when I made my comeback in 1988. I boxed Hanlon in the semi-final, put him down, but he came back well and won the last round. McLeod beat Ashton in the other semi-final and got the verdict over me in the final. I thought it was a very rough decision again. Three bad verdicts, and each time they stopped me from standing on a rostrum with a gold medal round my neck.

Around that time I had a letter from Mickey Duff. He said something like, 'I can count on one hand the number of fighters I have written to, to ask if they'd turn professional with me. But you are one of the most promising fighters I've seen.'

I had already been over in London, training with Terry Lawless, and he too had said, 'If you're going to turn pro, would you go with me?' This was in early 1978. I had won the Ulster Senior bantamweight title, and went to London to stay with my Uncle Leo, out at Wood Green. Every day I'd get the tube to Mile End, to Lawless's gym. Later, in May, Danny McEntee suggested I go over there for a while with Frank Mulligan and spar with Charlie Magri. I did the first night with Magri, and the second and third with Ray Cattouse, who became the British lightweight champion.

I'd brought big gloves, but Lawless said, 'No, we don't use those — we spar with small gloves,' so I had to go and buy a set of moulded gloves instead of the big puffy ones. Magri walked out, the British flyweight champion, and *bang*, I sent this jab right to his nose, and his head jarred back. Lawless called, 'Stop!' He said, 'We don't spar hard in this gym — we spar light. He won't go hard with you, so don't you go hard with him.' So we sparred nice and light, jab for jab, but I had already done his nose and it cost him five months of his career. One jab, and I didn't even know that I'd done any damage. In fact, he had to have numerous operations to get the cartilage out of his nose.

Next day I sparred with Ray Cattouse. I was nervous — I was only an amateur, after all — but I hit him with a right and then another and Lawless says, 'Stop! What the hell's going on? I told you yesterday, no hard sparring.' Later, in the changing-room, he was looking at me. 'How old did you say you were?' 'Sixteen.' 'Well, you're the best-built sixteen-year-old I've ever seen.' I did four rounds with Cattouse the following day, and I felt I was getting on top of him even though he was a lightweight, and was probably at that stage ten-four or five.

After Magri had finished his workout he sat under a blanket for five minutes, and then weighed himself. He was eight stone six – and this was after he'd done his work! And I thought to myself, 'He's a flyweight, and here I am worrying about my weight.' I watched Lawless's fighters closely, and they all seemed like clones; they all did exactly the same things in the ring. I watched Magri, Austin Owens and Cattouse spend fifteen minutes shadow-boxing in front of a big mirror, throwing precisely the same sequences of punches. It was all a bit regimental for me, but I was never a cheeky boy, so I just watched and picked up as much as I could.

In between the two trips to London I went up to Derry with my father and my Uncle Peter, to spar with Charlie Nash. Charlie came out and set about me. He was the British lightweight champion, and I was only an amateur bantam, and he tried to give me a duffing. I lasted the four rounds, although I was tired, but I promised myself that I'd get my own back for what he'd tried to do to me. It annoyed me – and it wasn't the only time something like that happened to me. Gerry Hamill, who won the Commonwealth Games lightweight gold medal, went really hard on me in sparring. He was a bit better than me, and a lot bigger and stronger. I promised myself that I would pay them both back, and I did.

*

Mickey Duddy, who sparred regularly with Nash, was in the gym that night waiting for his turn. He had been friendly with McGuigan since 1977, when they had competed (at different weights) in the National Juvenile Championships in Limerick, where Duddy won the 9st 7lb title. He would later become a pro lightweight, boxing down on the bill on a few early McGuigan promotions, and also earn some hard money serving as an occasional sparmate for McGuigan himself.

'Charlie Nash was the nicest fellow you could want to meet,' Duddy remembers. 'What he did to McGuigan was completely out of character. All I can think of is that Barry had been getting a lot of attention from the press, and maybe that annoyed Nash – maybe he wanted to remind everybody that he was still the number one man in Irish boxing.

'But whatever the reason, he gave McGuigan a terrible hiding. Afterwards, we could see that Barry was very upset. There was an old store-room at the back of the gym, and I saw him go in there.

I think he had a wee cry to himself. Charlie was always a very competitive type – if he was playing darts, he'd want to nail you to the wall.'

*

The next time I went to spar with Nash I was a featherweight with plenty of top-level international experience. He was a fully-fledged lightweight; he had trouble making lightweight, so I'm sure he was weighing ten stone-plus. But he could only do two rounds with me. I gave him a good pasting; he didn't do any more sparring that night at all.

I paid Hamill back one night up at the All Saints club in Ballymena. He was around ten stone, but wanted to turn pro. I'd had two fights, and was training to fight Peter Eubanks. But after a couple of rounds with me he'd had enough, and dropped the idea of turning pro. In fact, he never boxed again.

My next visit to Lawless was in the autumn of 1979, a year after I'd won the Commonwealth Games gold medal, and I sparred with Jim Watt. He had just won the world title, and was training to defend it against Roberto Vasquez. I did six rounds with him, good fast stuff. I couldn't believe that I'd held my own with the lightweight champion of the world.

Anyway, I'd had enough of amateur boxing by now. Lawless wanted me, I'd had the letter from Duff, and other managers like Eddie Thomas, Ron Gray and Tommy Gilmour were after me too. Charlie Gray, from Barney Eastwood's office, had given me his card after I'd won the Ulsters. I had never heard of Eastwood before. He was the biggest bookie in the north of Ireland, with betting shops all over the place, but he didn't operate south of the border. He had been running professional shows in the 1960s, but that was before I was old enough to take an interest in boxing.

Gray told me that Eastwood had loads of money, and could do this and that for me. I said 'Fine', and put the card away, never thought about it again. And then Gerry Storey mentioned him to me in 1981, after my last amateur fight. I'd boxed one more time in the Ulster Seniors: I fought Damien Fryers, and broke two of his ribs. I was supposed to box Herman Henry the following night in Dublin, but after beating Fryers I had a big meal and a lot of liquid, and I thought, 'What's the point of fighting Henry? I'll weigh in heavy, and have to train it off. It's not worth it.' So I pulled out.

Storey, through Charlie Gray, set up a meeting for my father and me with Eastwood at the Ballymascanlon Hotel near Dundalk, out on the Carlingford road. Eastwood came in looking very suave, in an expensive Crombie coat. He had Davy Donnelly with him – 'Davy the Hat', they call him. We had a bite to eat and talked it over. Eastwood seemed to be exactly what we wanted. He appeared to know his boxing and obviously was a man with a lot of contacts. More importantly, he was Irish, and this was a big point in his favour: if I signed with him I would not have to leave home.

He told me about what he could do for me, so we agreed to meet him again at his house in Holywood. We sat there talking most of the night, and at the end of it I said, 'Right, this is the man for me.' We signed contracts at the Royal Avenue Hotel in Belfast. It was the last function ever held there. All the local boxing writers were there, and Harry Doherty, one of the top amateur officials, was witness to the signing. Somebody asked me, 'Are you sure you're doing the right thing, Barry, turning pro?'

But I was happy enough to be signing: my amateur days were over, and I was sure I had made the right move.

Chapter Five

'If you had what I owe, you'd be a wealthy man.'
Barney Eastwood

Bernard Joseph Eastwood has had an almost lifelong love affair with boxing. Born in 1932, the youngest of eight children of parents who owned a hardware store in Cookstown, County Tyrone, he first came into contact with the sport through watching American soldiers at a wartime army base near his home. Two decades later he would become rather more directly involved in the fight game, drifting into small-time promotions at the tail end of the Belfast boxing boom of the second half of the 1950s and the early 1960s, the days of the unrelated John and Billy Kelly, and of Freddie Gilroy and Johnny Caldwell before drifting away from the game for almost twelve years.

That was not the first parting of the ways for the man all now refer to simply as Barney.

The future manager of Ireland's first world boxing champion in almost a quarter of a century (since Caldwell lost his only partially recognized share of the bantamweight title in a 1962 unification meeting with Eder Jofre of Brazil) had been a fee-paying boarder at St Patrick's College in Armagh. And it was from there, in 1947, that he set out to make his way in the world. Not because he wanted to or was quite ready to at the time, but because, as he told Deirdre Purcell of the *Sunday Tribune* in 1987, he was 'asked not to return to St Patrick's'. The reason was a relatively frivolous one: he and a group of other students protested against the poor quality – and quantity – of food provided for the boarders by breaking into the kitchen the night before a dinner in honour of Cardinal MacRory, the then Archbishop of Armagh, and eating their collective way through the bulk of the elaborate courses that had been prepared for the Cardinal's visit the following day.

There was, however, a more positive achievement during his

college years: a star role in the school's All-Ireland Colleges Championship (Gaelic Football) success in 1947, when St Patrick's became the first team to bring the title north of the border. A year later came even greater success, when he filled the left half-forward position on the Tyrone inter-county team that won the All-Ireland Minor Championship, the national title in the Under-Eighteen grade. Shortly afterwards, however, came yet another parting of the ways for the young Eastwood: under a then existing 'Foreign Games' rule – 'The Ban' – he was expelled from the sport for playing soccer.

After leaving college, Eastwood's first job was as a van driver for a shoe shop owned by his eldest brother, Tommy Joe. He was married at nineteen to Frances, an office clerk who also worked for Tommy Joe, and with his new wife moved to the Antrim coastal town of Carrickfergus. There, with a £3,000 bank loan, they bought a public house. It was a purchase that, indirectly, was to prove the foundation stone of the present-day Eastwood business empire.

It all began with modest bets taken over the bar counter. Over the years it developed into a chain of betting shops that currently exceeds thirty and has an annual turnover of around £20 million. Along the way Eastwood was responsible for other growth areas: he and Frances had six sons and a daughter.* His other interests expanded apace: by the early 1980s the Eastwood portfolio included extensive property interests in and around Belfast and a network of homes – in which most of his sons reside – in the city's stockbroker belt that is the County Down seaside village of Holywood. Estimates of his personal wealth vary, some people putting it as high as £40 million. His Christmas cards are illustrated with paintings 'from the private collection of Mr & Mrs B J Eastwood', and he is also a knowledgeable and enthusiastic collector of antique furniture and clocks.

Yet he has always been decidedly coy on the subject of money. 'You know,' he once told a journalist who enquired about the true extent of his wealth, 'I've never actually given it a thought.' And, answering a similar question on another occasion, he responded by telling his interviewer, 'If you had what I owe, you'd be a wealthy man.'

Eastwood has always, in fact, had a decidedly mixed attitude

---

*One son, Finten, died in August 1990.

towards the media. On occasions, such as when he withdrew all advertising from two Belfast papers in support of striking journalists, he has earned the respect and gratitude of the press; at other times, such as when he has barred writers who happened to query either his benevolent godfather image or the true status of his relationship with McGuigan, he has earned extensive criticism. (One hack incurred Eastwood's displeasure for no more serious a crime than the revealing of his 'secrets' in relation to upcoming McGuigan fights, an act of crass temerity that brought an intriguing – and revealing – rebuke from a fellow scribe: 'Where, when and against whom Barry is fighting next is irrelevant; what matters is that you don't alienate yourself from the number one man in boxing in this country [Ireland].')

He did, however, rapidly prove himself to be an unrivalled master in the art of media manipulation, a talent that worked to both his and McGuigan's benefit for over five years.

Chapter Six

'Teams develop when talent and personalities mesh.'
Bill Bailey, New York Knicks baseball player

The McGuigan Team

Boxers are, by the nature of their trade, the most isolated of all professional sportsmen. Team players are free to spread the blame for defeat, and even some solo performers may seek solace in the shortcomings of others. Athletes might blame jostling competitors, or imponderables like the weather or the state of the track; tennis players can rant about myopic line judges or badly strung racquets. But when a fighter loses – barring injury or the temporary insanity which sometimes afflicts ringside officials – whatever excuses he devises are irrelevant. All that matters is that, on the night, he went up against a man who was better than he was.

Outside the actual competition ring, though, a boxer needs a solid team around him. McGuigan had better back-up than most. Some, like his brother Dermot and his wife, Sandra, were of his own choosing, while others, like Eddie Shaw and Paddy Byrne, were Eastwood's selections.

Dermot McGuigan is unmistakably Barry's brother, but has a gaunt intensity about him that contrasts oddly with his brother's wise-cracking, extrovert personality. He was there at the very beginning of it all, the first day Barry ever knew the feel of a boxing glove, and he was in Manchester in May 1989, on the night it ended. To some who undervalued his role, Dermot was a peripheral figure in the McGuigan entourage. But the truth was very different.

*

Dermot is only a year older than me, so we both got into boxing at the same time. He didn't like the training, and soon shelved it, but he still had a great interest in boxing, especially when I started doing well. He spent long hours in the gym with me. In the late 1970s Dermot began to do a lot of pad work* with me, and because I was an international he would go to all my fights and watch the opposition for me. He watched national coaches like Gerry Storey on the pads, and watched Frank Mulligan training me, and he did a bit as well, helping Mulligan. It wasn't very long before he became very good at what he was doing.

He also played a lot of golf at the time, and worked for Tunney's Meat as a factory butcher. He was a very competitive golfer, playing off two. He was the best golfer in the Clones club, with the lowest handicap, and he still holds the course record there. He was accurate at any ball game, and was very good at boxing too; he had a lot more natural style and technique than I had, but he didn't have the same determination.

I often did fifteen rounds a night on the pads with him in the gym at home; once we even did thirty rounds on the pads in one day, fifteen in the afternoon and fifteen at night. Dermot would come and do the pad work and the bag work, and then he would leave me to do the tedious work on my own. He only came in for the technical work.

When I turned pro he was always there. We spent hours developing my left hook. If anybody gets the credit for that, he should. He came to all my fights and often went to training camp. He enjoyed coming to the gym, but hated all the hanging around between the training sessions, so he would only come down for a couple of days at a time. Barney knew that he was very good, but I got the impression that he didn't like anybody who was close to me.

He particularly disliked Dermot getting into the ring before anybody else at the end of a fight. Dermot used to have an ejector seat – you'd see him bulleting through the ropes the moment the fight was over. I remember when I fought Julio Miranda in my

---

*'Pad work' is a gym exercise in which the trainer dons large pads, the size of a tennis racquet's hitting area, and, hands up in a boxing posture, moves around the ring while his boxer throws punches at the pads. The routine develops the boxer's timing and accuracy.

comeback in 1988, he was sitting at the ringside. He was on crutches after shooting himself in the toe, and John Douglas, one of the boys at home who's a very dry wit, asked him, 'How are you going to be first in the ring this time?' Dermot says, 'I don't know.' John says, 'Sure you could always just throw in the crutches.'

Eddie Shaw was my trainer, and was in charge of the gym, and Dermot sometimes got on Eddie's nerves when he came to watch me sparring. Normally he wouldn't interfere, but sometimes he'd be sitting at ringside and shouting bits of advice to me, just simple things like, 'Use the jab more' or 'Pick the speed up', 'Double up the left hook', 'Switch from the body to the head.' Barney would nudge Eddie, and every time he nudged him Eddie would say, 'Dermot, shut up!' Dermot would do what he was told, but he got very angry at times. He'd walk to the back of the gym seething, because he wasn't allowed to say the things I was doing wrong and they weren't telling me.

Yet Barney knew that he was a great help to me, and often said, 'That Dermot fellow can really work well on those pads.' But he never liked to encourage him, because his attitude was always to keep everybody that was close to me away from me, so that if I needed help he would be the only one I could turn to. But Dermot stuck it out and stayed with me through thick and thin.

We would look at opponents together, although it was always Barney who had the last word. I have to say that he did a great job, too: he managed me well in that way. Dermot and I knew the records and styles of the top fifty featherweights in the world, everything there was to be known about them. Each week there'd be a race to see who got *Boxing News* first – he got one from the newsagent and I'd get mine through the post. Dermot is a boxing nut who knows his history far better than I do. He watched all the old fights, and knew boxing inside out.

We used to read all about old-time training methods, about Joe Louis, Benny Leonard, John L Sullivan. John L, for example, would never run; he used to walk a while, stop and shadow-box, and then walk another while, and he'd do ten miles like that every morning. I'd read about how many rounds they did on the bag, about how José Napoles would shadow-box for ten rounds in front of a mirror. I'd even look at pictures of him doing it, to see what he was wearing.

I'd watch good pros hit the bag, and study how they did it. I watched Alexis Arguello taping his hands. He used mounds of tape, and of course I copied him for a while. When I went to Gleason's Gym in New York I'd watch the guys there, how they talked, and whether they'd be relaxed before they went into the gym, to know what their mental approach was to a workout. I watched John Collins (then a world-ranked middleweight) in Chicago. After he'd done his couple of rounds sparring he'd go on the bag, and as he'd hit the bag he'd be talking to the other guys. I said to myself, 'How can this be a world-class fighter when he's doing this?' My attitude was that you never open your mouth to anybody until your gym session is finished. Maybe when you're skipping you can talk to somebody, but not when you're doing your heavy work.

When Howard Davis came over to fight Jim Watt he'd put on music and turn it up really loud, and I thought, 'How can he concentrate on his sparring when he's listening to this?' It would be like going out to fight somebody, and turning on disco music. I used to listen to music a lot, but I would never have it on until I'd finished skipping. I would never turn it on when I was punching the bag, the pads, the overhead ball or even when I was shadow-boxing, so that I could concentrate on thinking my moves out. I even used to read about amateur kids and what they did.

I would discuss it all with Dermot, and try it out with him. If it was no good it would go in one ear and out the other, but if it was good I would try and remember it. Frank Warren offered Dermot a job working with his fighters, but he wouldn't take it, which annoyed me because I thought it would be perfect for him. But maybe he'll become a trainer yet: all that knowledge and ability shouldn't go to waste.

*

Two of Eddie Shaw's charges, McGuigan and flyweight Dave McAuley, won world titles, yet until he was recruited by Barney Eastwood to work with McGuigan, Shaw had never trained a professional fighter. But he knew boxing from the bottom up, and he too had his role to play in the moulding of a champion.

*

Eddie Shaw, who trained me throughout the time I was managed by Barney, boxed for Ireland as a bantamweight, and won an Ulster Senior title. He turned pro towards the end of Freddie Gilroy's career in the early 1960s, but wasn't very successful. He had nine fights between 1962 and 1963 but cut easily, and so he packed it in. He had the same manager as Gilroy, Jimmy McAree, and I remember him telling me about sparring with Gilroy a couple of days before Freddie fought John Caldwell. Gilroy had terrible trouble making the weight: he was sparring in plastics and he was absolutely drained. He was so weak that Eddie knocked him down and, as he said, 'I could never even knock the cap off your head!'

He worked in the Irish Forester's club. He used to train at the Immaculata club, at the bottom of the Divis Flats, a really rough area in West Belfast, until he lost a bit of interest in the amateur game. He had one son and four daughters.

How he and I got together was that Eastwood was looking for someone to train me. Gerry Storey, who had introduced me to Eastwood, had hoped to train me himself. But Gerry worked for the Ulster ABA Council, which was a paid job, and the people on the Irish ABA said that he was really a professional. He was a completely dedicated guy, who gave his whole life to the fight game. If he gave up his job with the Ulster Council, he would want some kind of payment to train me and the other fighters, as Eastwood's stable progressed.

Eastwood said he would build a gym for us, but that didn't happen for a long time. We used to train like gypsies; we would go to the Holy Family, the Immaculata, the Holy Trinity, the White City. He arranged for us to meet Eddie in the Immaculata one day, not long after I had turned pro. Old Ned McCormick was there; a great old skin, who had been in the fight game for years, training professionals and amateurs, and really knew his boxing. He used to train the Immaculata, where Shaw was helping out occasionally, and I think Eddie had got a bit disillusioned with the amateur game.

I came along there, and did about five rounds on the pads and five rounds on the bag. It was a basement gym, very cold, and with quite a strong stench about it, but I liked it: it was a lovely authentic gym. Anyway, we trained away and I remember thinking initially that I wasn't very impressed. Shaw was good, but he wasn't showing me anything I hadn't seen before. Eastwood was impressed, though: Shaw was a different type to Storey, who was a very level-headed guy with strong ideas on how you should train and so on.

Eastwood then assigned Eddie to train me, and old Ned came along as well. I thought Ned was very good. He didn't come on the pads, or the like, but he had sound ideas and taught me a lot of moves. He spoke a lot of sense. He was also a very wily old guy.

I used to be fairly close with Shaw. I would go round to the Forester's to pick him up, and after training we'd have a drink there. Occasionally I'd go up to his house and meet his wife, Mary. I liked her, and the family – they were lovely people.

Anyway, his training developed and got better, but we were still waiting for our own gym. I began to wonder if Eastwood was ever going to build it, but he did in the end, at the back of his offices in Castle Street, and it was a grand place. Eddie liked it. He used to be very heavy, liked a drink, and wore a rubber suit during the workouts. Barney would take in people like Gerald Hayes, Teddy Atlas, Bobby McQuillar and Ken Buchanan to train with me, and it always used to hurt and annoy Eddie.

Barney would say, 'Ah, you're all right, Eddie, it's only to help the lad,' and he would play it down, but I knew Eddie was upset many, many times because the play was taken away from him and these guys got the limelight and the praise, although he always felt that he was the one doing all the foundation work.*

In fact, Dermot did all the foundation work with me down in Clones. I only came up to Belfast two or three weeks before the fight, as the fights got more important. In the early days I would stay in Eastwood's house, but after a while the atmosphere became very sharp, very tense, so when he suggested that I stay in Jean Anderson's guest house in Bangor I jumped at the chance.

Barney Wilson, the referee, and Eddie went to school together – they were very friendly. He had a couple of other friends at the Forester's that I really liked and enjoyed, who would come along to the fights and support me because of Eddie. I even travelled to my first professional fight with one of them. Skull, they called him – they always have great nicknames in Belfast.

As time went on we got close. I had a lot of faith in Eddie, but Dermot annoyed him because he could do the pads so well, and of course he knew me better than Eddie ever could.

Barney used to talk about 'the Eddie Shaw left hook'. But I developed the hook myself, from throwing it thousands and thou-

---

* 'Foundation work' is the achievement of basic physical fitness and the practising of routine gym exercises, including bag and pad punching. It precedes the 'fine tuning' period in the build-up to a fight.

sands of times at the bag at home. I worked it and worked it. I watched other fighters throw left hooks; I'd watch the Americans throw double hooks, to the body and then to the head. But then I saw a photograph of Alexis Arguello in *Boxing News*. He was throwing a body punch, and I saw the way his elbow was turned outwards, and I realized then and there that *that* was the way to throw a body punch.

Before, I'd always catch guys on their elbows with the body shots. No matter how well I threw the body punch, I'd always clip them and never get through properly. So I said to myself, 'I've got to disguise it right', so I used to bring it up the middle. I practised it. Instead of throwing left hook to the body, left hook to the head, I'd go bang-bang-bang, all to the head, and then rip it to the body. It was the reverse way of doing it, and I caught them every single time. Of course, when I started going up in class I'd find the Americans were used to that, going head to body, but it worked over here. Even with the Americans I'd throw it the normal way, then throw it in reverse again, and throw it the other way again, and it worked.

Dermot and I spent hours and hours watching old fight films, and it was he and I who perfected that left hook. Nobody else throws that punch. Dave McAuley does something similar, and so does Paul Hodkinson, but Hodkinson was doing it before he ever went pro.

Eddie worked hard in the gym, but he tended to push you a bit too hard. He would never say, 'OK, you've done enough.' Barney would come into the gym and sit there watching, and he would tell Eddie, 'That's enough on the pads' or 'That's enough sparring', or whatever. But you had to depend on Barney, otherwise Eddie would work you to death. I learned from being around the Americans that I was the best judge of my own condition. If I felt bad I would moan at Eddie for three or four rounds, so that he would know to take it easy on me.

Eddie was the head buck-cat in the gym, and when we took on other fighters Eddie controlled them. Give him his due, he worked hard and did his bit, but he was never the 'Irish Angelo Dundee' that Eastwood called him.

*

His name, properly, is Nicholas, but for over forty years nobody has called him anything but Paddy. In his time, Paddy Byrne has filled just about every role in the professional boxing business. He had a brief and unsuccessful career as a lightweight – Ernie Fossey, many years later a rival matchmaker, knocked him out in six rounds on his debut – and since then he has been promoter, agent, manager, second, cuts man and confidant to an army of fighters of varying accomplishment, from world champions to six-round preliminaries.

*

Paddy Byrne was involved with Barney back in the 1960s and 1970s, but I didn't meet him until my second pro fight, at Wembley against Gary Lucas. He lived in Brighton, and he arranged my third fight there, with Peter Eubanks. He came to pick me up at Gatwick in Jack Solomons' old car – he used to work for Solomons, and Jack left him the car in his will. Paddy promoted the Eubanks fight, and after that he was part of the team. He was there in case I got cut, although once when I was cut Paddy was actually working in the other corner. It happened when I fought Sammy Meck in Navan, my first appearance as British champion. Paddy was the agent responsible for Meck, so he was working in his corner, but the understanding was that if I got cut Paddy would leave Meck and come across to see to me. Roger Bensaid, his old manager, was in the corner with him. Bensaid was very frail – he was about eighty-five and used a walking-stick, so Paddy did all the running up and down the steps while the old fellow would lean through the ropes and do the talking.

The cut I got wasn't too bad, so they told Paddy to stay where he was – but in between rounds Paddy would be staring across the ring to see what kind of a job they were doing on my eye. In the sixth round Meck was really knackered, and Paddy got a big sopping spongeful of water ready to douse him when he came back to the corner. But he was really more interested in what was happening across the ring, and he was so distracted that he sprayed the water all over poor old Bensaid instead.

Paddy would spend the last couple of days before a fight with me. He was really the heart and soul of the party, great fun. He was full of jokes and funny stories: I remember him telling me about Dennie Mancini, the London manager, ringing up Coe McConnell, from Doagh who looked after the Turkington brothers, Henry and Willie, in the 1960s. Dennie was making the matches for a sporting club at the time, and he wanted Henry for a ten-rounder. The show was a sell-out and his top of the bill had pulled out, so he was desperate to get Turkington.

There was a flyweight McConnell used to look after as well, so Mancini said, 'Bring him along and I'll do you a favour and put him on the show too, in a six-twos.' This was on the Friday and the fight was on Monday. Sunday night, Mancini rang him to make sure everything was all right.

'No bother,' says Coe, 'we'll be there tomorrow.' So Mancini went out to the airport to pick them up, and here's Coe walking down the steps with the flyweight. 'Where's Turkington?' says Mancini, who of course has built the whole show around Henry. 'Well, do you know,' says Coe, 'the bugger wouldn't come!'

Paddy kidded that he could speak French, Spanish, Italian and anything else, but he'd start off in French and finish up the sentence in Italian. The bits in between he'd do with his hands and his shoulders, and Eastwood would be saying to us, 'Look at him, the oul showoff!' Paddy had plenty of style: he always dressed well and could talk as easily to an archbishop as to a barman.

When the split between Eastwood and me finally came, Paddy stayed out of it. He had worked well with the pair of us, and he never started throwing any shit. He just said, 'I'm not going to say anything – I'd rather just remember the good times.' Today, I can still walk up to Paddy and shake his hand and throw my arms around him. I have great respect for him, because he could have earned well from slagging me off in the papers, but he wouldn't do it.

*

Even more important than a fighter's choice of manager is his choice of wife. The wrong woman can ruin a champion quicker than any contender ever could: ask Mike Tyson. Sandra McGuigan, though, is the other side of the Robin Givens coin.

*

I met Sandra when I was three and she was a couple of months older, but she doesn't like being reminded of that. My parents had moved into Clones and bought a grocery shop on the Diamond, and a family called Mealiff, Sandra's parents, owned a hardware shop and hotel across the street. I became friendly with the Mealiffs right away. Sammy and David were Sandra's brothers. Sammy was about a year younger than me and David a year and a half older. They used to hang about with me and Dermot, and sometimes I would give their father, Jim, a hand in the shop.

Sandra and I went to different schools. She was educated in the North, at Newtownbutler and then Lisnaskea in Fermanagh. When I was eight I found a wedding ring somewhere and gave it to Sandra, but we didn't start going out seriously until I was seventeen. It came as a big surprise to both our families. We'd always been friends, and I used to show her how to do weightlifting and things like that – I'm sure she was very impressed. I'd fancied her for a good while, but it took me a long time to realize that maybe she fancied me too. I'd been out with girls before, but nothing too serious. I didn't have time for girls, really, and that was the great thing about Sandra: she understood the commitment that I had to give to my boxing.

We spent most of our courtship in the gym. She kept a record of all the rounds I did every session, how many on the bag, how many skipping, and so on. She recorded everything, written out in scrupulous detail, two sessions every day. We went out occasionally to discos, but not very often. Later on, when I started getting invitations to award dinners and so on, she would come with me and we would use those as our nights for socializing. Sandra was perfectly happy with this kind of relationship. She was as dedicated to me as I was to my training.

By 1979 we knew that we wanted to get married and spend the rest of our lives together, and when I came back from the Olympic Games the next year I took the pocket money I'd got left from Moscow (I had hardly spent anything there) and bought her an engagement ring in Dublin. In late 1981 we decided to get married. I was just kicking off in the pro game when we married, on 14 December 1981. We stayed with my mum for six months while I was trying to sort out a house.

We got married in the Church of Ireland, with the Canon from the Catholic church sitting in on it, and afterwards there was a short service in my church. It was all very amicable, and it kept everybody happy.

Eventually we got our own house, with a bridging loan from Barney. Sandra put up with him for my sake, but sometimes his real feelings would come out. I honestly believe I got closer to him than anybody else ever did, or ever will again. I think I was the one person that he kind of liked. He tried to get on with Sandra, but it was like feeding a child something it can't stomach: the child might take it down, but it will spit it straight back up again. A lot of the time, Barney didn't even realize what he was doing, or how hurtful he was being. For instance, when we'd be watching the videos of my fights and my father came on to sing 'Danny Boy', Barney would fast-forward the film.

Sandra trained as a hairdresser, and won the British championship for first-year stylists. She set up a hairdressing business in Clones with my sister Sharon, and they did very well until Sandra left work in 1984. We always wanted kids, as soon as we could, and she gave up a very successful business to concentrate on the family. Blain had arrived, and I was starting to earn some decent money, so she didn't need to work anyway.

When I was in camp, Sandra would come up to Bangor and spend the weekend with me. She lived in a room at the back of the house, well away from me. There was never any creeping along the corridor in the night. We both took my career too seriously for that. One time, she came to the gym to say goodbye to me and wish me luck for the fight. Barney met her at the foot of the stairs. 'Have you not gone home yet, Sandra?' he said to her. It was the first time she'd ever stood up to him. 'If Barry wants me to go home, he'll tell me,' she said. 'Go up and ask him if he wants me to go.' He came up to the gym, but never said a word to me.

She is a very calm person; what I lack she has got, and what she lacks I have. We've had Blain, Danika, Jake and Shane; my father has died, and we've come to England and moved house twice. Through all those traumas, we have probably become closer. After what she's had to put up with so far, she can put up with anything. We had to spend a lot of time apart, even though we were able to see each other at weekends in camp, but absence made the hearts grow fonder.

Sandra's the backbone to me. She's been there all the time, and I just hope that in twenty years I'm as happy as I am now. She has had to change a lot and adapt a lot. Maybe it's even worse for her now than it was when I was boxing, because I'm away from home so much. But we have an awful lot in common, and that helps. We're very compatible, four children later.

Chapter Seven

'We don't want to make a big thing about being Irish, and maybe alienate the people over here.'

Barney Eastwood, on why new pro Barry McGuigan would not wear green in the ring

My first pro fight was at Dalymount Park soccer ground in Dublin, on 10 May 1981, against Selvin Bell. Ned McCormick was in my corner, Eddie was there, but Barney was away in the Caribbean. The fight was made at nine stone two, and I had been training hard and going around like a gypsy dog, sparring in different clubs. We drove down to Dublin the day before with a couple of Eddie's friends, and stayed in a little hotel off St Stephen's Green. When I got on the scales next morning, I was actually under the featherweight limit – eight stone thirteen and three-quarters – and Bell was nine stone two and a bit. I knew nothing about him, other than that he had had a lot of professional fights. But the matchmaker assured me I could beat him, and I was in great shape.

We were supposed to go on early on the bill, but the TV cameras were there to show the main event live – Charlie Nash getting a terrible hiding from Joey Gibilisco, an Australian-based Sicilian, for the European title. I was actually running towards the ring, wearing plastic bags over my boots to keep the wet grass off them, when a TV guy with a headset stopped me and said, 'You can't go on now – there isn't enough time.' So we had to go back to the dressing-room and listen on the intercom as Nash got knocked out in the sixth. Old Ned was brilliant. He had trained with a good many professionals, and really knew the business. He would have been great to have had on the team, but Barney dropped him after the first five or six fights. If Barney said something that didn't make sense, Ned would tell him, 'That's a lot of rubbish.' Barney never liked to be told what to do, or told that he was wrong. I asked what had happened to Ned, and was told, 'Och, he was too difficult', and I left it there – I didn't want to get involved.

*

Defeat was not exactly a novel experience for Selvin Bell, the squat little Jamaican who was hired as McGuigan's first professional test-piece: he had been beaten forty-two times in fifty-eight fights, and had won just four of his previous twenty engagements. Bell, who was based in Manchester under Irish manager John Gaynor, was a professional fighter in the purest sense of the words. He fought for money, nothing else; at his level there is no room for illusions.

*

When I took my gown off in the ring, I was cold – I missed the amateur vest. Bell was the ugliest man I'd ever seen. He had these great long arms, and I thought to myself, 'Jab first, you've got to hit him with the jab.' So I walked out and hit him, *bam, bam*, with the jabs. He fluffed up like a duck, and his eyes doubled in size. I stepped back and thought, 'My God, what's this guy doing?' I knew he was either clowning or else I'd hurt him, so I rushed in again and hit him with another jab. I could see that he was frightened of me, but I was aware that he was very experienced and I didn't want to fall into any traps.

*

Bell's ungainly ring style, based around his extraordinarily long flailing arms, made him an awkward target for the six-round fighters of limited proficiency who were his customary opponents, but McGuigan had no difficulty in drilling hard, precise punches through his defences. A right under the ribs late in the opening round made Bell wrap his arms around the youngster and hang on grimly, and McGuigan resumed the onslaught in the second.

A stream of left hooks to the body doubled Bell over and sent him staggering backwards towards the ropes. Uppercuts and hooks to the head straightened him up, and a final left hook sent him sprawling inelegantly through the ropes on to the ring apron. He hauled himself back into a semblance of fighting order, but referee Bob McMillan spread his arms to signal the end. Immediately, the ring was engulfed by McGuigan's family and friends, who danced with the fighter in uninhibited, exuberant jubilation. Harry Mullan, at ringside for *Boxing News* and doubling as the BBC's inter rounds summarizer, observed sourly that, 'You would think he'd just won the world title, instead of becoming the forty-third man to beat Selvin Bell.' But it was a beginning, even if fewer than two thousand people had turned out on a miserably cold evening to watch the torch of Irish boxing pass from Charlie Nash to Barry McGuigan. The stadium's capacity was forty thousand.

The show was an unmitigated disaster for promoter Philip McLaughlin, an effusive and fast-talking Derryman who had hoped to match Nash in a world title fight with WBA champion Sean O'Grady, provided Nash retained his European title against Joey Gibilisco. Instead, Nash was pounded to sixth-round defeat, and never again boxed at top level. He spent the night in hospital with suspected concussion, and the young McGuigan was appalled to learn that, of Nash's pre-fight entourage, only his faithful trainer, Tommy Donnelly, had bothered to go there with him. Much later, in a Las Vegas hospital, McGuigan would himself experience the desolation and loneliness Nash endured on the night when, on several different levels, McGuigan learned what professional boxing was about.

Gary Lucas, a tall, straight-backed jabber from Liverpool with eleven wins in thirty-two fights, was McGuigan's second opponent. It was a six-rounder, buried down the bill at Wembley on 20 June 1981. In the main event, Jim Watt would fight with dogged resolution in a lost cause against the magnificent Nicaraguan Alexis Arguello, who sought to add Watt's WBC lightweight crown to the featherweight and super-featherweight titles he had already won.

That afternoon Eastwood phoned Harry Mullan at the *Boxing News* editorial office with an invitation to afternoon tea at the party's hotel, the Piccadilly. McGuigan was there, a quiet, shy and awkward boy who sat through ten minutes of small talk, staring constantly at his outsized hands. He seemed ill at ease – not on a social level, but as someone who had many better things to be doing and who begrudged the time spent away from them.

When he had gone, the conversation turned, incongruously, to sartorial matters: Eastwood wanted Mullan's views on whether the boxer should wear blue or green trunks for his first professional appearance in London. Eastwood favoured the blue. 'We don't want to make a big thing about being Irish, and maybe alienate the people over here.' Mullan, a Derryman, opted for green: 'He's Irish, so flaunt it. Wearing blue shorts won't make him any the less Irish, and anyway we have little enough to be proud about at the moment.'

McGuigan, predictably, wore blue. At least it was the shade worn by the Monaghan county Gaelic football team, although the Scots fans whose noisy presence enlivened Wembley that night were probably puzzled why a Catholic Irishman was fighting in Rangers blue.

*

That was typical of Eastwood; he would ask people's opinion, and make his own mind up at the end of the day. All the time I boxed for him, he would never let me decide what colour togs I wore. I suppose he was right. I never wanted to hurt anybody's feelings, to upset one side or the other. All I wanted was for people to come and see me fight, and enjoy themselves.

Lucas was an easy fight, but I was pleased with the way I boxed. I thought I showed some nice professional moves. He didn't go down, but it was very one-sided and the referee, Bob Galloway, stopped it in the fourth. Lucas came into the dressing-room and told me that I'd go a long way, and I was very pleased about that. Afterwards, I got dressed as quick as I could and went out to the front of the hall to watch Watt and Arguello. Watt showed a lot of heart: he hadn't a chance of winning, but he stuck it out bravely. He had a lot of pride.

CHAPTER EIGHT

'I'd had my fill of bad decisions in the amateurs and I thought that in the pro game at least that wouldn't happen.'

Barry McGuigan, reflecting on his first professional defeat

Peter Eubanks' career pattern was already set by the time he fought Barry McGuigan at the Corn Exchange, Brighton, on 3 August 1981. He had boxed seven times as a professional, winning three and losing four, and the surprise verdict he gained over the young Irishman did nothing to break the cycle of win a few, lose a few. As this chapter was being written the twenty-eight-year-old Eubanks had launched a comeback after almost two years away from the ring. He lost on points, bringing his overall record to fourteen wins from thirty-three starts. Like his twin brother Simon, he is known and respected in the trade as an honest journeyman who tests the best but rarely beats them ... with that one, shining, exception.*

*

After the Wembley fight I went back to Clones and trained until it was time to go to Belfast and prepare for the next one. Eastwood knew that I was an ardent trainer, but he preferred that I come and stay with him. Maybe he didn't trust me; maybe he'd had bad experiences with other fighters.

Paddy Byrne promoted the Eubanks fight. He drove me down to Brighton in Jack Solomons' old car, and told me about Jack leaving the Board of Control a penny in his will because he'd always said they weren't worth tuppence. I asked him about Eubanks, and he told me he was tough. I trained that evening in the gym under the Metropole Hotel – I always worked out the day before a fight –

---

*Another brother, middleweight Chris, was rather more successful: he won the WBO version of the world middleweight title in 1990.

and when I'd done I strolled down to the seafront. I'd heard about the nude beaches, but there wasn't a naked woman to be seen!

At the weigh-in Eubanks was half a pound over the weight, so his manager, Tony Brazil, took him into the next room to do a bit of skipping. When they came back, he was under the weight. The match was made at nine-four, but he looked really big – a well-muscled guy.

The crowd was poor, only a few hundred, and the show lost money. But they got great entertainment. We had brought along a young kid from Ballymena, Tony Dunlop, who fought a draw with Mickey Durvan in a thriller. Eubanks and I had a great fight, eight fabulous rounds of action, but I won it by miles. The fight was over eight-twos, which I had never boxed before. I'd been used to three-minute rounds, and found these were like sprinting rounds. I was so disappointed, because I'd had my fill of bad decisions in the amateurs and I thought that in the pro game at least that wouldn't happen. I put him down, landed dynamite punches, but could he take a shot! I hit him with real quality punches, right on the money. I boxed really well, outboxed and outpunched him, but Roland Dakin, the referee, gave it to him by half a point, $78\frac{1}{2}$–78.

That night I walked along the seafront with Eastwood, crying. He said, 'Don't worry about it, you won the fight.' But at the back of his mind he must have been disappointed too. I had fought beautifully; I boxed like a champion that night.

*

Twenty-one years to the very day after Jean Renard travelled from Belgium to test a future world featherweight champion, Howard Winstone, in a routine eight-rounder, his son Jean-Marc took the same road. The young Belgian was unbeaten in a brief pro career, but was not expected to trouble Barry McGuigan unduly when they were matched at the Ulster Hall, Belfast, on 22 September 1981.

The show marked Barney Eastwood's return to boxing promotion after a fifteen-year gap, since Wally Swift ended a memorable comeback by Al Sharpe, a local middleweight veteran of 120 fights, by outpointing him in a British title eliminator. There had been a handful of shows in the city since, but none that made any money. For a while in the 1950s the Ulster Hall had hosted boxing twice a week. Wednesdays were 'novice nights' and Saturdays featured established, good-class performers.

The tradition was there, and so, Eastwood was convinced, was the potential market. All that was needed was the catalyst...

*

Paddy Byrne was responsible for bringing Renard over. He put most of Eastwood's shows together for him; he'd make the matches, sort out the money, arrange the hotels and so on. The Belgians said Renard was *'fantastique'*. He'd won all six of his fights, and they said he was going to be great. The Ulster Hall was bursting.

In my first few fights we'd used gloves made by Bailey's, but the new gloves the Board of Control were using now were very soft and you could feel the knuckles coming through them. I'd had hand trouble, so I used as much bandaging as I could.

I boxed brilliantly that night, never took the jab out of his face and kept out of his way. I'd jab my way in, and then rip him with a left hook. I couldn't catch him cleanly, only on the top of the head, but he had a lot of lumps and abrasions around his head after the fight.

He was good, though. Every time I'd go in and throw a right hand, he'd hit me with a left hook – every single time. They weren't knock-out punches, but they stung. In the seventh I jabbed twice and tried the right, but I didn't bring my hand back quick enough and he hit me a great left hook and I went down. Harry Gibbs, who was refereeing, must have assumed I'd tripped over his foot, but it was a knockdown. I thought, 'What are you doing down here?' and jumped up immediately. I went straight at him with a right hand, but it had no effect.

When I came back to the corner Ned asked me, 'Was that a trip or a punch?' I was up without a count, but it was a punch all right, and the first time I'd ever been down. I thought I had him going late in the seventh, but he came out in the eighth and finished like a storm. It was a real good fight, and the crowd loved it. I got it by 79–78, and they showered the ring with nobbins.

*

Losing to McGuigan did Renard's career no harm at all; he went on to win European titles at featherweight and super-feather, and challenge unsuccessfully for the International Boxing Federation (IBF) world title. He had been a tougher opponent than anyone anticipated and, for that heart-stopping moment in the seventh round, Eastwood must have feared that he had killed the Golden Goose before it had laid its first egg. But the very fact that McGuigan's Belfast debut had been such a competitive and thrilling affair augured well for the game's revival there. Now Eastwood knew that he was building on a solid base.

But after the Renard scare, opponent number five in the Ulster Hall on 26 October had to be someone less demanding. Byrne came up with Sylvester Price, an American from Muncie, Indiana, who had lost three of his ten fights. A week before the fight Price withdrew and was replaced by Terry Pizzaro from Florida.

The brash American's boasting and baiting of McGuigan helped sell the Hall out again. 'They tell me the crowd really get behind their man over here,' Pizzaro said. 'Well, they'll need to get in the ring with McGuigan to hold him up.' He talked a great fight, but delivering it was something else.

*

Terry Pizzaro was a joker, a complete piss artist. He frightened me – boy, could he talk. He came to a press conference and said everything, made me feel a prat. He said to my father: 'Say, are you Mr McGuigan? I'm sorry, but I'm gonna have to knock your son out.' Freddie Starr was staying in the Europa, where Pizzaro was, and he told me that two nights before the fight he had your man up half the night drinking vodka.

Pizzaro was awful, really dreadful. He ran about the place for a couple of rounds, and then I hit him in the stomach in the fourth. He let a waach! out of him, and his left knee shot up in the air, and referee Bob McMillan stopped it.

*

The Eubanks verdict nagged at McGuigan, and Eastwood recognized that the revenge angle meant another Ulster Hall sell-out. He rematched them for 8 December.

*

The Hall was jammed, packed out again. Eubanks came over six days before the fight and decided he wanted to spar with his manager, Tony Brazil, who'd been a pro lightweight twenty or thirty years earlier. He gave Tony two big black eyes, two lovely shiners. I saw Brazil when I walked into the hotel for the weigh-in, and I couldn't believe it.

It was a great fight. Eubanks did well for four rounds, but then I took over. In the sixth I hit him with a cluster of punches and he was all wobbly. He went back into the ropes. I hit him again and the referee looked at him and then said, 'Stop!' He thought he'd heard the bell, but when he checked with the timekeeper there were still twenty seconds left in the round.

Eubanks came back well in the seventh, but I got him going again in the eighth and this time McMillan stopped it. But it had been a great fight for the crowd, and revenge for me.

Six days later, on 14 December 1981, I got married. Barney was invited, but didn't come. That morning, the doctor took the stitches out of my eye, from where Eubanks had clashed heads with me just before I stopped him; my father-in-law had a horrible sty in his eye as well. We went to Tenerife for our honeymoon, which was cut short after eight days when, tragically, Sandra's Uncle Gordon was killed in a car crash.

Barney had fixed me another fight at the Ulster Hall for 27 January, against Don George of Wales, and I trained all through the honeymoon. I remember skipping on a beautiful marble floor on a verandah in the apartments where we were staying, and a German woman complained about it. She thought I was crazy and called the security guards in, and they made me stop. I had to shadow-box in the room instead, sweating like a pig, so I wouldn't put any weight on.

George pulled out, and I fought Luis de la Sagra of Spain instead. He'd been around and boxed for the European bantamweight title a couple of months previously. He was a real old spoiler, who kept claiming that I was hitting him low. He even did it after I'd hit him a right hook to the chin! De la Sagra had never been stopped in twenty-three fights, and he took me the distance as well, the last man to do so until I fought Juan Laporte.

Two weeks later Paddy Byrne, who was the matchmaker for the World Sporting Club, fixed me up with an easy job against Ian Murray of Manchester. Eastwood told me, 'Don't do him in the first round', so I deliberately let him last. I could have taken him with one punch, and when I went to work I put him down six times and stopped him in the third. That was the first time Eastwood deducted any money from me. The purse was to be £800 but he cut it to £600, and I was really gutted by that, although I didn't have much say in it.

Angel Oliver of Spain was next, back at the Ulster Hall on 23 February. I was supposed to fight Juan Francisco Rodríguez, the former European bantamweight champion who'd won and lost title fights with Johnny Owen, but he had a car crash on the way to the airport and Oliver was sent over instead. Oliver had only been stopped twice in forty-eight fights, but I put him down in the first and twice more in the third, and Bob McMillan stopped it.

I had done a deal with Barney for £5,000 for my first ten fights, and the last of them was against Angelo Licata, a tall, dark-haired, good-looking Italian who had gone ten rounds with Renard for the Benelux title. Renard fought on the same bill, and stopped Ritchie Foster in five rounds. Licata had a decent record and moved well enough in the first round, but in the second I hit him a terrific left hook to the body – wham, and he went down. He got up at five, but I walked in with a jab that splattered his nose before I put him over again and it was stopped.

My left hook to the body was dynamite in those days, and still was when I fought Laporte, though I didn't get through with it later against Pedroza or Taylor, who were as cute as foxes. It's very difficult to land a left hook to the body on a moving target, especially on a cagey guy.

Next time around I boxed Gary Lucas again, at the Lakeland Forum in Enniskillen, and knocked him out in the first round this time. That was some show – Hugh Russell won in the first as well, Danny McAllister [boxing as Young Patsy Quinn] in the second, and Eddie McDermott in the third. But Davy Campbell, a local light-welter, saved the show by boxing the full six rounds.

The body punch I hit Lucas with was probably the second best of my career, or maybe even equally as good as the one I would beat Bernard Taylor with. He came running out as if he was going to have a war with me, but I hit him a right hand that must have dented his ribs. The bell rang to end the round while he was on the floor, but Bob McMillan carried on counting him out. I was impressed with the way I'd improved since I last fought him.

Chapter Nine

'It was as though six months had passed, and the world had stopped for me.'

Barry McGuigan, on the long months while Young Ali lay in a coma.

McGuigan's twelfth professional fight, at the World Sporting Club in London on 14 June 1982, should have been against Steve Farnsworth, a journeyman performer who had won ten of his sixteen pro fights. But Farnsworth pulled out and Paddy Byrne, who also made the matches for the WSC, needed a substitute in a hurry. He booked Asymin Mustapha, a young Nigerian who used the ring name of Young Ali.

Ali held the Nigerian and West Africa bantamweight titles and, while he had yet to box in Britain, his record showed him to be a competent pro who knew his trade thoroughly enough to give McGuigan a decent test, without actually beating him.

*

We weighed in at the Board of Control offices. Because I was approaching a British title fight I had to show that I could weigh in at or around nine stone, to prove that I could make the championship weight. I weighed nine stone and half a pound. Ali got on the scales in fawn-coloured crimplene trousers, and made eight stone thirteen pounds. But he looked lighter, more like a super-bantam or a heavy bantam than a feather.

I never liked boxing in Grosvenor House [the WSC's dinner-boxing shows were held in the Park Lane hotel]. The atmosphere was flat, and I didn't care for it at all.

Ali had Al Phillips, the former European featherweight champion, and Guinea Roger, the old Nigerian light-heavyweight, in his corner.

He was really tough, and in the first round he was fast and lively.

Africans are always tough, and even the skinny ones are very durable. I'd just been feeling him out in the first round, but in the second I stepped the pace up and hit him a lot of solid punches. I was well on top in the third, and in the fourth I hit him hard around the temple. I was digging my heels in when I was hitting him, but he could take a tremendous punch, like another Peter Eubanks. Three or four times I thought he was gone, but he always came back with something. He was fighting like a Trojan. Paddy Byrne was in the corner with me, along with Eddie and Barney. Byrne was good, telling me to be patient.

In the fifth I took an easy round, and his cornermen said to him, 'There you are, he's tired now, you're back in the fight.' I came out for the next round and I hit him four punches, bang, bang, bang-bang, right on the nose. I looked at him and his legs wobbled, and he went down to be counted out.

Eastwood said to me, 'He's hurt, he's badly hurt,' but they got him up and half-carried him to his corner. They helped him through the ropes and I thought, 'Thank God, he's recovered', and I got out of the ring as quick as I could. But as soon as he'd got out of the ring he collapsed again, before he'd walked a dozen steps, and they laid him down on the floor between the dinner tables.

I went up to the dressing-room, and Jarvis Astaire and Mike Barrett came in and told me the kid was away to have an operation.* As soon as they said that I thought about Sandra: Jesus Christ, if that had been me. This poor man's wife was six months pregnant.

People were telling me that it had been a brilliant performance, and that I was a legitimate contender for the British title. Ray Clarke, who was then the General Secretary of the British Boxing Board of Control, came in, and I asked him if Ali was going to be all right. He said, 'I don't know, but he'll get the best possible attention.'

So I went home, and sat around thinking about him and trying to keep in touch. Eastwood was in contact with Ali's people, and I rang him constantly to find out how he was. I wasn't interested in fighting at that stage. I wasn't communicating with anybody. The months dragged on with Ali still in a coma, and eventually they

---

*Astaire, Barrett, Mickey Duff and Terry Lawless comprised the four-man group which dominated British professional boxing for most of the 1970s and early 1980s.

took him home to Nigeria. It was as though six months had passed, and the world had stopped for me. I never thought something like this could happen; I had always thought boxing was just a sport, just a game.

I remember ringing Eastwood and asking what I should do, and he said it wasn't my fault. I used to go down to the handball alleys on my own for hours, just hitting the ball up, trying to get it out of my system. I had an old dog called Bandit and this wee black and tan terrier called Boss, and I used to go ferreting out in the fields.

I was hoping against hope that he would come out of the coma. Bobby Neill [the Scottish featherweight who was British champion in 1959–60] came out of it: lots of fighters had. I was trying to pretend that it wasn't really happening. He was such a young, fit, strong, kid – that's why it affected me so much. He'd given me such a hard fight, and then with that one punch he fell on his face and that was the fight over, everything over. Jesus Christ, I couldn't fathom it.

When he was taken back to Nigeria it made a bigger gap between us, and it became easier to blank it out. It was a horrible time, but eventually I decided that I'd have to get back in training again. Sandra was a great help to me. She was bewildered for a long time; she knew I was going through a trauma, but didn't know how to cope with it. But I suppose nobody really knows ...

I didn't spar very well, or very often. I trained, and then I fought Jimmy Duncan. He was a good, game opponent, very awkward and fought out of a crouch. I moved and boxed all right, but I didn't feel the same fire in my belly. I stopped him in four rounds, with body shots; I'd done a bit of bobbing and weaving, that sort of thing, and got him out of the way, but I wasn't myself.

I fought Paul Huggins after that. It was a British title eliminator, the most important fight I'd had so far, and I stopped him in five rounds. I felt then that I was getting back to myself, getting over it – until, on 13 December 1982, Ali died in Nigeria and that brought it all back again. The post-mortem showed that he had an abnormally thin skull, and it could have happened in any of his fights, but that wasn't really a consolation. I couldn't believe that I could kill somebody, with my own hands. His wife had had a son, and I was hoping to have a son too. It meant even more now; I live for my kids, for my sons and my daughter, and I was glad for Ali's wife that she had a son.

I spent months moping. Sandra was working five days a week to keep us. People were trying to get in touch with me, but I didn't want to talk to anybody. I had hurt my right hand against Huggins, and it was an excuse for me to keep away from training, to stay at home and isolate myself. I was hoping it would all just disappear, I suppose. Eastwood was trying to organize me as if nothing had happened. He was going ahead and I was standing still.

He was saying, 'Do you want to fight for the British title?' and I was saying, 'Yeah, yeah', not really even taking it in. At the end of the day I said to Sandra, 'I'm going to have to go on.' I wanted to be a champion, so that it wouldn't be just another fighter who had killed that young fellow . . .

CHAPTER TEN

'I reckoned that there was no harm in doing them a favour because maybe they could do me one back at some later stage; that's the way this business works.'

Frank Warren, on his early dealings with the Eastwood family

McGuigan's bid to become the first Irishman to be crowned British featherweight champion since Billy 'Spider' Kelly back in 1955 was originally scheduled for the King's Hall, Belfast on 2 March 1983. Steve Sims had relinquished the title in mid-January on being nominated for an ultimately unsuccessful meeting with Loris Stecca of Italy for the vacant European championship, so McGuigan, instead of challenging Sims for the British crown, was now to meet Vernon Penprase for the championship.

This bout was to have been the top of a bill that would include a second British title fight, an all-Belfast bantamweight contest between champion Hugh Russell and challenger Davy Larmour. In mid-February, however, McGuigan was hospitalized with a serious flu bug and was compelled to pull out of the King's Hall promotion.

But all was not lost from the Eastwood standpoint. Russell's title defence against Larmour provided him with an immediate and worthy top-of-the-bill replacement and all that remained to be arranged was a suitable chief support bout. To find one, Eastwood turned to Frank Warren.

Warren, a thirty-one-year-old Londoner, had only been in the boxing business some three years at this stage. The licensed side of the business, that is. A dropout from Highbury County Grammar School at the age of fifteen, Warren had, in rapid succession, sampled a range of jobs that included diverse if brief careers as a clerk in a solicitor's office, a runner for an on-course bookmaker, a porter in a meat market, a partner with footballer Frank McLintock in a London restaurant, a pool-hall owner and then a slot-machine operator. Only at the age of twenty-seven – 'I grew up a bit late' – did he take his first tentative steps into the world of professional boxing. Even then, he did so on the wrong side of the sport's 'law': promoting unlicensed shows around the Finsbury area of London and setting up the National Boxing Council as an unofficial rival body to the long-established (1929) British Boxing Board of Control.

After promoting five such shows Warren, on the mutually recognized principle that if you can't beat them you join them, was granted an official BBBC licence to promote in late 1980 and promptly lost £25,000 on his very first show, an all-American light-heavyweight headliner between Jerry (The Bull) Martin and Otis Gordon at the Bloomsbury Crest Hotel. Undeterred by this potentially crippling setback, and boosted by the proceeds of the lucrative sale of his slot-machine interests, Warren set about taking on the firmly established promotional and managerial hierarchy of British boxing, the Jarvis Astaire–Mickey Duff–Mike Barrett–Terry Lawless alliance.

One of Warren's favourite ways of doing this was through recourse to the courts to break what he – and others – deemed were obvious monopolistic practices resulting from then current BBBC rules. Two Board rules in particular were targeted by Warren: the decree that no British title fight could be televised live, and the one that required a minimum of fourteen days between any two promotions which were to be shown on television, even if the showing was to be on a delayed-transmission basis. Warren's rivals were already the beneficiaries of a lucrative contract with the British Broadcasting Corporation and the Board rules in question, Warren felt, therefore compelled him to suffer unfair restrictions in his trade as a fight promoter.

By carefully scheduling marginally less than four weeks between each of their shows, Duff and his associates could make it impossible for Warren to observe the fourteen-day rule even if he did manage to secure TV backing, while the ban on any live coverage of a British title fight made it virtually impossible for a newcomer such as Warren to attract any television support in the first place.

Warren would ultimately succeed in having both rules overturned, a twin triumph that opened the door for him to his own exclusive promotional package with the Independent Television network. But in fighting his court battles with the British Boxing

Board of Control, he had widened the already deep gulf between himself and the sport's 'establishment'. And with Barney Eastwood by then firmly an establishment figure, Warren and McGuigan's mentor found themselves unavoidably on opposite sides of the British fight game's political divide, even though they had never up to this point had any direct dealings whatsoever with each other.

But Warren, even by early 1983, had put together a rapidly growing stable, a stable that could hardly be ignored at any time and most certainly not by a promoter desperately trying to save his show. Thus Eastwood, in his quest for a back-up contest to the Russell–Larmour bout, included the Warren stable in his search area. One fighter therein who soon attracted Eastwood's interest was Keith Wallace, a Liverpudlian who only a month previously had won the Commonwealth flyweight title with a ninth-round stoppage of Steve Muchoki in London. To fill the number two spot behind Russell's title defence, Eastwood sought to match Wallace with Pat Doherty, a London Irishman who six years later would briefly hold the Commonwealth lightweight championship.

Paddy Byrne, Eastwood's regular matchmaker, was asked to approach Warren about the availability of Wallace. After discussing the matter with his fighter, Warren agreed to let Wallace take the bout at four days' notice and Wallace duly extended his unbeaten record to ten successive wins by taking an eight-round points decision over Doherty. What happened then, though, was to have consequences that few could have imagined at the time.

'I didn't even try to take advantage of their situation by arguing about money,' Warren insists. 'I simply let Keith go ahead and fight to help them save their promotion. I reckoned that there was no harm in doing them a favour because maybe they could do me one back at some later stage; that's the way this business works.

'But, after Keith had beaten Doherty, the Eastwoods disputed what I understood was the agreed purse figure. There was an argument in the dressing-room and in the end I basically told Barney Eastwood to piss off. I had done my best to help them out, yet they were arguing over pennies. And by getting involved with them in the first place I had caused problems for myself because the fight went out on BBC and Wallace's fights were shown on ITV.'

The relationship between the Warren and Eastwood organizations, which up to that point still fell some way short of the boozing buddies category, had instantly crossed the point of no return. Open warfare between Frank Warren and Barney Eastwood had been declared.

Chapter Eleven

*'There has never been a question mark over my identity.
I know who I am: I'm Irish, and I'll always be Irish.'*

Barry McGuigan, on his decision to take out British
nationality in order to contest the British title

It had been twenty-seven years since an Irishman last held the British featherweight title, and the Ulster Hall was crammed on 12 April 1983 to watch McGuigan's attempt to emulate Billy 'Spider' Kelly, the Derryman who was champion for thirteen months in 1955–6. It was two days and twenty-one years since the last Irish challenge – and that, by a remarkable coincidence, had been by another naturalized Monaghan man, Derry Treanor. He had had the misfortune to go up against Howard Winston, a boxer of sublime artistry, who stopped him in fourteen rounds.

McGuigan's task was rather less formidable. Vernon Penprase, a baby-faced twenty-four year-old from Devonport, had never quite fulfilled the potential of his amateur career, which he crowned by contesting a memorable ABA final with Jackie Turner. As a professional, under the guidance of his ex-fighter father Tony, he had won seventeen and drawn one of his twenty-four fights. He was a neat boxer in the classic left-jabbing British mould, and his courage was unquestioned; in his last fight, five months earlier, British bantamweight champion John Feeney had made a painful mess of Penprase's nose but Penprase had endured, stoically, and finished the eight-rounder bloodied but defiantly upright.

The question marks were more against McGuigan than Penprase. Had he completely recovered from the draining, debilitating virus which had sent him to a hospital bed only weeks earlier? And, despite the impressive stoppages of Jimmy Duncan and Paul Huggins, had he put the Young Ali trauma behind him? The answers were emphatic, and convincing.

*

Penprase had a nice jab, but it was never going to be enough to keep me out. I came inside the jab, belted away to the body, and then switched back up again. By the end of the first round there was blood all over the place from his nose, and as soon as the second round started I put him down with a left hook. He was brave, though: he didn't take a count, and tried to fend me off with jabs. But I felt really strong that night, and I battered him with combinations all through the round.

I put him over again with a perfect right-hander, against the ropes in his own corner. He should have stayed down, but he stood up at four. He was in a shocking state, blood everywhere, and referee Harry Gibbs took one look at him and said, 'That'll do.' Getting that Lonsdale Belt strapped around my waist was a wonderful moment.

*

In order to qualify as a contender for the British title, McGuigan had taken the difficult and not universally popular decision to seek British nationality. He had been able to represent Northern Ireland in the Commonwealth Games because he boxed in the Ulster championships, which embraced the historic nine counties of the province rather than the partitioned six counties of 'Northern Ireland', but the professionals were not so easy-going in these matters.

*

Of course, when I took out British citizenship I got a bit of stick from the Republican side. It used to get to me, hurt me and annoy me, because there is nobody more Irish than I am. At the time, I didn't see anything complicated about taking out citizenship. It was just a quick way to get through the red tape, and get to the top: win a British title, then a European, and then the world.

*

Harry Mullan remembers Eastwood phoning him to discuss the move. 'I advised him against it. My view was that McGuigan was so good that the British title was an irrelevance. At that stage, he could have gone straight for a European title, and won it without the risk of upsetting or even alienating his own people.

'Eastwood argued that fighters like Pat and John McCormack* from Dublin and Mick Leahy from Cork had become British without encountering any problems, but I responded that they were men whose potential was limited to British titles anyway, whereas McGuigan was likely to go all the way. Furthermore, the McCormacks and Leahy were known only within the narrow world of professional boxing, whereas McGuigan, even then, was becoming a national figure.

'But Eastwood's mind was already made up, and he dismissed the whole issue by saying, "Sure it's only a piece of paper, anyway."'

*

Looking back, it wasn't worth the trouble. I didn't even get the Lonsdale Belt. Ray Clarke, who was the Board of Control secretary at the time, promised me one but I never heard any more about it. They gave Charlie Magri a Belt because he didn't have a worthwhile challenger. I held the British title for a couple of years, and defended it once, but they never gave me one.

With hindsight, perhaps I shouldn't have taken British nationality. But at that time I was making such progress, and the Irish Boxing Union didn't amount to much. That was why Barney opted for the other route. It was never a big deal to me; I didn't think anything about it.

Certainly, Barney and I never had any major discussions about it. I talked it over with my father, and he wasn't entirely for the

---

* Not to be confused with his Glasgow namesake, who held the British middleweight title for forty-seven days in 1959 and was European champion in 1961–2. The two actually came together in 1966 when the Dublin McCormack won a points decision in an eliminator for the British light-heavyweight title at the Royal Albert Hall, a fight that produced an amusing postscript.

In a sequel which members of the anti-boxing lobby would never appreciate, the two shared a shower and a friendly conversation minutes after they had spent ten rounds attempting to outwit and outpunch each other. After a short while 'Glasgow John' said, 'Hold on a wee minute,' and hastily left the shower. Returning two or three minutes later he handed 'Dublin John' a bottle of beer and then, pulling the shower curtain half-way across, added, 'I'd like you to meet my father.' Handshakes were exchanged and then, without warning, the Scot pulled the curtain the whole way open and added, 'and this is my wife Margaret!' Dublin John, with one hand holding his beer bottle and the other covering his private parts, felt unable to exchange handshakes in this instance and mumbled an apology to that effect. 'Don't worry,' said Margaret McCormack, 'when you've seen one John McCormack you've seen them all!'

idea. But he never had any say in my career, and promised me and Barney when we started out that he would never interfere. He told me, 'If that's what you want to do, then go ahead', but inwardly I felt he didn't like the idea. My mother's attitude was 'Whatever gets you there, do it!'

Even after I'd fought for the British title, though, I still got fabulous support from the hardened Republican areas in Belfast. There were never any threats, or any hate mail. Any rational person could see that it was a career move for me, nothing more. The fact is, I am Irish, and everybody knows that, and nothing changes that. When I walk down the street, people don't say, 'There's that little English fellow.' At the time, the 'Barry The Brit' taunts really hurt me, although I can laugh at it now. There has never been a question mark over my identity. I know who I am: I'm Irish, and I'll always be Irish.

Of course, not everyone in Northern Ireland thinks the way I think, and that's what I couldn't understand. I didn't make the moves, and I didn't make the decisions, but at the time I thought it was the right move. Three of my four children were born in Ireland. When they grow up they can make up their own minds about what they are: my only concern is to give them a good moral and religious background, and after that it's up to them.

*

Sammy Meck should have met McGuigan seven months earlier, but he pulled out a week before the fight and Jimmy Duncan took the job in his place. The hard little African, by now a French national, was booked instead for McGuigan's first appearance as British champion, at Navan Exhibition Centre, roughly equidistant between Dublin and Belfast, on the afternoon of Sunday, 22 May. It was designed to test the water for a big-time promotion involving McGuigan in the Republic; boxing, south of the border, has traditionally been of the amateur variety, but the attendance – estimated at over two thousand – was encouraging.

*

Meck was tough, as hard as nails. His head was in my face the whole time, and I concentrated on not getting cut. But it was inevitable, and in the fourth he banged his head into me and cut me over the left eye, but luckily it wasn't too serious.

I set about him in the fifth, hurt him to the body and rocked him with a left hook. He nearly went from a right in the sixth, and I kept hammering away at him until he finally wobbled into a corner and fell down. He beat the count, but [referee] Freddie Teidt stopped it. There were only two seconds left in the round.

Chapter Twelve

'You fight like a brother, not a white man.'
Puerto Rican Tony Santana to Barry McGuigan, after
sparring with him in New York

A few weeks after beating Meck, McGuigan was off to America for his first taste of the transatlantic fight scene. Eastwood had arranged for him to appear on a BBC-televised show from Chicago on 9 July featuring two other British fighters, Lloyd Honeyghan and Frank Bruno. It was a low-key, low-budget affair, and drew no more than a few hundred spectators – yet they saw two future world champions and Bruno, who would challenge twice for the heavyweight title.

*

We flew into O'Hare Airport; Paddy Byrne, Eddie Shaw, Barney and myself. The idea was to have two fights, one in Chicago and the other in Atlantic City. I wasn't too sure about the second one, as Sandra was heavily pregnant with Blain and I didn't want to be away for too long.

The second night we were there, there was the worst thunderstorm I've ever seen. I was sharing the room with Eddie, and it had big, heavy, black curtains at the window, but even so the lightning was lighting up the whole room, and the thunder was like bombs going off. Next morning Eddie said to me, 'I've never said so many Hail Marys in my whole life!' and I was the same. At breakfast, the old woman who served our table said, 'I think the Big Man must have been trying to make you feel at home.'

We were driven around by a fellow from the west of Ireland called Tony Monaghan, who had been friendly with my father since the 1960s. You'd swear he had never left Connemara – he still had the accent intact. We trained in a Spanish part of the city, in a huge gym with sparse facilities. There was an overhead ball that was very slow, and one big, heavy bag that was hung twenty feet from the ceiling, so that when you'd hit it you would have to wait half an hour for it to come back to you. I sparred first with Dominic Fox, a lad from Belfast who had turned pro in America.

After a couple of days they got me a Mexican called Parajito Marquez, who had fought Jackie Beard and claimed he'd been robbed. He would arrive at the gym with his party, and the ring would be surrounded with Mexicans. Every day it was a real macho thing, to see who would back off first. We did four rounds a day, but they were tougher than eight rounds of ordinary sparring. He would try to batter me, and all round the ring the Mexicans would be hissing and spitting at me. He was hard; every time I'd think he was hurt, he would come flailing back at me with with these long, wide punches, and lots of them. If you'd put a camera in that gym you'd have seen top-class fighting, every day.

The Americans were very impressed with me. They thought I was world class even then, in 1983.

The fight was in a place called DaVinci Manor, an old opera house. The place was empty. We'd got no press coverage at all, but Cedric Kushner and Mickey Duff [the show's co-promoters] weren't too bothered. They had sold the show to the BBC, and they were happy enough to get the TV money. Frank Bruno and Lloyd Honeyghan were on the bill with me, though I didn't see them until the day of the fight. I had a substitute opponent, Lovan McGowan. He'd won four and drawn one of nine. He was a tall, rangy black guy, slender rather than skinny. It's a perfect fighter's build, like Alexis Arguello's.

I kept stalking him. He was snapping out left jabs, hands high. He had a nice style, but I jabbed with him. I always did that, no matter how big a guy was, because if you can outjab a jabber, what has he got left? I have the reach of a man five feet ten, although I'm only five feet six, so I was able to jab up at him. Even if they didn't hit him, they were keeping him occupied. I hit him a couple of right hands and a left hook, then dummied a jab and hit him with one of the best right hands I ever threw. He dropped like a stone. He got up, but was staggering about. I went after him with a couple of body punches and one to the head, and then I rattled a left hook into his guts and I could hear him groan. He fell to the floor and spat out his gumshield, and that was it.

The referee was Italian, very dramatic, and he was on one knee bellowing the count into McGowan's ear like it was a Rocky movie.

But he was wasting his time – all poor McGowan wanted was somebody to help him, for he'd no plans to get up again.

Next day we headed for New York, and stayed at the Ramada Inn on 39th Avenue. We went to Gleason's Gym the first day, just to see what it was like and what was going on. I watched the way the other guys trained, and one of my workouts would have killed them. But they were so relaxed, everything they did.

The place was like an assembly line. There were queues for the punchbag, queues for sparring, queues for the lockers. I found it exciting just to watch. I met Bobby McQuillar and Teddy Atlas there, two great trainers who worked with me later on. Billy and Vinnie Costello, Carmelo Negron and Henry Brent were working out, and a lot of other fighters I didn't know, and the Viruet brothers, Edwin and Adolfo, were helping with the training. The place was an absolute dive, and the stench would have knocked you sideways, but I loved it and wanted to do my work there too.

I started working there the next day, and the day after that I sparred with Vinnie Costello and Tony Santana, who was one of the best junior lightweights in the world at the time. Costello tried to take my head off, but I beat the shit out of him, punched him to pieces. I did two rounds with him, and was tired at the end of them. It was stifling hot in the gym, in the middle of the day, with these big sparring gloves on and Costello trying to do a murder job on me.

I sparred Santana next, and was well able to handle him too. Afterwards, Santana said to me, 'You fight like a brother, not a white man.'

This went on for four or five days, and the sparring was always hard. One day Santana wasn't there, and Vinnie Costello was getting ready to go into camp with his brother Billy, who was training to fight Bruce Curry for the WBC light-welterweight title. Victor Valle, Costello's trainer, said Vinnie wouldn't be sparring, so I shadow-boxed, worked the pads and moved around for a few rounds with Henry Brent. I'd finished the workout, nine rounds altogether, when Valle came over and said, 'Vinnie'll spar with you after all.' He was trying to do a job on me again, and he had Billy at the ringside shouting at him. But I battered him again, and when I got out Billy said to me, 'Man, you whipped his ass good! You're a world-class fighter.' Coming from him, a guy who'd soon be a world champion, that was a great confidence builder.

But anyway, the fight in Atlantic City didn't seem as if it was going to materialize, and I was getting anxious to be with Sandra. Eddie had already gone back to Belfast; he was a real home bird, always. We'd been away the best part of a month, so Barney and I talked about it and decided we'd done enough for one trip. But I'd enjoyed it, and the experience was worthwhile.

*

Most fighters encounter substitute opponents from time to time, but Barry McGuigan seemed to be making a career out of it. He was scheduled to meet a Puerto Rican, Hector Sanchez, at the Ulster Hall on 5 October 1983, but Sanchez pulled out at short notice and Ruben Herasme was hustled in from the Dominican Republic as a replacement. He was hardly worth his air fare, let alone the £5,000 which Stephen Eastwood told the *Sunday Mirror*'s Scottish edition (9 October) Herasme's brief appearance had cost him. It was a vintage McGuigan performance, and the left hook to the body which dropped the Dominican for the full count in the second round reassured Barney Eastwood that his gambler's instinct in arranging McGuigan's next fight had been sound. For on 16 November the King's Hall would reopen to championship boxing, with McGuigan topping the bill against Italy's Valerio Nati, and the vacant European title on the line.

*

I didn't know much about Nati, only that he'd given Loris Stecca a good run for the European title. We asked Stecca to come to Belfast, but he relinquished the title and the European Boxing Union nominated Nati instead.

Nati had moved up from bantamweight, where he'd beaten John Feeney twice in European title fights. He'd only lost twice out of twenty-eight fights, and he'd never been stopped, so it looked as if he would be a tough opponent. The Hall was about 80 per cent full, and I had my first taste of the King's Hall atmosphere. When I saw the place first, I thought it was a big old barn with no atmosphere at all, but that soon changed when I started fighting there.

I tried to box-fight him, rather than storm into him. For a couple of rounds I outjabbed him, popped his head back. He was very defensive, and fought out of a crouched-over, crab stance. He kept complaining that I was hitting low, and the referee [Kurt Halbach of Germany] warned me a few times and even threatened to disqualify me. I was always guilty of throwing punches to the top of the foul-proof cup, but I never in my entire life hit a boy deliberately low. The punches were always around the top of the cup, because the target area is so small.

I used to aim for a four-inch square behind the guy's right elbow. There's no point in hitting him in the solar plexus, because he's got three layers of muscle there, upper, middle and lower abdominals, and that's just a wasted punch. I'd give him one up the middle, to bring his arm across, and then I'd bury the hook in that four-inch square just to the right of his elbow. The ribs are there to protect the lung, and if you hit them right they'll go in and semi-paralyse the lung. It's like getting hit in the stomach when the muscles are relaxed; you can't get a breath, and you have to wait until that feeling of paralysis goes. That's how to wind a person, and I perfected it.

But Nati was cute enough to block a lot of them, and as the fight progressed and he sweated a lot, the punches were slipping off him and on to the top of the cup. But even if ten of them fell short, one would get through, and he was being worn down.

He neither came forward nor went back, and I didn't know what to do with him. When I attacked him he'd cage up like a crab, so I had to be patient. Eventually I got him in the fourth and hurt him quite a bit [Nati was later found to have three cracked ribs], but then I eased off, because I was a bit uncertain how I would cope if the fight went into the later rounds. He came back well in the fifth, and fought better than he'd done before. He opened up on me, but I blocked and slipped a lot of them. He had a bit of power there, but nothing exceptional, and by the end of the round I was on top again.

I battered him in the sixth with body shots and right hands to the head, until finally he went down. He didn't make an attempt to get up; he had lost heart entirely.

There was great excitement afterwards. I felt really fantastic, to have won the European title in the same ring where Freddie Gilroy and John Caldwell had fought. I was proud to be alongside them.

Chapter Thirteen

'[Barney] *said he was a very rich man, who wasn't doing it for the money, but for the love of the game.*'
Barry McGuigan, on his early financial dealings with Eastwood

In the beginning Barney and I got on very well together. My first impression was that he seemed to be a very sincere and genuine kind of man, and also very suave and sophisticated. He told me at our first meeting that he felt sure I could go all the way and that between the two of us we'd be able to get professional boxing going again in Belfast. He also said he was a very rich man, who wasn't doing it just for the money, but for the love of the game. My father, I think, was a little bit dubious and perhaps felt he was too sweet to be wholesome, but he never got involved in the relationship or interfered in any way.

The deal he offered in the beginning was that I would be paid £5,000 for my first ten fights. When you're less than a month past your twentieth birthday a figure like £5,000 seems a lot of money, but as things turned out it was very, very little. I didn't know at the time, for instance, that I would be topping the bill in the Ulster Hall in only my fourth pro fight, and that within another fight or two there would be a full house every time I fought. Barney has since claimed that he had to give away tickets for my fights to make it look as if we had a good crowd, but anybody who was going to shows in Belfast in those days knows that I had no trouble filling the Ulster Hall any night of the week. Maybe he did hand out a few tickets to one or two of the very early shows, but once I stopped Peter Eubanks in our return fight there was never any problem in getting a full house.

The problems between us really started coming thick and fast when that first ten-fight deal ran out after I had beaten Angelo Licata [a year to the day after the contract had been signed and just ten months after McGuigan's professional debut], because then we had to negotiate a purse for each separate fight. And it didn't take me long to find out how totally helpless I really was.

He has said somewhere since we split that I would always leave the money to just a few days before a fight and then start arguing over it. In fact, he was the one who would put the subject of money on the long finger. It's obvious that I'd want to know as soon as possible exactly how much I'd be getting for a particular fight, but I could never pin him down on it. He'd announce the fight first and only then, a couple of weeks later, would he even discuss money.

He usually tried to fob the money situation off on his son Stephen, saying that Stephen was the promoter and that the reason I couldn't have any more money for a particular fight was that he – and not Barney – wouldn't give it to me. But Stephen was never much more than a figurehead. When he dropped out as promoter after the Pedroza fight he was replaced by Al Dillon, who worked in Barney's office. But Barney still called the shots, regardless of whether Stephen or anybody else was the promoter of record.

And even if Stephen had been the promoter in the true sense, how could Barney be expected to be able to get the best possible deal for me – which, as my manager, he was obliged to do – when the promoter he was negotiating with was his own son? And if he was not a promoter, then how come he shared in the benefits of Eastwood Promotions, as he later acknowledged?

When I bought my first house in Clones, when Sandra and I were getting married, I got a County Council loan but I needed bridging finance until it came through. The house cost £18,500 and the bridging I needed was £14,000. Barney said he would help me and, in fairness, he did. He gave me the £14,000 until the loan came through from the Council. It should have been only six weeks, but it ended up at something like twice that. When the money from the Council eventually arrived, I went up to Belfast to pay Barney back. He wasn't there so I gave it to Stephen. I thought that was all there was to it, but Stephen pulled out a calculator and began adding up figures. Then he said to me, 'The interest on that comes to £616. I don't want it but the oul fella will.' I know that strictly speaking there was nothing wrong with Barney looking for interest, but he was always telling me how rich he was and how well he'd look after me, so I never dreamed that he'd charge me for the loan – and £616 was an awful lot of money to me then. I told Stephen that I'd need a while to pay it, but then he said, 'We'll forget about it.' But, just to let me know that he had done me a big favour, he added: 'I've just given you £616. Remember that.'

When I beat Paul Huggins in an official final eliminator for the British title in November 1982, in my fourteenth fight, all I got was £700. I was paid the same for the fight before that, the one against Jimmy Duncan; and for the two previous ones, my second one with Gary Lucas and then the Young Ali fight, I got £600 and then £750. I was paid £1,500 for winning the vacant British title against Vernon Penprase. That fight was in April 1983 and it meant that by then I'd been a professional for exactly two years and had had fifteen fights, from which I had earned a total of precisely £9,250 – a long way short of the kind of money that people assumed I was making.

After becoming British champion, I had four more fights during 1983. The money improved slightly, but it still wasn't what anyone could call great. I earned £10,000 altogether for the four fights [against Sammy Meck, Lavon McGowan, Ruben Herasme and then the European title-winning one against Valerio Nati]. All my fights had both sponsorship and television money by this time, yet by far my biggest purse was the £3,500 I got for the Nati fight, and that was the one that opened up the King's Hall again with its capacity of seven thousand. By the end of 1983 I had been a pro for two and a half years, had won all but one of my nineteen fights and was the reigning European and British champion and, with total earnings of £19,250, had averaged fractionally over £1,000 per fight. Yet even then the papers were carrying stories about how much money I was supposed to be making; one Dublin paper, for example, said that for winning the British title against Penprase my purse was £10,000 and that I got twice that for the Nati fight.

*

On 26 April 1983 Eastwood wrote a single-sentence letter to Ray Clarke, the General Secretary of the BBBC. Citing section 6 of the manager and boxer Articles of Agreement, Eastwood invoked his option 'to renew my manager's contract with Barry McGuigan, when it expires, for a further three-year period'.

Section 6 of the standard BBBC contract is headed 'Duration' and, in clause 2, says: 'If at any time during the continuance of this Agreement the Boxer shall become British, European, Commonwealth or World Champion as recognized by the BBBC, the

Manager shall be entitled upon giving not less than sixty days' prior written notice ("the Extension Notice") to the Boxer and the Board to extend the duration of this Agreement for such further period as is specified in the Extension Notice.' Even allowing for the required sixty days' advance indication, Eastwood exercised the Extension Notice a full nine months earlier than necessary ... and within exactly two weeks of McGuigan becoming British champion.

Within six weeks of McGuigan winning the European title with his victory over Valerio Nati at the King's Hall, the financial differences between fighter and manager had reached a previously untouched nadir. McGuigan, his determination fuelled by mounting frustration and resentment at what he was coming to regard as a deliberate attempt by Eastwood to keep him in the dark about business matters that directly concerned him, crossed a threshold he had always shied away from in the past and hinted that if he could not get the information he wanted regarding his financial affairs, then he would hire somebody who could.

He arranged for Leo Rooney, his mother's brother and a chartered accountant then living and working in London, to talk to Eastwood on his behalf.

'I had been home in Clones for a few days over the Christmas of 1983,' Rooney explained. 'I returned to England on 27 December, but a few days later Paddy McGuigan phoned me and said that Barry was concerned about the whole structure of his financial arrangements with Eastwood and that he, Paddy, wanted somebody – preferably somebody with a financial background, as I had – to talk to Eastwood on Barry's behalf. I flew back over to Ireland the following day – I am pretty certain it was 30 December – and then had my first-ever meeting with Eastwood, along with Barry and Pat McGuigan, in his office over the bookie shop in Castle Street.

'Even then I expressed my concern that fighters were traditionally the easiest prey for mismanagement as far as finances were concerned. I was not, I might emphasize, referring to their managers in general and certainly not to Eastwood in particular; I was speaking of the fighters themselves from their own point of view, of getting a lot of money and losing it, and of falling foul of the taxman – Roberto Duran or Joe Louis probably being the classic examples.

'My primary concern was that Barry McGuigan should get on an even financial footing and that a proper *modus operandi* with Eastwood be established. What worried me most of all was the possibility that, perhaps three years down the line, McGuigan would have a massive tax bill slapped on him. McGuigan at this stage was clearly on the move; from a commercial standpoint he was obviously "good stuff" (he was marketable) – and that was why we wanted to get together.

'In addition, Pat McGuigan, both because he had spent almost his entire working life in show business and because he was well read and knowledgeable about what had happened to countless other boxers down the years – he always, for instance, talked of Randolph Turpin and what had happened to him – felt that Barry should be protected from many of the managers and promoters in the boxing business.

'I mentioned to Eastwood that now that McGuigan – already European champion – was going to be a big-money fighter, I was concerned that the money should be regulated. I said that we should have to look at the whole situation from a tax perspective, that Barry might have to set up a company to look after his tax affairs.

'At this stage McGuigan had never seen a contract or details of the accounts for any of his fights. Under the Board of Control's Regulations, any fighter is entitled to ask his manager for the full details of his purse and how it is made up, of the television and sponsorship aspects and of the individual fight contract. But McGuigan never knew anything about any of those figures. He not only never saw any of them, he had never even asked to see them, because he did not know what he was entitled to see or know about. That's how green he and the rest of us were then: we were all virgins in the boxing game. But we learned, and we learned damned quickly.

'My number one concern then [at the end of 1983] was to ensure that McGuigan's financial affairs were not going to be wide open to an attack by the Revenue Commissioners. To that end, I insisted to Eastwood that McGuigan be paid at all times by cheque. Prior to this, it had mostly been done by cash. Barney seemed to want it that way but, as I said to Barry, "One man's cash is another man's problem."

'As an accountant, I wanted all cash payments to be kept as small as possible – and every amount, however small, was declared by us to the Inland Revenue.'

Chapter Fourteen

'All boxers accept that they have to get hit with punches, but there is a very thin line between taking enough punches and taking too many.'

Barry McGuigan, on a tough fight with Charm Chiteule

McGuigan ended 1984 as European and British champion, and was voted Britain's Boxer of the Year by the readers of the trade paper, *Boxing News*. He had arrived as a major force on the international scene, a position which Eastwood aimed to consolidate with another King's Hall appearance, on 26 January 1984. The opponent this time was a veteran Zambian, Charm Chiteule, a globetrotter who divided his time between Africa, Germany, London and America. Chiteule was thirty, and on the wrong side of the hill, but McGuigan was about to learn that he was still a formidable performer.

*

I knew Chiteule would be a tough job. Shortly before I fought him he went twelve rounds with Refugio Rojas for the USBA [United States Boxing Association] super-featherweight title, and he'd been leading Azumah Nelson for ten rounds before Nelson caught him with a right and knocked him out. Chiteule had been around for a long time, and had a great reputation, but Barney judged the time was about right to take him.

It was a final eliminator for the Commonwealth title, which Nelson still held.

I felt a bit ponderous that night. I tried to box with him, which was wrong; to beat him at his own game, which was sharp counterpunching, instead of going straight at him. As the fight progressed he hit me in the right eye a few times with his thumb, and from the fourth onwards the eye started to swell and close. I don't know if it was deliberate or not, but his thumb kept poking into the eye and I complained about it to Roland Dakin, the referee.

I was taking a fair bit of punishment that I shouldn't have taken. I tried to be a bit macho with him, stand there and let him hit me, which was a silly thing to do. If I'd been sensible I'd have stayed on top of him, rolling and bobbing. I was wearing boots that had no resin on them, to help me slip and manoeuvre across the canvas. It felt as if I was anchored to the ground, stuck to the canvas. I couldn't slither forward the way I liked.

But that's not an excuse. I just went about the job the wrong way, used the wrong tactics. He was a very accurate puncher, who never missed. Any time I gave him an opportunity, he was in there. He was a solid rather than devastating puncher, but he kept sticking the thumb in my eye.

Eventually I said, 'Here goes, boy', and I went for him. I threw a lot of low punches, but not deliberately. My eye was closing rapidly and affecting my range, and besides, I always aimed the body punches close to the borderline. He had such pinpoint accuracy that he was picking me off as I came in, and I couldn't get my shots in. Between the frustration, the lack of accuracy and the bad vision, I was throwing a lot of borderline punches – and quite a few that weren't even borderline, but were low. Roland Dakin warned me twice, and came to the corner before the tenth to say, 'Once more and you're out.'

I had got right on top in the ninth and in the tenth I pounded away at him until Dakin came in to stop it with forty-five seconds left in the round. I got a lot of criticism for that performance, but the fact was that I'd done exactly what Nelson had done, the only difference being that I didn't lay him out the way Nelson had. Although Chiteule had been doing well and hitting me a lot, I was coming forward and winning rounds with my aggression. But Nelson was losing all the way, until he hit Chiteule in the tenth. I had won five, maybe six rounds, and felt that I was dominating the fight.

I was disappointed afterwards, but I put it down to a learning experience. I was young, and if I'd fought him again six months later I would have knocked him out much sooner than that. I knew that I'd made mistakes and used the wrong tactics, and that I couldn't afford to make mistakes like that again.

All boxers accept that they have to get hit with punches, but there is a very thin line between taking enough punches and taking too many. If you step over that dividing line, you are gone; your reflexes are slower, you lose that little bit of awareness of punches coming towards you, that inbuilt radar that enables you to see punches coming and avoid them. You lose that, the more punches you absorb.

On the way up through the ranks you have to fight good opponents at each different level; top fifteen, top ten, top five and then the world title. All the way through those stages, you have to pick opponents who can give you a test, yet you must have the ability to beat them without taking too many punches. It's a vicious circle; if you want to progress like that, learning without being hit, you have to be defensive-minded, but if you want to attract the crowds, you have to be aggressive, and when you're aggressive you're going to get hit.

It's very difficult to come forward and entertain the people, beat all these punchers and world-class fighters, and yet not take punches. It is hard to create a balance, but the ones who manage to do so are the ones who get there, the champions. Thank God I still have plenty of savvy, but I have to admit that I suffered a certain amount of damage. My memory is not as reliable as I'd like it to be, and there are times when I say silly things out of context, that I'd prefer not to have said. People will say, 'Sure we all do that', but they don't, or at least to the extent that an ex-pug would.

It's the price we have to pay, and we budget for it.

Chapter Fifteen

'I knew I could get rid of them quickly, and could make it fairly painless if I got them right and knocked them out properly.'

Barry McGuigan, on fighting inferior opponents

I had got a bit of stick for the Chiteule fight from people who thought I had made heavy weather of it, so I was a wee bit concerned about fighting José Caba next. He had given Eusebio Pedroza [the WBA champion] fifteen good rounds, and I had watched him against Jackie Beard.* He battered Beard all over the place and put him down. He was a very dangerous puncher, and I wondered if we were doing the right thing, but I got myself in great shape for him.

Bobby McQuillar came over to work with me for the fight, and brought his light-welterweight, Ricky Young, to spar with me. They had watched me in Gleason's in New York the previous summer, and they saw a marked improvement.

I knew I had to change my tactics. I couldn't stand and trade with Caba because he was such a good hitter. I had watched the way Pedroza fought him, and decided on an in–out kind of battle. I outboxed him from the start, stayed out of the way and jabbed, jabbed, jabbed. He was lunging at me, but I was very quick and evasive.

McQuillar was very cool in the corner. He was brilliant, the epitome of the way a corner should be handled. Eddie wasn't too pleased at him being there, but McQuillar talked calmly and sensibly to me, leaning in from outside the ropes and whispering in my ear. He told me to pick Caba apart and take it from there, and that's what I did. I snapped his head back with jabs, and his eyes were all

---

*In October 1983, in his last fight before meeting McGuigan, Caba had been outpointed by Pedroza in a WBA title challenge at St Vincent, Italy.

watered from the jabs hitting his nose. I never took the jab out of his face.

I remember slipping all three of his punches in a combination, and then making him miss with two head shots and pulling my body back to miss the left hook to the body; I was pleased with that. I just wore him down, bundled him around. McQuillar told me at the beginning of the seventh round, 'You're doing a good job. He's ready to go.'

I punched him to pieces. I didn't really settle and punch him hard, I just took him apart, in and out without staying long enough to hit solidly. At one stage, in the seventh, I hit him with two and stayed there for the third, and he nailed me with a good right hand, so I got back on my toes again, bouncing in and out.

The referee was Jim Brimmell, and it was his last job before a terrible fall a week later that ended his career and left the poor man crippled. I was battering Caba along the ropes in the seventh, and Brimmell let him take it. I went in again, and Caba's head was going all over the place as Brimmell jumped in to stop it. Caba was actually in the process of throwing a left hook, and it hit Jim right up the balls. It was funny, although I'm sure Jim didn't think so.

I really felt pleased with the win. I'd done in seven rounds what Pedroza hadn't been able to do in fifteen. Caba had taken some stick from Pedroza and hadn't fought since then, but he was certainly a fresh guy and a lively opponent.

*

Caba had indeed been 'a lively opponent', but the same could not be said of the next man to face McGuigan. In one of those logic-defying decisions which have become their trademark, the European Boxing Union (EBU) nominated a Spanish bantamweight, Esteban Eguia, as the official contender for McGuigan's European featherweight title. The Spaniard had scaled only one and a half pounds over the bantamweight limit in his last fight, a ten-rounds points defeat in London by the Commonwealth flyweight champion Keith Wallace four months earlier.

In his own category, Eguia was not a bad fighter: he had won forty-one, drawn two and lost four of his forty-seven fights, and earned a draw in 1980 with Cecilio Lastra, whom Eusebio Pedroza had dethroned as WBA featherweight champion. Ominously, though, he had also been knocked out in five rounds by Valerio Nati, the man whom McGuigan had crushed in becoming champion. The BBBC protested about Eguia's nomination, but the EBU were adamant. Mickey Duff and Mike Barrett used the match to showcase McGuigan in his first major appearance in London, and the fight duly went on in front of a near-capacity crowd at the Albert Hall on 5 June 1984.

The pressure was on McGuigan for several reasons. He was keen to impress the London fight public, whose only previous chance to see him had been in a down-the-bill six-rounder against Gary Lucas three years previously. More importantly, he was about to make his American TV debut. Eastwood had concluded a deal with the CBS network to screen McGuigan's next fight, a ten-rounder at the King's Hall on 30 June against New Yorker Paul DeVorce, winner of all but one of his twenty-three fights.

*

There was never any problem motivating myself for a fight like that. It was just a matter of making sure that I didn't make any mistakes, because it was vitally important that I didn't screw up at this stage, with the American TV date coming up in three weeks. I was never worried that I might hurt people like Eguia or Farid Gallouze [an outgunned French challenger McGuigan would face nine months later]. I knew I could get rid of them quickly, and could make it fairly painless if I got them right and knocked them out properly.

I was always afraid that I would look crappy in that sort of fight. Eguia had given Keith Wallace a good fight, and Wallace had proved that he could take on featherweights when he beat Pat Doherty; he beat Doherty as easily as he was beating flyweights and bantamweights, so from that point of view I was concerned that Eguia could make me look mediocre, and bring me down to his level.

I didn't really want the fight, but I had to go through with it. Anyway, I had to make weight for Eguia the same as I would for a world title fight, which meant that I had to work just as hard in training. I tried to drill it into myself that this guy was a danger to me, that he was liable to cut me and beat me, and that my job was to get rid of him as quickly as I could and look good in doing it.

I had a look at him in the first round, then put him down twice in the second. He was game, though – he got up and came flailing back at me. I tried to nail him and bang him out of there, and I got him in the third. A long left hook and a right hand finished him; he bounced off the floor and didn't get up.

*

Paul DeVorce, twenty-eight years old, was a stocky, powerfully built black man from New York. He had been a fine amateur, beating Henry Brent in the 1977 New York Golden Gloves flyweight final and losing on points to Hector Camacho in the 1979 bantamweight final. But his pro career, while successful in statistical terms, seemed to be going nowhere in particular. His only loss in twenty-three fights had been on points against the world-rated Jackie Beard, in a North American Boxing Federation title challenge in November 1983. That fight, on the undercard of Marvin Hagler's middleweight title defence against Roberto Duran in Las Vegas, had been DeVorce's only taste of the big time, and the offer to fight McGuigan on live CBS TV was an unexpected second chance for him.

*

I knew how important it was to make an impression on American TV, and that gave an extra little edge of tension to the fight. The place was packed again – around 7,000 – and DeVorce got the crowd at it by doing a flashy warm-up routine, but once the fight started I found him surprisingly easy to hit. He was a little guy – five-three – and I kept banging the jab into his face and switching hooks up and down, head to body.

He didn't really start throwing punches until late in the third, when he stood and traded with me. The crowd were going mad; we couldn't hear the bell and carried on fighting, until Eddie Shaw jumped into the ring between us. DeVorce shook me at the start of the fourth with a right to the head and a left uppercut, but I backed him to the ropes and kept him there most of the round, working away to the body.

He looked like he was ready to go, and I went for him in the fifth, rattling in hooks to the body until finally he grabbed the top rope and half-turned away, making it obvious he wanted out, and [referee] Sid Nathan stopped the fight. The American TV commentators thought that he had been too hasty. Believe me, DeVorce wouldn't have lasted another round. He'd been soaking up the body punches, and he was completely gone. When Nathan came in he didn't protest, because he knew that he was ready to be taken.

*

Sid Nathan's answer to his critics was concise, and complete. 'Go and ask the boy if he thought I was hasty – he's not complaining. I know he hadn't gone down, but he was taking all the punishment he needed to standing up. He'd had enough, and he knew it.'

The build-up towards a world title challenge continued with another King's Hall appearance, on 13 October 1984. The scheduled opponent was Angel Levi Mayor of Venezuela, who had lasted the full fifteen rounds against Eusebio Pedroza in a foul-filled title challenge five months previously. NBC bought the match for live transmission, and were none too pleased when the Venezuelan failed to arrive in Belfast.

The replacement, though, was acceptable. Felipe Orozco of Colombia had been beaten only once in twenty fights, by World Boxing Council (WBC) super-bantamweight champion Jaime Garza in a title bid earlier in the year. At five feet eleven he was the tallest man McGuigan had faced. He was also the first southpaw the Irishman had faced as a pro, but intensive sparring with former WBC super-featherweight champ Cornelius Boza-Edwards, a classy southpaw who was featured on the King's Hall undercard, removed McGuigan's lingering doubts.

The Belfast fight crowd had no such reservations. They started queueing for tickets at noon that day and the show was another complete sell-out. The atmosphere they generated helped make NBC feel they'd had value for money, even if the action was decidedly abbreviated...

*

I thought Angel Mayor was going to be a bit of a dark horse, a tough old fight, so I'd trained hard to fight an orthodox opponent, and then at the last minute Orozco was brought in. I had no local southpaw sparring, so I worked with Boza – what a lovely fellow, but what a hard man! He had left his weight a bit late, so he was a big, full lightweight, nine-nine or heavier. We had a war for four rounds, and at the end of it I knew I could handle Orozco.

It was an easy fight – I knocked him out in two rounds. Some people said he was a mug, but he wasn't. He took Brian Mitchell the distance in 1990, and he went ten good rounds with Rocky Lockridge too. But I didn't think he was anything at all. I just walked through him.

He was a big guy, but slender. He'd been training in Florida for a fight, so he was ready. He boxed lively enough in the first round, but went to pieces when I caught him in the second. I hit him with a perfect combination – left hook, right hook, double left and right again, and he went down, sprawling on his side. I could feel the punches all the way up my arm, and I knew he'd had enough. Probably he could have beaten the count; he started getting up at nine and a half, and complained that he'd made it in time, but I don't think his heart was in it.

*

The impressive destruction of Felipe Orozco whetted American interest in McGuigan, and negotiations opened for a match against a world-class opponent in February 1985. But before that there was a little local difficulty to be resolved. For the first time since he had become British champion twenty months previously, a challenger had emerged – a smooth-boxing part-time cabbie from Slough called Clyde Ruan. McGuigan's European title would automatically be involved, which made it a more attractive package for BBC-TV, which screened the fight live from the Ulster Hall on 19 December.

Ruan, twenty-four years old, had covered much of the same ground as McGuigan. His twenty-three fights (only two defeats) included wins over Peter Eubanks, whom he stopped in eight rounds, and Paul Huggins, whom he outpointed in a Southern Area title fight. Both Eubanks and Huggins were floored by the crisp-punching Ruan, whose victims also included Steve Sims and Jimmy Duncan. But there is a painful gap between a good-pro craftsman and a world contender, as McGuigan was about to demonstrate with icy efficiency and a minimum of fuss.

*

Ruan was a time-wasting exercise, a water-treading fight. I only took it because if I didn't fight him I would forfeit either or both of my titles. I had everything to lose and nothing to gain. The press thought that he wasn't going to give me any sort of a test, so I was in a situation where if I knocked him out in a few rounds they would say, 'Well, we told you so', or if I took a few rounds longer than I should have, they would say, 'McGuigan's not really up to it.'

Three days before the fight, my grandfather Rooney died, and I was very upset about it. I remember driving back from his funeral, crying my eyes out. I had to spar that afternoon when I got back to the gym. I didn't feel like doing it, but I knew that I had to if I was to keep my weight in check.

The Ulster Hall was jammed, the atmosphere was tremendous, and I was very much aware of the fact that I wanted to give the crowd value for money. I thought Ruan was quick, having watched him win his final eliminator against Pat Doherty. He had fast hands that night, and a sharp right hand, but when our fight started he seemed as slow as a carthorse. I stayed right in distance, up close to him, and hit him when I liked.

He said after the fight that I 'was like a ghost', meaning that he would try to counter and I wouldn't be there, and that was exactly what I wanted to hear. That was what I had planned to do; give him something, and be gone when he tried to return the punches.

I intended to let the fight go a couple of rounds. I wasn't planning just to walk in there and blast him out of it. By the fourth, he was exhausted. He had thrown a lot of punches at me, but I had avoided them very well and kept out of the way. I went after him in the fourth and took the wind out of him with a body shot. He came back with a left hook and put so much effort into it that, when it missed, his own momentum made him fall over. I was on him as soon as he got up, with three jabs and a left hook that swept him clean off his feet. There was no way he was going to get up from that.

*

The dismissal of Ruan had been accomplished with economy and precision, and served only to underline the extent of McGuigan's superiority over the rest of the field at domestic level. At another time, Ruan might have been good enough to wear the Lonsdale

Belt, but this was McGuigan's time, and all that Ruan and the others could do was wait for him to move on to higher things and leave them to scramble for the British title. That day came closer with the announcement, early in January, that Barney Eastwood's son Stephen (who was nominally the promoter for McGuigan's fights) and his American agent, Mickey Duff, had secured an opponent of shining quality for McGuigan's US TV date in February: the former WBC champion Juan Laporte.

Chapter Sixteen

> *'The punch sent tingles all the way down to my feet, shock waves of pain right through my body. A big spark went off in my head, and it felt as if there were goose pimples inside me, pins and needles right down to my foot.'*
>
> Barry McGuigan, describing what it felt like to be hit by Juan Laporte

Juan Laporte was a hard man, and the New York-based Puerto Rican was still at the peak of his considerable powers when he signed to face McGuigan in the King's Hall on 23 February 1985. He had a pedigree far above anyone McGuigan had so far met. Still only twenty-five, he had already won three out of five fights for the WBC featherweight title, as well as surviving fifteen bitter rounds with Eusebio Pedroza in a bid for the WBA title. He took the magnificent Salvador Sanchez the full fifteen rounds in his first world title challenge in December 1980, and when Sanchez was killed in a car crash, Laporte stopped Mario Miranda in ten to win the vacant title. He retained it against Ruben Castillo and Johnny de la Rosa, lost a surprising non-title match to McGuigan's sparmate Gerald Hayes, and then broke his thumb in the second round of a title defence against the brilliant super-bantamweight champion Wilfredo Gomez. Even one-handed, he forced Gomez to go the whole twelve rounds to beat him.

The McGuigan match was made at nine stone two, mainly to protect Laporte's options. He had scored a two-round knockout over Rocky Lockridge for the United States Boxing Association featherweight title in 1981, and as Lockridge now held the WBA super-featherweight title, Laporte fancied his chances of a rematch. But a win over McGuigan would, of course, put him right back in line for a featherweight title chance. He came to Belfast as a winner, having outpointed Dwight Pratchett (another one-time sparmate of McGuigan's) in November 1984. That was his twenty-fifth win (thirteen inside schedule) in thirty fights.

*

Laporte was the last hurdle before the world title, and the biggest fight I'd ever had. I knew that every fight was crucially important, but this was a big step up in class. I wondered if I was good enough, or experienced enough, to handle Laporte. I am one of those people who are always pessimistic but also very, very self-confident. Outwardly very confident, but inwardly pessimistic, never showing what I really thought. I would worry to myself, 'Can I really beat this guy?' and then I'd tell myself, 'Of course I can – I'll destroy him.' I liked to have Dermot there, because his assurances would give me the confidence I needed.

It was always the same no matter who I fought, but particularly with Laporte. I knew he was a very dangerous right-hand puncher. He had knocked out Rocky Lockridge, and fought the last ten rounds against Wilfredo Gomez, when he lost the title, with a broken thumb. He went on to prove me right – he took Chavez to a whisker of beating him, and even in 1991 he's still a top-class fighter. The thing that I worried about was that I knew he was a laid-back counterpuncher, and there were times in previous fights when I had made mistakes through lapses of concentration. If I did the same thing two or three times, a cute guy would say, 'OK, do it again', and then bingo, he'd connect.

I knew there were two ways to fight Laporte: stay on top of him or outbox him. Punch fast and move out of the way or else stay with him, never give him a moment's rest. When he'd start punching, you'd stop, and as soon as he'd stop, you start, all the time rolling and slipping inside. When he starts throwing his big bombs, get your head out of the way, tuck up, but never exchange with him when he's throwing. Even when he's unloading, stay close to him, right up tight so that he can't get a fourpenny one at you.

CBS were covering the fight in America, and they arrived a few days beforehand with their commentator, Gil Clancy. He had trained Laporte and they were very confident. They were here to blow me out of the water. It was Laporte's chance to slip straight into another title fight by beating the McGuigan sensation, proving that he was just another European false alarm.

I invariably made a thing of shaking hands with my opponents when I met them and being nice to them. I would never spit or shout at them; I'd say, 'How are you doing? Nice to meet you. Hope we have a good fight,' and they would all look at me as if to say, 'What's this guy playing at?' But Laporte was different, and I remember it so well. We had passed each other three or four times when he was using the gym and I wasn't, and eventually one day he was coming down the stairs and saw me, and said, 'Ah, at last! It's really good to meet you,' and made a big fuss of me. And I was impressed; I thought, 'Now you're up in the real class', because he was doing the same thing I had been at. I already knew he could fight, but now I knew he was a classy individual too – and very smart.

Early in a fight, I liked to feel how powerful a guy was when I would go close to him. You can feel the physical strength, the power a guy has when you are right in beside him, exchanging. You know immediately if he's strong or not, even if he's not hitting you. I'd been popping Laporte with jabs in the first round, snapping his head back with them, but when I actually got right up beside him in the second I could feel he had loads of power. He was the first guy I'd faced since Jean-Marc Renard who really had that one-punch power. But I knew too that I had more power than he had, and when we got up close I could see in his face that he was really shocked by the amount of strength that I had. That gave me an extra boost.

As the fight went on I realized that this guy wasn't going to be stopped in a few rounds. When I'd gone close to other guys and started punching them and staying on top of them, they would get all tensed up and eventually they'd crack. When they got tired I'd start nailing them, because they'd slow down, and then I'd punch them to pieces. But I knew Laporte was different, and that this was going to be an all-night job. I was scoring points and slowly wearing him down, but I wasn't making any real impression on him. I hadn't gone the distance since Luis de la Sagra in my fourth fight, but I had done ten rounds of sparring many times and so had no doubts that I could last.

He couldn't believe that I could punch with him. He was thinking, 'This is a cheeky so-and-so, staying right up close to me when he knows I've got all this power.' He nailed me in the fifth round with a left uppercut and a right hook, a wee short one. It was a stunner of a punch, but there were two minutes gone in the round and I had to show him that I wasn't hurt. I moved back and kept out of the way for ten, fifteen seconds and then went in at him again. I didn't want him to gain a mental score over me. It was half-way through the fight and a psychological advantage at that stage was important, so I had to get back on top of him.

The seventh and eighth were my best rounds of the whole fight. I punched him all over the place, but although I was hitting him with good shots, I knew I was not going to knock him out, and that as I got tired he would still be around, and he'd still be dangerous. He had such a good guard that even when he slowed down he'd be able to nail you, and he did just that in the ninth round.

There are two ways you can throw a jab: you can flick it or you can step forward with it, like Mark Breland did to Lloyd Honeyghan. I stepped forward with it, hit him with one, and tried it again. I thought I had my hand half out, but in fact I'd missed him with it. The jab was just going past his head when he hit me with this right hand. I was coming forward at the time, so he hit me flush on the jaw with my nine stone and his nine stone behind it. My head snapped back, the spray went flying up in the air and my foot lifted maybe ten inches off the floor. As my foot came down he hit me again with a right hand, then lifted my jaw up with a left hook and then another right hand down again. It was a great combination: double hook and then the right hand, right down the pipe.

I had never been hit like that in my life before, and I remember thinking for a split second that I was standing in Keenan's toy shop, two doors down from us in Clones. I thought, 'What the hell am I doing in Keenan's?' Old Mrs Keenan had been very good to me when I was a kid and I loved going round to the shop. Maybe that was why it came into my head then. For a split second, he'd knocked me right back to my childhood.

The punch sent tingles all the way down to my feet, shock waves of pain right through my body. A big spark went off in my head, and it felt as if there were goose pimples *inside* me, pins and needles right down to my foot. The sensation only lasted for maybe a second and a half, but I was dazed for another thirty seconds. My left side was numbed and I felt I was looking out through clouds, trying to see him. It took me half a minute to get the clouds out of the way. Imagine you're driving a car with condensation on the windscreen. You put the fan on and for about ten seconds you can't see properly, and then the window begins to clear. That's what it was like; I was clouded by the shock of the punch.

At that moment I was past caring about winning or losing; I just wanted to survive, to get rid of the cobwebs. It wasn't late in the round either – I had at least a minute and a half to survive, which I did, and I came back well. I got back to the corner, and the sponge. Ned McCormick had shown me how to do it; he'd get a big sponge and saturate it with ice-cold water, and as soon as you hit the stool he'd smash you with this in the face – it was great. Ned was long gone from the corner, but I always told Eddie to have the sponge ready as soon as I'd hit the corner after a hard round. He gave it to me and it woke me up. Eddie told me I needed a big last round, not that anybody needed to tell me that.

We were fighting up close in the tenth and I hit him with a perfect hook. He told me afterwards it was the hardest he'd ever been hit, the first time that he'd felt as if he was gone. I hit him on the temple, in the danger spot, and his legs went off in different directions. I remember glancing down at the ringside and laughing to myself because Hugh McIlvanney (the distinguished *Observer* columnist) was on his feet, throwing the punches with me, and Harry Mullan beside him was bouncing up and down, banging his hand on the ring apron. I thought I had him and I rushed in at him against the ropes – and he hit me with another deadener, but was too dazed to follow it up.

Barney jumped in at the end of the fight, the only time he ever got there ahead of Dermot. He was so relieved.

That night, the Americans had to concede that here was a serious contender, a serious operator. They had watched me knocking out Orozco and stopping Paul DeVorce, but they said Orozco was nothing and DeVorce was stopped too early. But Laporte was a class fighter, and I'd beaten him fair and square.

*

Boxing News headlined 'He's got the whole world in his hands', but Harry Mullan drew aggrieved accusations of partisan bias for his report, which began: 'Winning the world title looks no more than a tiresome formality for Ireland's brilliant Barry McGuigan, who gave a performance of astonishing maturity to outscore former WBC featherweight champion Juan Laporte on a night of high emotion at the King's Hall. McGuigan's display was as close to perfection as I have ever seen in a ring, ten rounds of exhilarating quality and variety ... The most satisfying aspect of it all was that it answered, loudly and clearly, the last remaining question about McGuigan.

'We knew he could box, and could hit, but we wondered how he could take a top-quality punch himself. Now we know.'

Laporte endorsed Mullan's view as he announced his retirement afterwards. 'I did everything right for this fight, got myself in great shape and fought my best, but I couldn't handle him. So long as Barry is around I'll never be champion again, so it's time to get out. We knew Barry was good, but not *this* good.'

The retirement lasted fourteen months, before Laporte returned as a super-featherweight. Since then he has fought unsuccessfully for both the WBC and WBO super-featherweight championships, won four North American Boxing Federation title fights, and in early 1991 still commanded a top-ten ranking.

Chapter Seventeen

*'A McGuigan fight over here would make Irishmen out
of a hell of a lot of Americans.'*
Associated Press boxing correspondent, Ed Schuyler

Almost overnight McGuigan was hot property, very hot property indeed. His reputation, it is true, had been rising on the British and European scenes at a meteoric pace for over two years but, over and above the simple fact of his beating an opponent of the calibre of a former champion such as Juan Laporte, was the style in which he did it. Suddenly McGuigan made a real mark in the most important sphere of influence in the entire world of professional boxing: American television.

The CBS network had screened the Laporte fight live across America on the Saturday afternoon and, despite the counter-attraction of summerlike weather all along the East Coast, was more than happy with the viewing figures. But as Rick Gentile, the network's Assistant Director of Sports, acknowledged, CBS was even happier about the audience reaction to the contest.

'We always like to go where the atmosphere is,' Gentile said, 'and because of that we're ecstatic about McGuigan's performance. There is no other way to put it. We knew he was a first-rate attraction – that is why we went to Belfast in the first place – but Barry and the whole show surpassed even our highest hopes.

'We also do Billy Costello fights from Kingston in upstate New York. [Costello was WBC light-welterweight champion at the time.] Billy is a real crowd-puller, and we reckon now that McGuigan is another Costello. We'd certainly like to be part of his world title shot.' Gentile added that both he personally and CBS as a whole were so taken with what he termed 'the whole crowd scene in Belfast' that they had a definite preference for the King's Hall as the venue for any proposed world title bid by McGuigan. And, Gentile hinted, they 'might even be prepared to dangle a few financial carrots' to help ensure that their wishes in the matter were met.

'While we don't do the actual promoting,' he pointed out, 'we do call a few shots. The promoter signs up the fight and then we come in and buy the television rights; it is at this point that we can have a real say. We can, and often do, raise the champion's share by quite a significant amount in order to persuade him to defend in the other guy's territory, if that is what we would prefer for a given fight.'

With but one qualified exception, the reaction within the boxing business to McGuigan's display against Laporte was one of universal acclaim. Even to this day, there are many who hold that the Laporte fight remains, in the technical sense, the definitive performance of McGuigan's eight-year and thirty-five-fight professional career.

Among those smitten by the manner in which McGuigan overcame what was by far the stiffest test of his career up to that point was John Condon, then the president of the boxing division at Madison Square Garden. He made no effort to hide his desire to put together a McGuigan fight in MSG, the one-time undisputed Mecca of world championship boxing. 'He simply doesn't give the other guy a chance and he seemingly never stops throwing punches. That's his real trump card and it makes him extremely difficult to catch, let alone beat. McGuigan's non-stop style reminds me a lot of Willie Pep.

'There is little doubt in my mind that he has the beating of Eusebio Pedroza – but only after a classic fight. Pedroza himself throws an incredible amount of punches, but I think Barry's speed would win it for him.' Three months later Condon's assessment was to prove uncannily accurate.

And Pep, ruler of the featherweight division from 1942 to 1950 for all but a four-month period and widely regarded as the greatest nine-stone fighter of all time, was equally impressed. 'He's dynamite, and we all love him over here. He's quick and he's strong, he never stops chasing and he gives the crowd a real fight. Laporte may be an ex-champion but he's certainly no has-been. I was genuinely impressed with the way McGuigan handled him.'

Other trade notables shared the opinion of Condon and Pep as to McGuigan's new-found status. Bob Arum, his Top Rank matchmaker, Teddy Brenner and fight journalists Mike Katz (*New*

York Times), Herb Goldman (*Ring* magazine) and Ed Schuyler (Associated Press) all expressed laudatory views.

Bob Arum: 'I admit I had some reservations about him prior to the Laporte bout, but his performance in that fight completely wiped them out. I'm certain now that he is ready for any featherweight in the world.'

Teddy Brenner: 'The kid is delightful, a real breath of fresh air in a sport that thrives on new faces and attractions. He clearly gets into the ring to fight in the real sense of the word, and he certainly gives the fans value for their money.'

Mike Katz: 'He showed that he can really take a good punch as well as give one, and while I'm one of those who feel that Laporte is very definitely on the slide and that the fight was a brilliant piece of matchmaking by McGuigan's handlers, Barry did his job extremely well. McGuigan is definitely a legitimate world-title contender and I think I'd rate him as probably a better-than-even chance against either Azumah Nelson or Eusebio Pedroza.'

Herb Goldman: 'McGuigan certainly has to be taken seriously now. He showed against Laporte that he's not just the product of a well-oiled publicity machine.'

Ed Schuyler provided what he himself regarded as just about the ultimate accolade. He keeps individual files on all fighters he views as being of real world championship class. On the grounds that European boxers are not usually around long enough to make the effort worthwhile, Schuyler had but one such file open on an Old World boxer in the early months of 1985: Barry McGuigan.

'The Laporte fight proved once and for all that McGuigan is capable of tackling any featherweight in the world right now. His real strongpoint is his superb physical condition. It alone can help him go all the way, because in this day and age far too many fighters don't put in all the hard work and training that they should. Too many of them are only interested in the money and not the work that has to be done first.

'A McGuigan fight over here [in America] would make Irishmen out of a hell of a lot of Americans. If he ever fought either Pedroza or Nelson over here, the crowd would very definitely be on Barry's side.

'McGuigan fights in the American style in a way that I don't think any other European fighter ever did. He knows how to fight "dirty" if he has to.'

Bob Arum, in fact, was prepared to back his enthusiasm with hard cash. Two days after the Laporte bout, he contacted the Eastwoods with a $40,000 offer to McGuigan for a ten-round non-title bout on the undercard of the Marvin Hagler–Thomas Hearns middleweight championship fight in Las Vegas seven weeks later.

'Such a fight,' Arum reasoned, 'would mean incredible exposure in America for McGuigan, and the choice of opponents offered – Tommy Cordova, Freddie Roach or Adrian Arreola – should not pose too many problems for him, even though all were selected because of their ability to provide Barry with the type of fight that would show him at his best to the American boxing public.'

Arum's offer, however, was rejected out of hand by Barney Eastwood on the grounds that America was only of interest after a world title shot had been secured. It was a view shared by McGuigan, even though he was not informed of Arum's offer and therefore not given the chance of turning it down himself – a scenario that was to be repeated with more serious consequences one year later.

The only partially dissenting voice among the euphoria that followed the win over Laporte belonged to Oklahoma-based Pat O'Grady, the father-manager-promoter of one-time WBA lightweight title holder Sean and the guiding force behind yet another organization claiming jurisdiction over world-championship fights, the short-lived World Athletic Association (WAA).

O'Grady, never reticent about his Irish heritage, made no secret of either his overall admiration for McGuigan or his own personal satisfaction at the Laporte fight outcome, but he did wonder about McGuigan's real prospects of lifting a world title. And for one very specific reason.

McGuigan, said O'Grady, had one basic flaw in his technical make-up, the same flaw that had cost Joe Louis so dearly in his first fight with Max Schmeling in the summer of 1936: a tendency to drop his left hand fractionally on the way back after throwing a punch with it, thereby leaving himself open to a right hand over the top.

'Laporte is a good puncher,' said O'Grady, 'but he's not a sneaky one in that an opponent can usually see his shots coming. If Barry gets in with a really sneaky puncher like Nelson, he could really get blasted.

'Barry's left is very good, but it is when he is pulling it back that he creates problems for himself. When he is drawing it in he is inclined to do it just a little too slowly, and he also lets it drop a few inches.

'Those few inches could destroy his world championship hopes, for from now on he is going to be meeting the real pros of the boxing world. And a hell of a lot of them will be better able to take advantage of the situation than Laporte was.

'Otherwise he has everything it takes to be a champion. Louis wasn't yet champion when Schmeling destroyed him; he learned to correct the problem and McGuigan can too. Boxing has its very own version of Murphy's Law: if there is a flaw in your make-up, then you can be damn certain that some day some opponent will find it.'

By now, Pat O'Grady's question mark notwithstanding, all were in agreement that McGuigan was ready to bid for a world championship. The crucial question was, which one?

Aside from O'Grady's somewhat farcical WAA, which nobody ever took seriously, there were three other organizations claiming control over world championship boxing, each with their own champion. The WBA recognized Eusebio Pedroza of Panama, the WBC opted for Azumah Nelson of Ghana and the IBF regarded a South Korean by the name of Min-Keun Oh as the best featherweight in the world. The dilemma for the McGuigan camp was which of the three should become the prime target?

In reality, the choice had to be made from only two champions, not three. The IBF was very much a fledgeling organization in early 1985 – it had been founded less than a year and a half previously and at that stage its infant sphere of influence was largely limited to the Far East in general and to South Korea in particular. The prospects of luring Min-Keun Oh to Belfast (or even London) were decidedly slim and, with both McGuigan himself and Eastwood having worked so hard to get within serious talking distance of a world-title challenge, there was little inclination on the part of anyone in the McGuigan camp to jeopardize so much effort by journeying all the way to South Korea whenever the title chance did finally come.

Besides, the IBF simply did not have the degree of respectability or acceptance then that it now enjoys. If McGuigan was to have real credibility as a world champion, it was imperative that he should become such under the auspices of either the WBA or the WBC.

The easy way out of the poser for the McGuigan camp would have been just to sit back and do nothing; let the passage of time work to their benefit by simply sitting tight while those fighters ranked above McGuigan in the various ratings sorted themselves and their title chances out. McGuigan would, eventually, be granted a number one rating – and therefore a mandatory title challenge – by one or other of the two major organizations, the WBA or the WBC.

But any number of things could go wrong with such an approach. The time required, for instance, might well turn out to be considerable, as the plan would necessitate waiting in the wings for two ratings lists to unravel. Even then there was no certainty that one or more new championship contenders might not leapfrog over McGuigan in the rankings and therefore add still further to the waiting period. And McGuigan, in the interim, would still have to keep active with relatively inconsequential fights against opponents for whom he might find it difficult to retain the drive and concentration that had got him to the verge of a world-title opportunity in the first instance.

Further, even though McGuigan himself was confident of his ability to deal with whatever opponents he might come up against during any such waiting period, the risk of an unforeseen disaster would still be ever present. A clash of heads, a cut eye or even a single lucky punch, and the world-title dream would be in ruins.

And there was one other major impediment to the adoption of a wait in the queue policy: the not inconsiderable risk of purse padding. A mandatory championship defence – that is, one ordered by one or other of boxing's governing bodies against their recognized number one contender for a particular title – is put out to purse offers (a form of auction by tender) in the event of the champion's and challenger's camps being unable to agree terms for the contest. Since each side is always reluctant to concede home venue, mutual agreement is extremely rare and mandatory championship contests almost invariably have recourse to the purse-bid format.

But challengers are severely handicapped under this system. The promoter who 'controls' a champion and normally stages his fights, by means of either the always contentious options technique or an actual manager/promoter contract, simply comes to an accommodation with the title holder to inflate his purse for the purposes of the required bid; this greatly increases the chances of outbidding any rival offer from a promoter associated with the challenger, and which would usually be based in the latter's home territory. The cards are thus so stacked that a champion is almost always able to defend his title in front of his own supporters when it comes to a mandatory challenge for his crown.

Thus, if McGuigan and Eastwood were content merely to bide their time until a mandatory challenge for McGuigan was ordered by one or other of what *Ring* magazine has christened the 'Alphabet Boys', that challenge would, in all probability, have to be made not in Ireland or England but in either Central or North America. Eusebio Pedroza, it is true, had twice defended his title in Italy – but on neither occasion was he conceding home territory to his opponent; the two fights concerned were against an American (Rocky Lockridge) and a Colombian (José Caba), and thus in each case the challengers were just as far away from home as Pedroza himself was.

And Azumah Nelson, although a Ghanaian by birth, was based in America and had fought only once in his home country in the three years prior to McGuigan's win over Laporte. (It would, in fact, be the end of 1988 before he fought in Ghana again). And there was also always the possibility that either Pedroza or Nelson – or both – might lose their titles while McGuigan and Eastwood were playing out their waiting game. If that were to happen, there would simply be no way of telling how long they might have to wait, or to where they might have to travel if and when the waiting were to end.

No, realistically, the waiting tactic was never a serious starter in the list of post-Laporte fight options. Between the time, risk and travel factors, the only sensible course of action was to seek to secure a voluntary defence on McGuigan's side of the Atlantic.

To do that, to entice either Pedroza or Nelson into risking his championship in McGuigan territory – whether Belfast or London – was clearly going to necessitate paying somewhat over the odds. In short, neither champion was likely even to consider the prospect unless he were to be made an offer that, quite simply, he could not refuse.

All along, Eusebio Pedroza seemed the most likely target for

McGuigan's world championship ambitions. A genuine contender for inclusion in any top ten of featherweight all-time greats, he had nevertheless been perched on his WBA throne for seven years by this stage, surviving nineteen challenges to his crown. He had, in fact, been battling for world championships for nine long years – Alfonso Zamora had beaten him in two rounds in a WBA bantamweight title defence in Mexicali in April 1976 – and, at twenty-nine years of age, he had finally begun to show signs of the ravages of time.

He had, for instance, been taken the full fifteen-round distance (as it then was) in each of his last six world championship fights (a series that included his being held to a draw by Bernard Taylor in Charlotte, North Carolina), after having won all but three of his previous fourteen featherweight title bouts without having to resort to judges' decisions.

And, in what was ultimately to prove the final successful title defence of his seventy-four-month reign as world champion, against fellow Panamanian Jorge Lujan (himself just two months short of his thirtieth birthday), Pedroza had struggled to what was a far from impressive points win in Panama City. A ringside spectator at that contest was Juan Laporte's manager, Howie Albert. Two weeks later, in a telephone interview with an Irish journalist only days before leaving America for Belfast and the Laporte–McGuigan bout in the King's Hall, Albert insisted that Pedroza's days as champion were numbered.

'Jorge Lujan has never been what you could call a great puncher, yet he still caught Pedroza with an awful lot of right-handers. If either Juan or Barry had been fighting him and had done the same thing, Pedroza would be an ex-champion by now.'

Pedroza, by general consensus, was therefore the prime candidate. The only real alternative, WBC title-holder Azumah Nelson, who had won his title by stopping Wilfredo Gomez in eleven rounds in San Juan ten weeks before McGuigan beat Laporte, was contracted to Don King and at that time King was reluctant to do business with Eastwood's ambassador-at-large, Mickey Duff. Furthermore, as Nelson was then only twenty-seven and, like McGuigan, just coming into his prime, common sense suggested that an eleven-year veteran of ring warfare would be a more suitable choice.

That, however, did not mean that Pedroza was the soft option;

merely the more sensible one. And there were many acknowledged boxing experts who were convinced that Pedroza was still in a class above McGuigan. The late Jim Jacobs, for instance. Dining with a friend in London shortly after the announcement of the fight, Jacobs (then co-manager of Mike Tyson) accused his companion of getting carried away by McGuigan's win over Laporte. 'McGuigan,' said Jacobs, 'is too raw yet. Pedroza is one of the best world champions of recent years at any weight and he'll know far too much for McGuigan.'

*

Pedroza became our target after Barney went to watch him box José Caba. He brought a tape of the fight back with him, and I thought he boxed Caba very well. And then I watched a tape of Caba boxing Jackie Beard and I thought, 'Hey, this guy can fight a bit!' He looked great against Beard, knocked him down and punched the living daylights out of him for ten rounds. Then he fought Pedroza, and Pedroza just played with him for fifteen rounds. He hit Pedroza a few really good smacks, but Pedroza was able to take them and outbox him. I think that was the stage I realized I was going to go for him.

After I beat Caba I fought Esteban Eguia, and three weeks later I got the chance to fight on American TV. Some fight had fallen through and they came over to film me fighting Paul DeVorce. I had a couple of months' break, then boxed Felipe Orozco on the same show as Cornelius Boza-Edwards against Charlie Brown. I was closing in on Pedroza all the time, and I was watching for any flaws in him – not that I got too many films of him, but I was reading the reports of his fights in *Boxing News*.

I used to say to Eastwood, 'What do you think? Can I beat this fellow yet?' And he would say, 'Well, I don't know. I watched his last fight, and he's looking a bit frayed. Maybe give him six months.' But from watching the Caba fight, and other little bits of film I'd seen, and from reading about the other guys who'd fought him, I always knew that I would have a great chance against him, although he was still a magnificent fighter.

*

Within three days of McGuigan's victory over Juan Laporte at the

King's Hall, Frank Warren re-entered the McGuigan picture. And did so amid considerable controversy.

Warren announced that he had signed up Eusebio Pedroza for a summer title defence against McGuigan and that the sole stipulation made by the champion's manager, Santiago Del Rio, was '*No Irlanda*'. That same day Warren sent the following telex to Eastwood's office in Belfast:

HAVE AGREED TERMS WITH SANTIAGO DEL RIO, PEDROZA'S MANAGER, THAT HE WILL DEFEND HIS TITLE IN LONDON IN MAY OR JUNE. PEDROZA WILL NOT BOX IN IRELAND. OFFER MCGUIGAN ONE HUNDRED AND TWENTY-FIVE THOUSAND DOLLARS TO BOX PEDROZA. REQUIRE TWO OPTIONS ON MCGUIGAN. GUARANTEE MCGUIGAN FIVE HUNDRED THOUSAND DOLLARS FOR THE TWO FIGHTS IF SUCCESSFUL AGAINST PEDROZA. BOTH FIGHTS TO TAKE PLACE IN UK.

The following day, Wednesday, 27 February 1985, Warren upped his title-fight purse offer to McGuigan significantly in a second telex to Eastwood, and also threw in the additional carrot of a share of the promotional credit for the proposed title fight.

MCGUIGAN PURSE FOR PEDROZA NOW 150,000 STERLING. JOINT PROMOTION FRANK WARREN AND STEPHEN EASTWOOD.

The Eastwoods, father and son, were indignant. Saying that Warren 'had no mandate' to negotiate for them and that they 'didn't need' him, the promoter/manager duo accused their London rival of merely jumping on the bandwagon, a charge Warren accepted with unique honesty: 'Of course I am. That's what I'm in business for.'

A month later, on the Saturday prior to McGuigan's defence of the European title against Farid Gallouze at Wembley, Eastwood senior took his rejection of Warren's bid a stage further. In an interview on the BBC 'Grandstand' programme, he asserted that Warren's claim to have reached agreement with the Pedroza camp was 'a lie'. That represented a shift in the Eastwoods' stance on Warren's claim; until then they had merely dismissed his proposal out of hand, but now they were insisting that it was no more than a figment of the Londoner's imagination.

This was a rather strange allegation in view of the fact that

Pedroza's promoter, Luis Spada, could confirm the existence of Warren's agreement to one of the authors on several occasions. 'But,' said Spada, 'it takes two to make a fight, doesn't it?'

'I've only one question for the Eastwoods,' said Warren, when it became clear that the Belfast organization was simply refusing to do business with him. 'I offered McGuigan £150,000 to fight Pedroza. Will they show what they are paying him?'

Chapter Eighteen

> *'Santiago Del Rio turned out to be one of the hardest and most difficult bargainers that my father has ever met in business, and he has been in business quite some time.'*
>
> Stephen Eastwood, on the negotiations for the Barry McGuigan–Eusebio Pedroza fight

From the sublime to the ridiculous: Barry McGuigan followed the toughest fight of his career with the easiest, as the EBU compelled him to defend against an obscure Frenchman, Farid Gallouze. They had originally nominated Gallouze the previous autumn, and the British Board protested strongly on the grounds that he was simply not good enough. Their objections seemed to have been vindicated when Gallouze took a fight in Thailand in November and was stopped in four rounds. It was his fourth stoppage defeat in his last eight fights, hardly the stuff of contenders, and it brought his overall record to fifteen wins and four draws in twenty-five fights.

The Board renewed their objections but were overruled. The mismatch was put out to purse bids, which were won by Stephen Eastwood. He came to a private arrangement with the Mickey Duff–Mike Barrett alliance, who staged it at Wembley on 29 March, in a show which also featured Frank Bruno against another Frenchman, the former European champion Lucien Rodriguez. Bruno knocked him out in the first. It was not a good night for the paying punters.

*

I always tried to give the public value for money in mismatches like this, as far as it was possible, but Gallouze was just so bad that I couldn't look good against him. I deliberately let him get through the first round, to see what he had to offer, and then I got rid of him. Two knockdowns, and his corner threw in the towel when he went down for the second time. There was no pleasure at all in beating him, only relief that I'd got it over quickly and without him getting hurt.

But it had been difficult enough, in a way: all I had to do was lose, and I'd blow everything. I was very conscious of that; I didn't want to do anything that might diminish my chances of the world title.

*

The real drama that night was played out, not before the 7,000-odd spectators at the Wembley Arena, but in a third-floor hotel room a ten-minute drive away. Two hours before McGuigan began his summary dismissal of the hopelessly inept Gallouze, his world title dream came within seconds of an abrupt death.

Eusebio Pedroza, in company with his wife, Rosa, and his manager, Santiago Del Rio, had flown into London the previous Sunday morning. Eastwood, with the financial assistance of Smirnoff boss Trevor McClintock, had persuaded the Panamanians to attend the Wembley bill because, as Santiago Del Rio publicly put it, 'It was good for the promotion.' Nobody, however, was buying that: Pedroza and his travelling companions were in town to talk turkey for the world title fight.

But things did not go quite according to plan. On arrival in London, the Panamanians immediately checked into the Curzon House Hotel and retired to sleep after their marathon journey. Then, somewhat refreshed, they played their part in helping to hype the forthcoming Wembley promotion by going along to a mid-afternoon press conference at the Holiday Inn Hotel. They returned to the Curzon House directly after the conference ended ... and had no further word from the Eastwoods until Tuesday night, over fifty hours later.

Then, at ten minutes past seven on fight night, Santiago Del Rio, in Room 205, received an ominous telephone call. The caller was the party's assigned interpreter, known to them only as 'Gerry', and he asked if the Panamanians could get a taxi to take them to Wembley Arena.

Del Rio was incensed and made little effort to hide the fact. He and the Pedrozas had travelled almost six thousand miles only to find that, having been left to their own devices in a strange city for two whole days and nights, they now had to make their own way to a fight in which they themselves had no interest whatsoever.

'Not only will we not get a taxi,' said Del Rio, 'but we won't even go to the fight', before abruptly terminating the conversation with a message for Gerry to pass on to his lord and masters: 'By the way ... get f—ed.'

Just over forty-five minutes later, almost on the stroke of eight o'clock and at just about the precise time that the opening bell for the Wembley card was ringing, an 'obviously distraught' Stephen Eastwood presented himself at the door of Room 205, accompanied by the same Gerry who had earlier roused Del Rio's ire.

'Perhaps,' explained Gerry, attempting to smooth the troubled waters as Stephen Eastwood watched silently, 'my Spanish isn't good enough. Maybe I didn't explain the message properly; what I meant to say was that we would be collecting you in a taxi.'

But, far from placating Del Rio, this seemed only to intensify his sense of outrage. Already agitated, he rapidly grew even more furious.

'Your Spanish is perfect,' he assured Gerry. 'I understood you perfectly on the telephone and I understand you perfectly now.'

The unfortunate Gerry then said that he had phoned the hotel 'three or four times' with messages for Del Rio, whereupon Del Rio checked with the reception desk and was informed that not a single message had been left for him. 'I didn't leave my name,' explained Gerry, a response that did nothing to mollify Del Rio.

Stephen Eastwood then apologized to Del Rio for not having contacted him or the Pedrozas since Sunday evening. He and his father, he explained, had both been so completely wrapped up in the business of preparing for the fight that they just had not had time for anything else. And besides, he added, both he and his father had been under the impression that 'somebody else' had been looking after the world champion's party.

Del Rio remained markedly unimpressed. 'The least I expected,' he said, 'was that some professional courtesy would have been shown.'

Aware that the conversation was not following its hoped-for course and fearful of exactly where it was heading, the younger Eastwood then enquired if the 'misunderstanding' meant that the world title fight talks were being abandoned.

'No,' said Del Rio, 'but we are not going to tonight's fight.' The less than harmonious meeting had been brought to an abrupt end and Stephen Eastwood, escorted by his interpreter/driver, set off for Wembley Arena.

Thus it was that having (ostensibly, at least) journeyed all the way from Panama to London to see McGuigan clear the final hurdle to a world title showdown, the Pedroza party refused to travel the final eight miles from the Curzon House to the Wembley Arena.

There was, of course, a public explanation – the champion had a stomach upset and was forced to watch the fight on television in the quiet of his hotel room.

'Unfortunately,' said Barney Eastwood, 'he wasn't feeling too well last night. That was the reason why he wasn't at the fight.' But few believed it. Most regarded his non-appearance as an insulting piece of gamesmanship by Pedroza; few were aware that, as far as the champion's camp was concerned, it was they who had been insulted.

And there the matter was to remain for over four hours, stalled in an unsatisfactory limbo until a little after midnight, when Del Rio was awoken by a second party of visitors to Room 205 – Mickey Duff and Mike Barrett.

With Gerry again acting as interpreter, Del Rio resumed where he had left off with the previous delegation. Pedroza, he complained, had been herded along to the Sunday press conference like a prize bull and then totally ignored for over forty-eight hours. That, he insisted, was no way to treat a world champion of his standing.

'We haven't,' said Del Rio, 'seen much gentlemanly behaviour since we arrived in London.'

'We are gentleman,' insisted Duff.

'Well,' was Del Rio's unenthusiastic reply, 'you certainly haven't behaved like gentlemen.'

Finally, though, the two sides did get down to business, the real business for which the Panamanians had travelled half-way across the world. The talks lasted for three hours, broke for a similar length of time, and were finally concluded at seven o'clock on the Wednesday morning. Even then, however, the agreement reached was an incomplete one: the negotiated document contained no specification as to venue or date other than that the fight would take place somewhere in London and not later than 10 July.

'Santiago Del Rio,' Stephen Eastwood told the assembled media in a bookshelved room in the Holiday Inn a couple of hours after the contract signing, 'turned out to be one of the hardest and most difficult bargainers that my father has ever met in business, and he has been in business quite some time.

'The stumbling block to the deal was options. Pedroza wanted them on Barry's services if Barry were to beat him. We had to pay him, and pay him very dearly, for them – but if Barry can beat Pedroza he will be a free agent.'

*

I've always objected in principle to options and multi-fight package deals, which is just another way of creating the same situation of total control. The options system is one in which a world title challenger has to sign away a share of his money from his first two or three defences if he becomes champion and is also committed to having those fights for a particular promoter. It is probably the biggest curse in professional boxing today and, more than anything else in the game, is reponsible for the monopolizing of the sport by a small handful of promoters, who often behave more like dictators.

And, make no mistake about it, it is the promoters who benefit from options, not the fighters – and not even the champions.

Barney Eastwood has publicly acknowledged that when I fought Steve Cruz in Las Vegas he acquired options on my challenger. Cruz subsequently defended and lost the title against Antonio Esparragoza, but while Barney claimed that he had to pay option money to Pedroza for each of my first two defences, I was not paid one penny out of Cruz's first and only title defence.

A middleweight friend of mine thought that he'd found a way round the system. He was offered a shot at one of the world titles, on condition that he signed a multi-fight deal to cover his first three defences in the event of his becoming champion. Under the terms of the package, his purses would be fixed at $50,000 for each of the first two and $75,000 for the third.

My friend complained about this and pointed out that his second or third defence could conceivably be against somebody like Sugar Ray Leonard, Roberto Duran, Michael Nunn or even Marvin Hagler. In other words, it could turn out to be a real megabuck fight in which his opponent – who, if he didn't hold a rival version of the title, would merely be a challenger for *his* world title – could have a purse of several million dollars, while my friend would be contractually bound to go through with the same fight for a miserable $50,000 or $75,000.

Eventually he negotiated a three-word insertion in the contract. The words were 'in excess of', and they were put in before the specified purse figure for each of the fights. My friend was delighted with this, because he thought it meant that he was free to negotiate a separate purse for each fight, including maybe a two or three million payday if he was involved in a superfight.

But then he realized that the freedom to negotiate was an illusion. In reality, all the revised contract meant was that the promoter could offer him *one dollar* in excess of the originally specified $50,000 or $75,000, and he would be legally bound to accept it, even if his opponent was getting perhaps $3m for the same fight.

*

Barney Eastwood, recalling his thirteen hours of hard bargaining in Panama, described Del Rio as 'a very difficult guy to work with'.

But neither Del Rio nor the Pedrozas were present to hear Stephen or Barney Eastwood's public assessment of the Panamanian manager's business acumen. All three, more than a little peeved, had flown out of Heathrow Airport at quarter past ten that morning.

'Pedroza and his manager,' Trevor McClintock told the packed press conference, 'would have loved to be here now but, unfortunately, Santiago had a very big business meeting in Washington. He sent his best wishes and apologies before he flew out. I can't say it in Spanish, but that's the interpretation.'

But was it the correct one? And would the agreement, so dramatically reached, hold up? Santiago Del Rio, for one, had his doubts. He and the Pedrozas had been flown to London on one-way tickets and, in their haste to depart on that Wednesday morning, had purchased and paid for their own tickets home. The total bill for the three seats back to Panama came to $4,678 and Del Rio insisted that until that amount was paid back in full, neither he nor Pedroza would have anything further to do with the Eastwoods.

The problem of the outstanding $4,678 was subsequently cleared up, and while the agreement reached in the early hours of 27 March did hold firm, Farid Gallouze's rapid capitulation encouraged the belief that the fans who had paid up to £50 to witness win number twenty-six for McGuigan had been cheated. Not only did they pay to see the wrong fight; they were even in the wrong arena.

*

The night of the Gallouze fight is one that I'll never forget as long as I live, and the Pedroza talks had nothing to do with it – I didn't even know about them until the following morning.

What I remember about the night is something a lot more serious. I hadn't seen my father for an hour or two but, when we were driving back to the Holiday Inn from Wembley (I can't even remember who was in the car with me; I know Sandra and Dermot were there and somebody else, maybe just a driver) and passing Marble Arch, I saw my father walking along the footpath. I called to him to get into the car but he just waved me away with his hand and kept on walking.

I knew there was something wrong, so I got out of the car and ran over to him. 'Come on,' I said, 'get in the car with us.' But he wouldn't. All he'd keep saying was, 'Leave me alone.' I kept asking him what was wrong; for a long time he wouldn't tell me, but eventually he did.

He'd only just come back from America for the fight, and while he'd been there he'd taken a bit of a fall while doing a show in New York. He went to a hospital for what he thought was just a precautionary check-up, but while he was there the doctor said he had spotted something and wanted to do further checks. At the end of the day he told Daddy what it was: he had a rare bone disease, a form of cancer, and the doctor told him he'd be dead in two years.

When we came back home I sent him to a couple of other doctors in Belfast and Dublin. They said that the guy in New York was making a mistake and that there was nothing wrong. But the New York doctor turned out to be right after all; that was late March 1985 and in the end he was only out by three months. My father died in June 1987.

*

What had yet to be resolved in relation to McGuigan's world title challenge to Pedroza was perhaps the most important detail of all: when the fight would actually take place. The initial announcement of 'before 10 July' was little more than a holding clause, and now the agreeing of an exact date had to be worked on by the rival management teams. And the scheduling of the bout was crucial for an additional and equally important reason: the chosen date had to suit American TV if the promotion was to attract the often considerable financial backing offered by the various networks.

But, as by now appeared to be the case with almost everything even remotely connected with the setting up of the fight, getting the respective camps to think in unison was no easy task. Pedroza, at the time of the signing of the fight contract, was weighing in in the region of ten stone nine – a remarkable twenty-three pounds over the featherweight limit, but his more or less customary weight between fights – and was clearly going to need quite some time to get down to the required nine stone. The champion, in effect, was thinking in terms of making his twentieth defence of the title some time in the latter half of June while, largely for television purposes, Eastwood and Mickey Duff were hoping to get the bout on almost a full month earlier than that.

About ten days into April, one of the authors received an intriguing telephone call at his office. The caller asked for the author by name but then would not believe that he was talking to him. His byline, the caller maintained, was merely a *nom de plume* 'for some of the big London boys' because, he said, 'a lot of that McGuigan material is pretty close to the bone'. Only after he had been given the author's home number as verification of identity – and had put it to the test later that evening – did the caller give his reason for making contact. It was to be another three weeks and several calls later before he would reveal his own identity: thus was born Fight Fan.

'You are the only one putting forward what I call "the alternative view",' he said. 'It is a view I happen to agree with and, from time to time, I might be able to help you get it across. You know they have problems, I know they have problems, but nobody else knows or apparently even wants to know it. I am in a position to, from time to time, pass the odd of bit of information your way.'

'What sort of information?'

'How about, as an indication of my bona fides, the date of the Pedroza fight?'

'You've got it?'

'I am pretty certain that I have. Ignore all the talk about it being in late May; it looks very much like it will be 8 June. Check it out.'

One other telephone call was enough to confirm Fight Fan's tip. Luis Spada was then a great deal more accessible than he would later become.* Asked about the likelihood of Pedroza's title defence against McGuigan taking place on the date in question, Spada acknowledged, 'That was the *only* date under consideration,' and that he expected it to be finalized 'within a day or two'.

And it was. McGuigan's world title challenge was set for the Queen's Park Rangers ground at Loftus Road in west London on Saturday 8 June.

*The relationship between Spada and Eastwood would subsequently develop to the point where the latter, a life-long racing enthusiast, would name one of his horses 'Lou Spada'. Other horses owned by Eastwood and/or his inseparable racing associate Alfie McLean, in the aftermath of the split with McGuigan, would include 'Desert Excuse'.

Chapter Nineteen

'While my father was singing Pedroza stared across at me, and Dermot was shouting to me, "He's looking at you! He's looking at you! Stare at him." He didn't have to tell me that. By that stage I was gone, the old pupils staring like a terrier that's got hold of a fox.'

Barry McGuigan, recalling the final seconds before the first
bell of his world title challenge

As the time closed in Pedroza fought Gerald Hayes down in Panama in a ten-rounder, and Hayes floored him with a right hand. I had worked with Hayes for the Laporte fight, and then Hayes came back to Belfast after he'd fought Pedroza. He was good sparring for me; in sparring you can kid a bit, but in the ring you can't. He was able to kid me, stay for a couple of rounds, but I had dropped him in sparring with body shots and knew he was very impressed with me.

He came back to work with me for the title fight. I knew at that stage I had a good chance against Pedroza, and Hayes told me that, 'He's open to the right hand, try the right hand.' But we'd been practising the right anyway, because against Caba it looked as if he dropped the left hand a bit, and pulled out of the road of punches, leaving himself open to Caba's overarm right. I knew the difference between me and Caba was that he was an aggressive fighter but didn't stay on guys the way I would stay on them, so I knew I would have a better chance than he did.

Pedroza came over to watch me defend the European title against the Frenchman Farid Gallouze, but didn't bother coming to the show. I would have felt a bit more pressure that night if he'd been sitting there watching me, but they told me before I went out that he wasn't there. It was an easy fight anyway; two rounds, a mismatch. But no matter who I fought I was nervous: I was always nervous, even if I'd been fighting a tramp out in the street. It was just the occasion that got to me. I suppose I had to be that way.

That very night the deal was done with Pedroza and his manager, Santiago Del Rio, and the next morning he was on the plane home. We had a press conference the following day to announce the world title fight. I never saw Pedroza, never spoke to him. I met him twice, in the Lonsdale gym in Carnaby Street two days before the fight. I smiled at him and shook his hand, and the only time I spoke to him was at the end of the fight, when I put my arms around him. I never saw him again – the man had been central to my whole life, and I've never spoken six words to him.

Barney found me good sparring for Pedroza. He flew two guys in from Panama, José Marmolejo, the Panamanian featherweight champion and number three in the world, and Ezekial Musquerra, the lightweight champion of Panama. We did loads of sparring with them, and with Dwight Pratchett, Davy Irving, Dave McAuley and the Harris brothers, Michael and Peter.

We sparred one day at the back of Brian Eastwood's house, where we'd set the ring up to get the feel of boxing outdoors. Marmolejo would be ten stone two, ten stone three when we'd *finished* training – I couldn't believe it. The other guy, Ezekial, was ten and a half, ten-ten. They would train in plastics, but Marmolejo never got below ten stone. There was a serious difference in size between us. Marmolejo would hit me with his head, his elbow, all the dirty tactics. Many a time I would lose my temper with him, while Barney was sitting outside the ring shouting at him to go on and do all the dirty stuff. I knew myself that I would put Pedroza under so much pressure that he couldn't fight me rough anyway, but it was just in case he did. I watched the Laporte fight – it was desperate. Pedroza hit him with ninety-eight fouls!

I really didn't start to get sharp in my sparring until the last fourteen days. Then one day I did twelve rounds, sparring with four or five different guys right through, and after that I didn't spar more than four or five rounds. All my heavy work had been done then.

We came over to London on the Monday before the Saturday. On Monday I was sparring with Davy Irving and Dave McAuley, and maybe one round each with Pratchett and Marmolejo, but at the finish of the fourth round I hit Irving with a long left hook. Whatever way I hit him, *bam*, I pulled all the ligaments in my elbow and I couldn't spar again until the fight. The injury didn't upset me, though: I was shadow-boxing and running every day. I had a physio come round every day to the Holiday Inn, where we were staying, to work on the elbow.

My weight was in control – I was always on the weight a fortnight before a fight, and I could hold it just by watching what I ate. Every day we'd go down to the kitchens at the Holiday Inn and check my weight on the massive big meat scales there.

We put it about that I didn't need to train because my weight was fine. Everybody was waiting for me to go to the gym, and they were mad to get hold of me, but every day at four o'clock I would push the bed out of the way in the hotel room, put on my gear and do twenty-five minutes straight without a break, shadow-boxing and skipping. Then I'd lie under the covers for half an hour, dry off, shower and weigh myself again. One day I tried to work on the pads, but the elbow hurt so I stopped. I worked out on the Friday and went down to the gym above the Thomas à Becket pub in the Old Kent Road to check my weight; it was fine. I knew the weight was OK, but we wanted to show everybody – it was a psychological thing, not that Pedroza would have been rattled if he'd heard about it anyway. He was too long in the tooth for that oul' crack.

Believe me, though, it was a struggle to make nine stone, and always was for me. Hard work was the only thing that got me down to it, bloody hard work.

I came back from the 'Becket and had chicken, broccoli, carrots and lemon tea, squeezing in a lot of lemon so that it would be a diuretic and flush out my system. I couldn't sleep that night. My friend Sean McGivern was with me, and Dermot. I was nervous about getting beaten.

In the morning I went down to the scales and checked the weight again. I was half a pound under, so when I went back up to the room I had a little drop of tea, with some lemon in it. I was very dry, but I only drank a quarter of the cup. By the time I got to the scales I was actually lighter again, because I'd peed.

We were late for the weigh-in at the Odeon, Leicester Square, but when the crowd – about a thousand – saw us arrive, the noise was tremendous. Pedroza had been sitting there waiting, and when the official time came for the weigh-in he got up on the scales, and there were none of us there to witness it. Stephen Eastwood didn't think that he had made the weight; he thought the scales hadn't settled properly, although it looked OK to me, as far as I could judge from TV. But Stephen was unhappy, and he said something to Del Rio, who started shouting.

Of course, Barney got on his high horse, yelling that, 'I'm not happy with this. I want to see him back on the scales.' Now there was no way the guy was going back on the scales: he'd been there too many times before. But what Barney was at was a kind of intimidation, or at least that was my interpretation of it. Eventually he came to the microphone, ranting and raving, 'I want him back on the scales', while the crowd were roaring, 'Go on, Barney', and the old WBA supervisor was sitting there with a big, long, wrinkly face on him, shaking his head and saying that he'd weighed him once and that was enough.

Every time the crowd roared, Barney would get more vexed. Paddy Byrne and Stephen were trying to get him to cool down, while I was sitting off in the corner getting ready to be weighed. Barney started shouting, 'There's no fight! There's no fight!' Then I calmed him down a bit and he said over the mike, 'I'm disappointed with the WBA, and I'm disappointed with the British Boxing Board of Control, but we're now going to continue. We've lost all the rounds so far, but we'll win tonight.'

So I got on the scales and they bleeped, and I jumped off. They asked me to get on again, and I did, and it settled below the weight, at eight stone thirteen and three-quarter pounds. Sean McGivern had got me a big flask of really sweet, milky coffee and as soon as I got off the scales I banged that into me. Then he came in again with two Big Macs, and I ate them with sweet water and milk. I was starving, but I could only get half-way through one; Sean and Dermot shared the other.

We called off at a little chapel on the way back to the hotel to say a couple of prayers. I always did that on the day of an important fight. We'd had Mass the night before. Fr Salvian Maguire was over, and Barney and I always used to have Mass with him before a fight. Sean McGivern would be there, along with my brother-in-law Ross, Dermot sometimes, and anybody else who wanted to participate.

We went back to the hotel and I ate something substantial: steak, minced really fine, with peas and beans and chips – lots of sloppy stuff that would be easily digested and fill me up quickly. I sipped sweet water all day long, nothing with too much carbonate in it. We walked around the block after the meal, around Marble Arch, and then I spent all the rest of the afternoon lying in bed. I was on my own in the room – I always preferred it that way. The room was as dark as I could make it, but I couldn't sleep. I don't think I ever slept before any important fight. I tried to think of everything but the fight, but my mind always came back to it. Finally, around half past five I ordered a piece of cheesecake and a cup of coffee.

Even at this stage, I had still not realized fully the impact the fight was having in the country, or how much it mattered to so many people. There was a profile of me on TV on the Wednesday, but I never watched it or read the papers. I would save them and read them all afterwards, and try and watch all the preview stuff from the TV, but never before. I remember Douglas Hurd, who was Secretary of State for Northern Ireland at the time, came up to the hotel room to see me, but the importance of it all still didn't register with me.

My routine was to arrive at a show after the first fight had started, so that there would be as little time as possible to wait. When we arrived we were hustled quickly through a side door into the dressing-room. Pedroza's man, Del Rio, came in to watch us taping. I had been so nervous all day thinking about the fight, about what would happen if I lost. I didn't know how important the fight was to other people, but I knew it meant everything to me. And yet when I went into the dressing-room I was probably the coolest guy there.

George Francis taped my hands, although I always made sure that the hands were done exactly the way I liked them. We had told Del Rio that he could use whatever tape he wanted, just so as he wouldn't bother us. Dermot went in to watch Pedroza tape, and told me he hardly put any tape at all over his hand, just a lot of wadding over the knuckles. Del Rio came in after we had done, and he made us take it all off and start again. Barney was furious, but we had to do it. That was when I got annoyed. My neck got all red, because I was really upset. I knew he was trying to disturb me, and he did. I got all worked up, and he walked out of there happy. He had done what he intended to do.

But we stuck the gloves on, checked everything, and five minutes later we were running out of there. I remember thinking to myself as we came out on to the pitch, 'There's not the noise here that there was in the King's Hall!' Of course, there wasn't a roof on the place, so the noise was just going up into the air.

We went to the wrong side of the ring, and all the way there people were battering and hammering on me and Paddy Byrne and Eddie Shaw. We all got a clattering, and the intensity of the crowd was incredible. There were two fellows looking after me, Danny McAllan and Vince McCormack. Vince and I had a custom, when we were going to the ring, of saying a prayer together. The noise and the roars of the crowd were deafening us, but Vince turned round to me and yelled, 'McGuigan, can you hear me?' I said I could, so he said, 'Come on, say the prayer.'

So we recited this wee prayer – it's a child's prayer really, but I always liked it.

> Angel of God, my guardian dear
> To whom God's love commits me here
> Ever this day be at my side
> To light and guard, to rule and guide.

We put plenty of emphasis on 'Ever *this* day' ... this day, now.

I got up in the ring, still thinking the noise wasn't too bad. The night air felt cool when I took off my top, and then I looked around at all those faces and *felt* the noise, and that was when it hit me, what this fight meant to everybody there. My father sang 'Danny Boy' but I was oblivious to it; I hummed the whole way through it, so that I wouldn't hear it, and could block it out. I was very emotional. I remember all these cards that my neighbours sent to me before the fight, with messages like, 'If you win the title you'll hear us cheering from the other side of the town.' I started reading them before the fight and I was nearly in tears. I couldn't take any more, so I put them all in a bag and read them afterwards. I deliberately blocked everything out so that it wouldn't get to me: I had to concentrate on Pedroza and nothing else. The feeling was so intense, you couldn't imagine it. I always prided myself on my ability to stay cool. I used to ask God that I would be able to stay cool, and think of what I had to do and only of what I had to do – that was the prayer I would say.

Barney had heard how, when Sean O'Grady fought in America, they'd had a dwarf dressed as a leprechaun get in the ring and jump around and carry on, so what did he do but decide that, on the biggest night for both of us, he would get this wee guy in. He thought the Panamanians would be very superstitious, so he got

Champion . . . the moment I heard I'd won the Commonwealth Games gold medal at Edmonton in 1978.

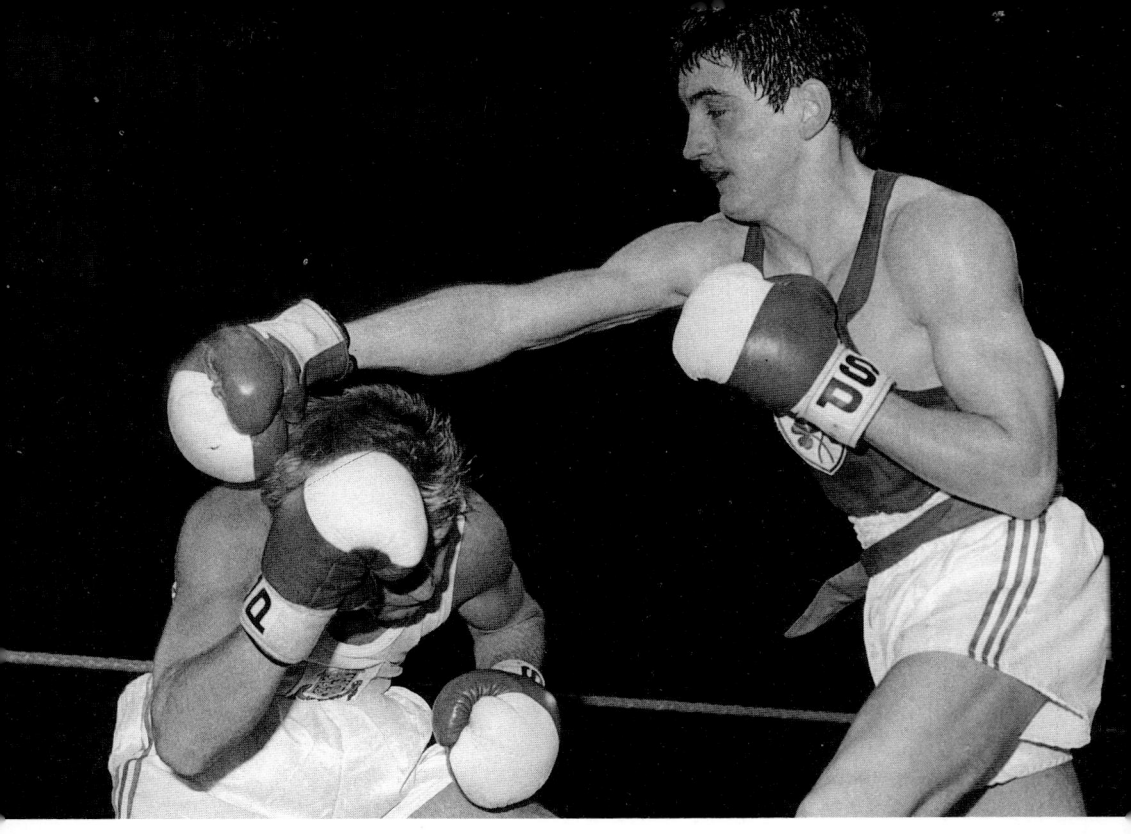

England's Pete Hanlon made me work to outpoint him in the semi-final of the Wembley multi-nations tournament in 1980.

Veteran loser Selvin Bell hangs on for dear life in my pro debut at Dalymount Park, Dublin.

Hard at work with brother Dermot in our home-made gym behind the family shop in Clones.

Home ground . . . the King's Hall, Belfast, one of the world's great fight venues.

The way we were . . . Barney and I in the early days.

Trainer Eddie Shaw prepares me for a sparring session.

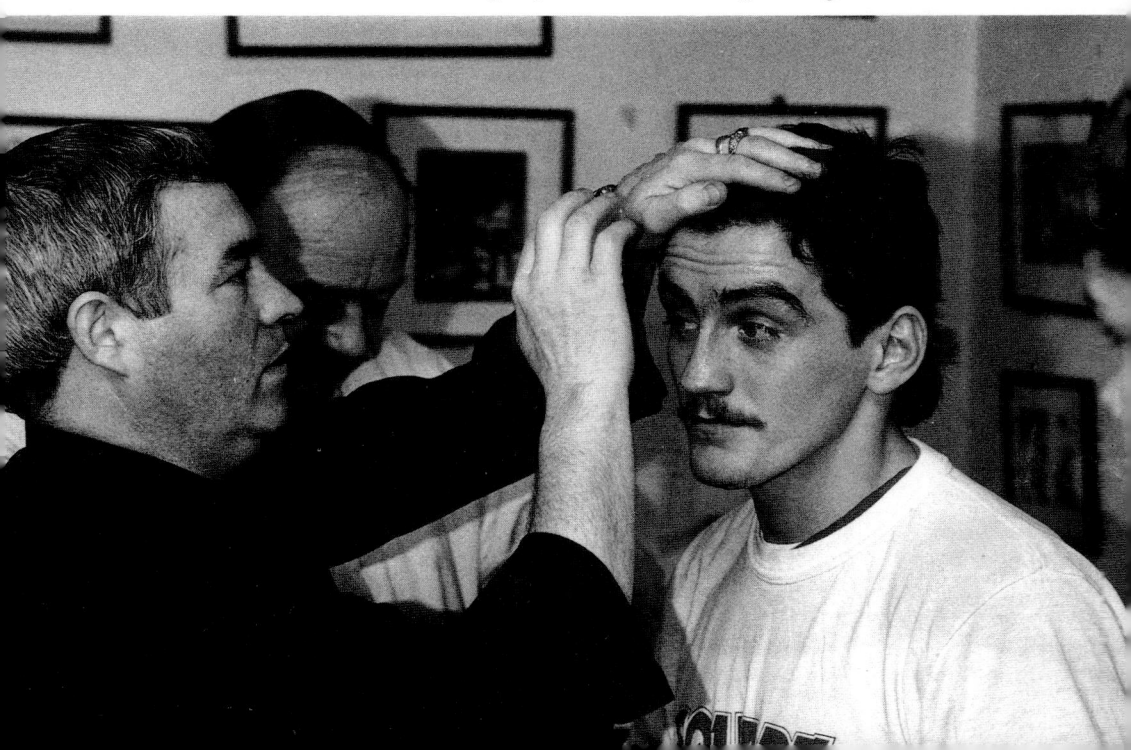

I'll always have a soft spot for Paddy Byrne, the wise-cracking Dubliner who was a central part of the team.

Playing shop with my sister Rebecca in the family grocery.

The row rages at the weigh-in for the Pedroza fight, as the WBA supervisor lays down the law to Stephen Eastwood, Barney and Paddy Byrne.

Pedroza was a lovely, elegant stylist, but he certainly doesn't look it as I have him under pressure.

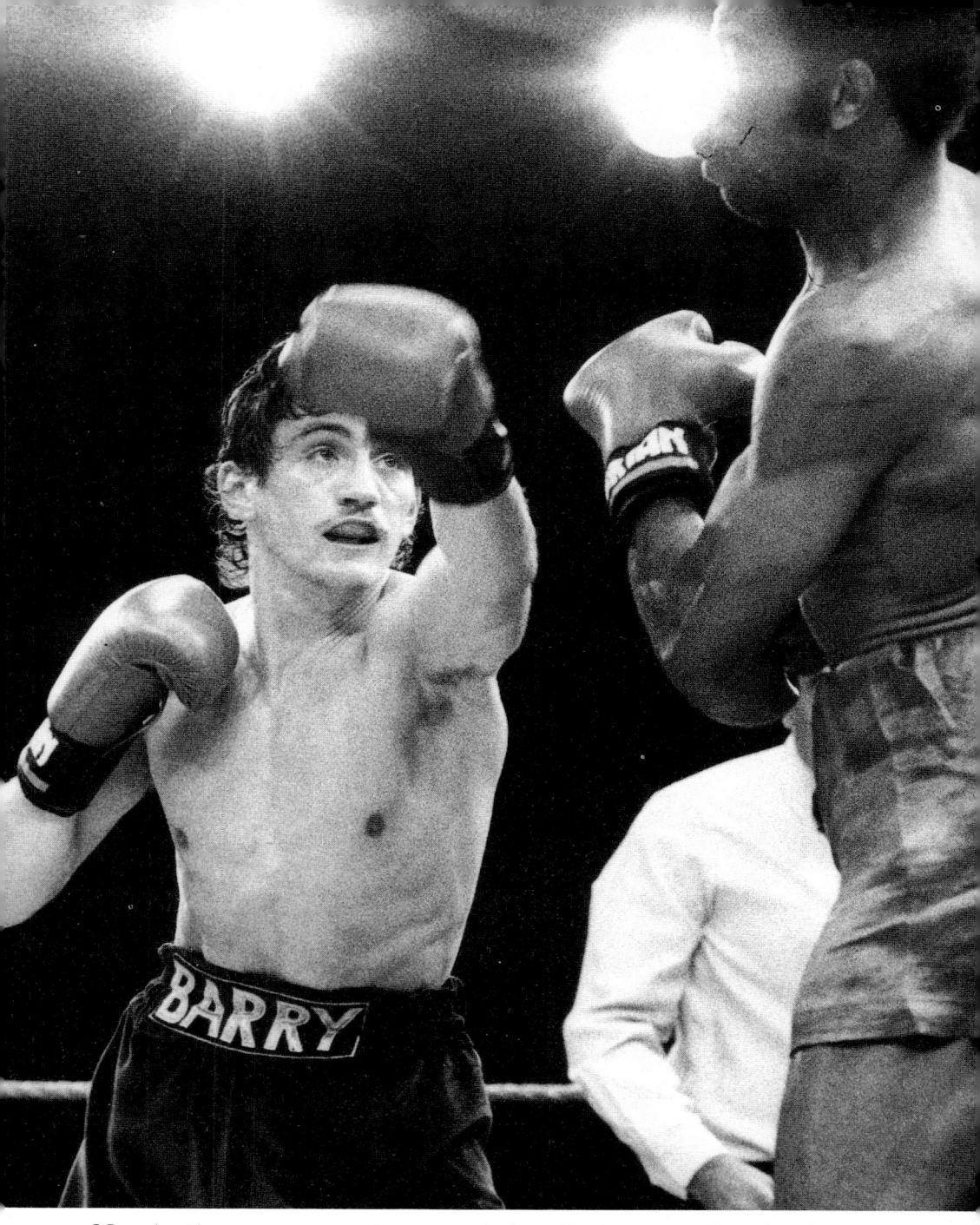

Nearly there ... one last attack has Pedroza reeling in the final stages.

A tender moment in the dressing room with Sandra and Blain.

What a welcome . . . the home-coming that brought Clones to a standstill.

the wee fellow to do cartwheels and throw 'magic green dust' at them. I didn't even see him, until I glanced around and saw him getting out of the ring. Barney had told me he was going to do it, but it had gone out of my head. I don't know what effect it had on Pedroza – probably not much. While my father was singing Pedroza stared across at me, and Dermot was shouting to me, 'He's looking at you! He's looking at you! Stare at him.' He didn't have to tell me that. By that stage I was gone, the old pupils staring like a terrier that's got hold of a fox.

Just as they were all clearing the ring, the oldest guy in Pedroza's corner came over to Barney and started saying, 'Fifty thousand! Fifty thousand my man win.' And Barney said, 'Get away to hell.' Maybe Barney regretted afterwards that he'd sent him away without taking the bet, but at that stage he was more psyched up than I was. And then Paddy and he got out of the ring, and there was just me and Pedroza, staring across at each other and waiting for the bell.

Chapter Twenty

'Enjoy it all, take it all in now and hang on to it, because believe me, it won't last.'

Phil Coulter to Barry McGuigan, the night he became world champion

My adrenalin had never been as high before, and never would be again. That's not to say that I was never as good a fighter again, only that the feeling would not be so intense.

I knew that I had to establish early on that the pattern of the fight would be me chasing him, and not allowing him to take the initiative. Farid Gallouze hadn't landed a punch on me, so I hadn't actually felt any punches since I'd fought Laporte. Pedroza came out and flicked a couple of jabs at me, I didn't feel him as powerful as Laporte, although he was much quicker and cuter than him. He would get his punches off just before me.

I would deliberately come close to guys and give them a target to fire at, so as soon as they'd miss I could counter, and then sometimes I'd give them the target and not do anything – be in position to throw punches but not throw them. It would lead them into a false sense of security; they would think, 'Well, he didn't throw anything last time so he won't this time either', and then I'd belt them. They never knew when I was going to throw punches, and that was why I always put myself so close to them. I'd show them punches and not throw, and then I'd throw, but I couldn't get away with that with Pedroza. Every time I got close to him, he nailed me.

I had been practising my right hand for months, but I remember thinking to myself, 'I'm never going to land this.' Gerald Hayes was sitting right on the ring apron, shouting to me, 'When he drops that hand, throw the right over.' He'd shout, 'Right hand *now*', and smack the canvas, and Pedroza was so cute that when he'd hear the smack he knew what was coming and blocked it.

Teddy Atlas had sent me a tape on which he actually demonstrated the way to throw it. He'd made the tape in the gym, on a little home video. I had worked it out for myself, anyway; we called it the Smithboro Special. I'd jab to the head, reaching for him because he was taller than me, and the next time I'd go *wham!* to the body. He'd block it – he was a great blocker – and then I'd throw another. He'd be thinking, 'He's not going to go to the body again', but I would . . . and then I'd switch it up to the head. I finally landed it in the ninth, but in the early rounds I was beginning to think that he was too smart for that. But I stayed on him anyway and tried to outjab him.

He was a master boxer and had a great record for going the distance. Barney was worried that he might use dirty tactics on me, but I planned on keeping him so busy thinking about defending himself that he couldn't fight dirty, and that's the way it worked out. Nobody had stayed on Pedroza; Caba did in little bursts, but I knew that was the way to fight him. I knew he would tire, and although he boxed very well on the retreat, I was sure I would get him if I stayed close enough to him.

In the second round I decided to see what he was like inside, so I came close to him. I was rolling and slipping, watching for openings. I was very accurate in close, and I hit him with a double left hook and could see him thinking, 'What's this guy at?' He was hitting me with his fair share, but I was landing much cleaner punches, harder shots. I had more power than he did, and at the end of the second round I had the better of him in close, even though he was outboxing me at a distance. He knew it too, and that gave me a psychological advantage.

In the third he didn't fight so much in close, but when he tried to take the play away from me by throwing quick ones round the side, I was still more effective. I really *wanted* the title and I was buzzing. All the time I was staying with him, hoping he would slow down so I could get to him. I was fighting the same pattern, jabbing and slipping under his punches, and even if I didn't jab, I'd show it so as to get inside. I was keeping my head moving as much as I could, so that I wouldn't get hit in return.

At the end of the sixth we were fighting in close again, and I hadn't landed a decent body punch yet. In fact, I didn't land a decent body shot on him all night; that's how good he was at blocking them. I had my back to the ropes. I threw a few to the head and missed him, then a left hook just grazed him and I stepped in with a right hand to the side. It really hurt him, and being that close to him I could hear him grunt, even among all the sound there was around us. When he was going back to the corner he gave his legs a little shake and my father, who was sitting across the ring from Dermot, jumped up and shouted, 'Dermot, Dermot! He's hurt!' A couple of boys behind him who didn't know who he was were shouting, 'Sit down, sit down!' and the next thing Daddy knew, somebody had thrown a full can of beer and hit him on the back of the head. He was ready to batter somebody, being pumped up enough with the fight already, but eventually my brother-in-law Sammy calmed him down.

Pedroza's corner must have told him at the end of the sixth to see what I was like going back. Now that was never my strong point, and they knew it. But Pedroza didn't come running out firing punches; what he'd do was hold the centre of the ring and then move in, throwing fast bursts. I thought to myself, 'I'd better do something here quick, or he'll take the play away from me completely.' I'd tried the right hand a couple of times before and it had just looked ridiculous. I'd tried the body shot too, but it was as if he could see it coming and he'd pull away. So he wasn't going to fall for that, but I thought I had a chance of landing it on him as he came forward. If he could see that I was bad going back, he'd try to back me up all the time.

Three times he came in with fast one–twos, and then moved back out again. And as I'd come trundling after him, he'd show a left and throw a right hand on its own. He must have become a bit complacent, because when he'd landed that right the last time I went after him with two jabs and then the right hand, bang on the chin. He lurched forward and I tapped him with a left hook to help him fall over. I ran to the neutral corner and looked over to my own corner. Paddy Byrne was the only one who wasn't excited; he was standing behind Barney and Eddie, signalling to me to stay calm, while they were going mad. I tried to think what I was going to do next. I knew he wasn't that badly hurt, because it felt as if the right hand had only glanced off him, and not landed really well. If I could land another on the side of the head, he'd be done, so I rushed over, firing hooks. But he was too cute to be caught again, and he pushed me back and hit me with a short little uppercut. He'd been doing that all night ... next day, I was all bruised under my chin where he'd been landing them. Of course, every time he threw an uppercut I could land a left hook, and I did.

The noise from the crowd was unbearable when I went back to the corner, even though I was well used to that kind of atmosphere. I could see everybody jumping up and down, and I said to myself, 'What are they all getting so excited about? This fellow's not gone, not by a long way.' But at least I'd made my mark and put him on the deck, so that he came out for the next round with a bit more respect for me. He was moving around instead of coming to me, so at least I'd stopped him pushing me back. He boxed really well in the eighth, and maybe even won it. I still felt in control of the fight, but that was his round.

I kept on top of him in the ninth, closing the gap. I had a lot of power at short range, and in the tenth I tried the right hand again. I pushed him back into his own corner against the ropes, and caught him to the chin. He was groggy and in trouble, but to shake it off he threw a few punches at me. We went round in a circle, ending up with my back against the ropes. As he came in, I hit him with the left hook and the right, to the side of the head, on the danger spot, and his legs went all over the place. I knew it was near the end of the round, but the noise was so incredible that we couldn't hear the bell and I hit him two clear punches after the bell. Santiago Del Rio came running into the ring, screaming at Stan Christodolou, the referee, but he hadn't heard it either.

Pedroza was in trouble again in the thirteenth and I thought the referee was going to stop it. I actually glanced at Christodolou for a second, took my eyes off Pedroza, and got clipped. He hit me the hardest punch of the fight in the fourteenth. I was pressing him and he stuck out his left. I came after him and walked straight on to a right. It hurt, but I wasn't going to give up then. I had no idea whether or not I was in front, but I could tell from the excitement in my corner that I was doing well. I had a general perception of the fight and knew that I was well in it, but I had no idea whether I was winning it.

I still had plenty of reserve, loads of it, but I had lost all sense of time and had no idea what round it was. In fact, the only time I knew what round was coming up was when Paddy Byrne leaned over to me at the start of the fifteenth and said, 'You've got three minutes to beat the best featherweight champion this century. In three minutes you'll be the champion of the world.' George Francis was in the corner too, and I heard him say, 'Go out and give it everything this round. You've got to have a big last round.'

I pushed him hard through the round, but I knew I wasn't going to knock him out. I was slipping his punches and working away, and I could hear Dermot shouting to me, 'Keep moving your head.' And then I heard the bell, and I threw my arms around Pedroza for the first and only time. I can't remember what I said to him, but I know what he said to me: 'You'll be a good champion.' People hustled me away from him and I never saw him again.

They hoisted me in the air, and I was saying, 'Hang on now – don't be counting your chickens yet.' When the verdict was announced, I tried to take it with dignity, instead of jumping around like a fool, but the whole place was a madhouse.

*

There was one more debt to pay, and McGuigan, in the supreme moment of his life, honoured it. In a voice choking with emotion, he told BBC-TV commentator Harry Carpenter: 'There's one thing I've been thinking about all week. I want to dedicate this world title to the young lad who fought me in 1982, Young Ali. At least it wasn't an ordinary fighter who beat him, but a world champion.'

*

When we got back to the dressing-room Dennis Taylor was there, and Pat Jennings. There was Jim Neilly and Harry Mullan, who'd done the radio commentary on my very first fight, and my father went back out to find Frank Mulligan and bring him in too. Garrett FitzGerald, who was Taoiseach at the time, came through on the phone. He told me I'd done the country proud, which was nice. After I'd lost the title he wrote to me as well, saying that I'd been a credit to Ireland in defeat as well as in victory, and I was very proud of that.

Phil Coulter, the songwriter, got in the van with us for the drive back to the hotel. All the way through Shepherd's Bush the crowds were banging on the sides of the van, throwing beer over it and cheering. It seemed as if the whole of London was celebrating. Coulter was sitting beside me and he said, 'Enjoy it all, take it all in now and hang on to it, because believe me, it won't last.' And boy, was he right.

When we got back to the hotel there was already a clatter of people there, but we just went straight up to our room. Maybe I came down for ten minutes or so, but no more. Next morning, when I got up, I was very stiff and sore, and I hadn't slept much. After Sandra and I had had our breakfast we had to get back into bed again, so the photographers could get their pictures of me reading about the fight.

It had been the night of all nights – and then next morning I heard that my parents' house had burned down. A TV had caught fire during the night and the place was gutted. My Auntie Brid had been staying there with my mother, and she woke when she smelt the smoke. She opened the window and shouted to a neighbour of mine who was walking past, still in a fair old state of celebration, 'Help! Help! We're on fire!'

'Never mind, love,' he said. 'We're all on fire tonight. You'll be grand in the morning.' But then somebody else a bit more sensible came along and got them out safely.

We stayed in London on Sunday, but Monday morning I decided I'd go home. The Lord Mayor of Belfast had arranged a civic reception for me. I had never realized how much was riding on the fight; I deliberately didn't read the papers or watch TV or anything, so that it would be just another fight to me. I never knew the full significance of it all until afterwards, but as long as I live I'll never see anything like that homecoming again. People who never were interested in boxing became caught up in the whole thing. People who were openly disgusted with the fight game were proud to say they were fans of mine. It all happened too quickly, just like Phil Coulter had said it would, but God, the memories!

I'd been in touch with Trevor Templeton, the car dealer. I wanted a Lotus Excel and I'd bought the registration BOX 1T. He had the car at the airport for me when I arrived at Belfast on the Monday. There were crowds of people at the airport – TV, everything – and Lord Mayor Carson too. It was the greatest thing that could happen to him, me winning the title in the year he was mayor, because he was a boxing fan and a big fan of mine as well. James Molyneux, the Unionist leader, was another fan – he wrote to me after every big fight.

Carson put the mayor's chain on me, and told me we'd drive into Belfast in his limousine. But there was my gleaming red Lotus parked behind him, so I told him I was going in that instead. I followed the mayor's car into town and parked in the back of the *Belfast Telegraph* office. There was an open-top bus waiting there, and the crowds were so thick we could hardly move. There were 75,000 people in Royal Avenue, hanging out of windows and on scaffolding – anywhere they could see. Everybody wanted to say 'Well done.' After the bus drive I went out on the balcony of City Hall and spoke to the people. It was a fabulous day.

Afterwards, I got a police escort to the border and the Gardai Special Branch were waiting to take me the rest of the way to Clones. Everybody was expecting me to come into Clones on the Monaghan road, but I got the Branch boys to take me the back way home. There was no milk in the house when I got there, so I drove into Clones to get some from my mother's shop and immediately the news was all around that I was back. So I drove out along the Monaghan road to meet the crowds, and they brought me back in a bus. There were 30,000 in Clones that evening and the population's only 3,500. They stopped out in the rain, a lot of them still half-drunk from two days previously. The town councillors all wanted to get up and say something, and I couldn't believe the patience of the people.

The first thing I did when we got to the Diamond, before I even got up on the platform, was to go and see the ruins of my parents' house. It cancelled out a lot of the joy of winning the title. The fire had done around £50,000 worth of damage, and they'd lost a lot of items of sentimental value. So had I: all my Irish medals were gone and the videos of my fights. I've never been able to replace the videos, either. But it was my mother I felt sorriest for, that the best night of her life should have turned into the worst night of her life. We have a saying in Irish, 'We saw the two days', meaning we knew the good times as well as the bad, but she saw them both on the one day.

Later that week we had a civic reception in Dublin, and it took us an hour and a half to get from the bottom of O'Connell Street to the Mansion House, which is only about half a mile. I'd outdrawn Ian Paisley in Belfast and the Pope in Dublin: not bad for a wee country boy from Clones.

Chapter Twenty-One

> *'Barney ... would always ask, "How much do you want?" ... I'd think, "Hey, you're my manager: how much can you get me?" But he'd always put the onus on me to come up with a figure, and then he'd give me all sorts of reasons why I would have to take a lot less.'*
>
> Barry McGuigan, on negotiating with Barney Eastwood

The public image was one of blissful harmony in the new champion's camp, but in reality the old problems had resurfaced long before McGuigan became world champion. The apparent understanding reached between Leo Rooney and Eastwood at the tail-end of 1983 had been but a temporary calm on the stormy waters of the McGuigan–Eastwood relationship. By the following November, McGuigan had stretched his winning streak to twenty-one fights and had firmly established himself as a legitimate world title contender. A planned defence of the European and British titles against Clyde Ruan, provisionally scheduled for the Albert Hall in London on 5 December, had been shelved because both fighter and manager were unhappy with the purse on offer from the promoters, Mike Barrett and Mickey Duff. (The fight eventually went ahead at the Ulster Hall in Belfast two weeks later than originally scheduled.)

On 14 November 1984, the day after a telephone conversation between fighter and manager concerning the collapse of the mooted title defence in London, Eastwood wrote McGuigan a letter that, in the light of what would happen between the two just eighteen months later, was decidedly ironic. (Copies of all correspondence that passed between both McGuigan and Eastwood and, later, between their respective legal representatives are in the possession of the authors. Legal constraints, however, prohibit the reproduction in full of the Eastwood side's letters, a restriction that impedes the authors' desire – as far as is feasible, given that only one side is co-operating in this venture – to present as balanced a view of the whole McGuigan–Eastwood controversy as is possible.)

In his letter, McGuigan's manager repeated a previously verbal insistence that Pedroza was 'not interested' in granting a world title shot to McGuigan in Belfast unless he could be guaranteed three options on his challenger; that is, a portion of McGuigan's purses for his first three championship defences should he succeed against the Panamanian. McGuigan had long rejected the notion of signing away his future in such a manner, but Eastwood attempted to persuade him to change his mind by informing him that unless he reversed his position on the options, his (Eastwood's) hands were tied and there was little prospect of securing a world title shot.

There were, in fact, twin ironies in the letter. To the public he presented a near idyllic relationship with the fighter and the later perception that all the problems in the relationship had followed McGuigan's decision to seek professional advice, and that the real breakdown had only occurred as a consequence of McGuigan losing the world title in Las Vegas was not discouraged by Eastwood. Throughout the letter Eastwood acknowledged that he and McGuigan had few areas of common ground; 'for that at least,' he had said of the abortive Ruan fight in London, 'you and I were in agreement'.

It was in the penultimate paragraph, however, that the real irony of the entire McGuigan–Eastwood saga revealed itself. Eastwood informed McGuigan that he would in future only negotiate on his behalf with the fighter's 'prior written consent'. This, it should be noted, was Eastwood's own suggestion; yet a mere year and a half later he would categorically reject an identical proposal from McGuigan himself, a rejection from which the 'partnership' between the two would never recover.

Eastwood went on to remind McGuigan that, under the terms of their existing British Boxing Board of Control contract, he, Eastwood, was in effect entitled to commit McGuigan to all or any fights he felt 'necessary', but omitted to add his own contractual obligation 'to arrange the Boxer's professional affairs with a view to the Boxer securing due and proper profit and reward therefrom, to negotiate in every transaction terms and conditions as advantageous as possible to the Boxer'. Eastwood did indeed have the right to commit McGuigan to specific fights, but it was not an inalienable right, it was a conditional one. If McGuigan were not allowed to see either fight contracts or accounts, then how was he to know if a particular fight proposal was 'as advantageous as possible' to him? Also, Eastwood informed McGuigan that he could not 'go to Panama without your agreement'; a year and a half later he would have no qualms about going either there or to Las Vegas without it.

Other points in the letter were of concern to McGuigan. He could see no merit whatsoever in committing himself to a five-fight package deal as suggested by his manager. There was simply no way of telling against whom or under what circumstances those contests might take place. (Eastwood also wrote in the letter that an American television network was interested in a McGuigan bout in 'late February' but that a chance for McGuigan to fight Juan Laporte had been missed because McGuigan had been unable to make up his mind about the fight offer and that Laporte had in the meantime signed for five fights and was therefore unobtainable as a McGuigan opponent. Laporte did, of course, subsequently fight McGuigan on 28 February.)

And, in view of subsequent developments and Eastwood's later comment outside the High Court in Belfast that McGuigan 'had more advisers than the Queen', his manager's written warning that there were 'too many people involved' would carry a retrospective irony for McGuigan: the fighter was still some months away from seeking advice from either James McSparran or Eamonn McEvoy, and the only 'people' involved were Eastwood advisers and associates, not McGuigan ones. That, indeed, was the kernel of their rapidly deteriorating relationship.

Five weeks after he had become the first Irishman to win a world boxing title since Johnny Caldwell had earned partial recognition as bantamweight title-holder in 1961, McGuigan attended a business meeting in a second-floor office at the Royal Avenue branch of the Bank of Ireland in Belfast. The purpose of the meeting was for the newly crowned world champion to hear suggestions from two English-based financial advisers. Among those present, as well as McGuigan himself and his accountant uncle, Leo Rooney, were Barney and Brian Eastwood and James McSparran, a barrister who had long represented the Eastwoods. Little came out of the actual meeting, but a significant development did take place immediately after the talks had concluded.

*

As we were leaving the building, Barney told me that he had what he said was great news for me. By this time we had stopped walking and were standing on our own on the actual steps of the bank, everybody else having moved on a little bit. One of the things that always annoyed me about him was that I always had to agree to something immediately and was never given any time even to think it over properly myself, let alone talk to anybody else about it. Now he told me that he could get me $600,000 for any next two fights. I thought that sounded fantastic, but I was very dubious about signing up for two fights at the same time. We already knew then that my first defence would be against Bernard Taylor, but at that stage there was no way of telling what the fight after that would be: it could, for instance, have been a two-, three- or four-million dollar fight with Azumah Nelson – and I would have been committed to taking it for just $300,000.

But, as usual, Barney was insisting on having his answer there and then, and I felt I had no choice but to give it to him. I said 'yes', of course, but I wonder how many people realize that the deals for both the Bernard Taylor and the Danilo Cabrera world title fights were actually concluded while we were standing on the steps of a bank in Royal Avenue?

*

About ten days later, on Monday 29 July, Barney Eastwood and Mickey Duff met in New York at a press conference organized by Bob Arum to publicize the forthcoming world middleweight championship defence by Marvin Hagler against John Mugabi. (The bout was scheduled for 14 November, but was later postponed for five months when Hagler was injured in training; the rearranged fight would also form a backdrop to negotiations for another McGuigan title fight, that in Las Vegas.) It was at this press conference that Eastwood and Duff opened formal negotiations with Arum for McGuigan's first world title defence, against the Arum-controlled Bernard Taylor.

The conference over, the trio adjourned to Arum's tenth-floor office at 919 Third Avenue, after which they continued their discussions over dinner in the Manhattan Café on the corner of 64th Street and First Avenue. The talks resumed in Arum's office early the following morning, and by noon a deal had been struck. McGuigan would make the first defence of his title before his own King's

Hall supporters on Saturday 28 September, in what would be Belfast's first world title fight since Rinty Monaghan's draw with Terry Allen in 1949.

Back in Ireland, a different story was being handed out. At the very time that Stephen Eastwood was confirming the Taylor fight in an RTE radio interview, the two Dublin evening papers were on the streets of the city with the same back-page lead: a categoric denial by the Eastwoods of a *Sunday Tribune* story two days earlier that McGuigan would meet Taylor on 28 September, as well as an insistence that Eastwood senior was really in New York trying to get agreement on a McGuigan championship defence against Juvenal Ordenes, a Chilean based in Miami. Fight Fan's tip-off had come good again.

Unknown to either Barney or Stephen Eastwood, something else had been happening while the New York talks with Arum were going on; McGuigan had finally been getting some legal advice. Ironically, he was getting it from Eastwood's own barrister, James McSparran – at the suggestion of Eastwood himself.

McGuigan's manager had suggested that now he was world champion, it might be appropriate for him to seek some professional advice about his business affairs. But McGuigan was thinking along different lines.

*

It was the two-fight deal on the steps of the bank that finally decided me. I had put it off for far too long. I was fed up with not being able to talk to anybody, with having nobody to turn to. What was I supposed to know about contracts? I had never even been shown one, let alone had one explained to me.

Barney had always told me that if I wanted advice about anything, about life, or money, or anything else, the man to see was Jimmy McSparran, so early in 1985 I went to see him. That was the day my whole life began to change, the day I started to feel free. McSparran was a barrister who handled a lot of work for Barney at the time, but he was a very moral man and I felt completely confident about pouring my heart out to him. We sat in his study for three hours or more, and I told him everything that was troubling me.

I tried as best I could to explain how I felt, the sense of helplessness and the feeling that I had to negotiate with Eastwood for myself, instead of him negotiating with others on my behalf. Barney, for instance, would always ask, 'How much do you want?' even when we were talking about a London fight that Mickey Duff was promoting. I'd think, 'Hey, you're my manager: how much can you get me?' But he'd always put the onus on me to come up with a figure, and then he'd give me all sorts of reasons why I would have to take a lot less.

I told McSparran all this, and for the first time ever I felt that I'd found somebody who really understood how I felt. Barney knew so many solicitors and barristers that I'd thought I would never be able to find one who could look at the relationship from my angle, and in my whole life I can never remember feeling as relieved as I did that day when I realized that at last I'd found somebody who could understand how imprisoned I felt.

James McSparran was a life-saver for me: I was going out of my mind with worry and frustration, but he pointed me in the right direction. He recommended me to Eamonn McEvoy, who had already crossed swords with Eastwood in a case involving one of Barney's betting shops. I felt comfortable with Eamonn right from our first meeting.

Barney obviously remembered him, and just as obviously didn't like Eamonn, because when he found out that I'd been to see him he was furious. But the Two Macs, McEvoy and McSparran, did so much for me. And McSparran did so at considerable cost to himself. Barney's relationship with McSparran went very cool after that. McSparran lost God knows how many thousands of pounds worth of Eastwood business by helping me, but he never let that stop him. If it weren't for him and McEvoy, I don't know where I would be now or what my life would be like.

Chapter Twenty-Two

'Soldiers should die on the battlefield, not in the trenches.'

The fighting philosophy of Pat McCormack, British light-welterweight champion in 1974

Within a couple of days of beating Pedroza I was back in the gym and training away, doing my usual workouts as if I'd had no fight at all. The problem was that I was in such demand, and not always for money; people were calling in their favours. There were a few paying jobs, though. Barney's son, Brian, who was acting as my commercial agent, arranged appearances for me in Kilkenny, Drogheda, Navan and a few other places. I also attended an anniversary greyhound meeting called after my grandfather Rooney, a small-time bookie who used to stand on his box at dog meetings.

But there never seemed to be anything big happening for me. We didn't have many deals coming our way, and I wondered why that should be. But I was quite happy to do these various appearances, and it was exciting, while it lasted.

Brian put me in touch with a crisp-making company, and we did a deal with them for a lump sum for two years plus royalties on the crisps sales. The company suggested that we start a fan club, with entry forms on the back of the packets. It seemed a good idea, so we agreed to it. I soon started getting letters from kids saying how disappointed they were that they'd joined the club and got nothing back, and I ended up writing cheques myself to refund their fee, and telling them how disgusted and sorry I was. It caused me nothing but embarrassment, and I never got a cent from it.

In November 1986 a piece appeared in an Irish paper about my 'so-called fan club' that made it look as if I had been responsible. In fact, I had nothing to do with it whatsover. I rang the company up numerous times, asking what was happening, but there was always some excuse or other. In the end, more people were unhappy with the club than ever got anything out of it. Members were supposed to get a monthly newsletter. One or two were produced, and then no more. It was a shambles, and I got the blame for it because my name was on it. It was a bad experience all round.

But we got a book deal, and the *Daily Star* contract. [The paper signed McGuigan to an 'exclusive' arrangement, which banned him from speaking to any other newspaper.] The *Daily Star* paid well, but from one point of view it was a mistake; it alienated us from the rest of Fleet Street, so that when the split came with Eastwood, the other papers owed me no favours and they didn't give me any.

I knew when I fought Pedroza that Bernard Taylor would have to be next, as he was the compulsory defence, but I hadn't realized that I would have to fight him so soon. I would have preferred a longer break between fights, but Barney wanted to push in as many defences as possible. I trained like a bastard for it. Barney brought in Bernardo Checa and Dwight Pratchett for sparring, and a Panamanian guy called Umberto Sosa. I ran more for Taylor than for any fight. John Doherty, a Garda in Clones who was a great friend of mine, used to do roadwork with me and we must have run hundreds of miles for that fight, sometimes ten miles a day.

I knew I would have to be fast on my feet for Taylor, who was a lovely mover. He'd been a brilliant amateur and had fought a draw with Pedroza for the title. That was the only one he hadn't won in thirty-four fights.

Barney wanted me to sign a five-fight deal with him, but I wasn't having that. Eventually I signed a two-fight package, with Taylor as the first.

I watched Taylor fighting Benji Marquez, Pedroza and a couple of others, and every time I watched him he got better and better. I stopped watching the tapes for a while because I was getting demoralized. I said to Dermot, 'How the hell am I going to beat this guy? He's brilliant!' He was so classy, although when he hit these guys with what looked like dynamite punches he didn't seem to be doing them any harm. He couldn't be banging that hard if he was staying on them, hitting them and not being able to put them away.

Dermot watched the tapes with me, over and over again, and told me, 'Stay on this guy, stick to him and don't let him breathe.' Others who'd fought him had stayed on him only in fits and starts.

I watched him against Tyrone Downes; he punched Downes to pieces. It encouraged me to see that he had Downes on the floor, but Downes got up and travelled the ten rounds. I told Barney how good I thought Taylor was, but he said, 'Ah, he's only a powder puff.'

All of the fighters I'd watched him against had goes at him, but never stayed on him the way I could. In some ways, it was the same approach as I had for Pedroza. Even Rocky Lockridge, whom I respected as a really good fighter, would only go at Pedroza in flurries, bang-bang-bang stop, bang-bang-bang stop. That suits boxers like Taylor and Pedroza. That's the way they love to do it, but I knew that I could put in the sustained effort that would be needed to beat him.

I'd sparred really well for the fight. Barney even had a ring set up in the Ulster Hall, so that I could get the feel of boxing in a hall again. Give him credit, it was a good move. I was sparring with Jeff Roberts from Guyana, a nice mover, and I put him down with a double left jab and a right. He had a headguard on, but he was gone. I knew then I was ready. I'd worked hard for the fight, brought my weight down gradually from ten stone plus. I was on the weight from a fortnight before the fight, and held it. I was sharp as a tack.

On the morning of the fight I made the weight easily, but when I looked in the gym Taylor was skipping in the ring. He'd come in from the States a bit complacent about his weight, because he knew he could do it, no problem, out there. There were rumours that he was two pounds overweight. Rubbish: he was twelve ounces over, that's all. He skipped for ten minutes, got his gear off, dried off and got back on the scales ... and he was still twelve ounces over. He skipped a bit more, walked around for a while, and made the weight on the nose.

He looked magnificent when he got in the ring. He was big as a house, built like a welterweight with a beautiful physique. He moved as well as Leonard or any of them, too. I expected Taylor to be fast, but I thought that TV can speed people up and make them look faster than they are. Not Taylor! When the fight started he was even faster than he'd looked on TV. I'd never met anybody who could throw punches or get out of the way so quick. He could throw a combination of five punches and be gone before you'd even get close to him. He was as fast as a light-flyweight, and I hadn't any time to place my shots or put power in them. He walked on to a few sucker ones, but I just kept banging away at his guts. I knew it would drain him eventually.

He was hitting me, OK, but only with one at a time. The rule is never to get hit with any more than one in a combination. If you get hit with one, don't get hit with the next two. He might land the second, but he wouldn't hit me with the first or the third, or he'd land the first and miss the second and the third. I was slipping and sliding his punches, and it was killing him. I could hear him panting and gasping, and I knew he was thinking, 'Come on, man, give me a break – leave me alone.' But I knew he was going to crack. I stayed on him, and I could hear the crowd going mad. I knew he was winning the rounds, but I wasn't concerned about it, nor was my corner. I had Teddy Atlas in the corner this time. His fighter, Chris Reid, a New York Irishman, was on the bill.

It was a fifteen-round fight. I knew that he would win the first half, but that he'd have to slow down to my pace in the second half. He won the first four rounds clearly, and maybe shared the fifth. The sixth was on level terms, but in the seventh I overpowered him and in the eighth I dug my heels in and whacked him.

I didn't really give him an enormous hammering, but I was definitely getting to him. Just at the end of the round, he pulled his left hand back and I hit him a body punch that went in up to my elbow. He was right on top of me, and I could hear the air leave him. It was the best body punch I ever threw. He lifted his head up to try to show me that he was OK, so I hit him a right hand and a left hook just as the bell went. He gave a little skip on the way to the corner, to shake himself up. I looked across at him, and I was thinking, 'Come on out for the next round, Bernard, because you and me are going to have some fun.' But then we heard the commotion and saw Taylor walking away to a neutral corner. That was it; he was done.

I felt sorry that he hadn't come out for the ninth round. It would have been hard to top the Pedroza night, but I'd have done it if he'd come out for another round. I felt a bit cheated, that he'd stolen my thunder by quitting. Pat McCormack, who loved a punch-up, used to say, 'Soldiers should die on the battlefield, not in the trenches.' From Taylor's point of view it was a wise move; he who fights and runs away lives to fight another day, and here he is, still fighting for titles five years later.

Beating him was a great relief. I thought I'd got the best one out of the way, and as it had been a compulsory defence I had six months' grace before the next was due.

That night we went back to Clones, and the next morning we went into the Lennard Arms, where they'd been drinking for three days. We watched the video of the fight in the ballroom there, but it was an anti-climax after the Pedroza fight. Johnny McCormack, who lived in a caravan beside the lake opposite our house at Kilroosky, was there with some of the boys, full as a po. He was a widower; his wife had died about ten years previously, and he'd come home to Ireland. We would go ferreting and fishing together: I'd hear a rap on the window at five in the morning, and it would be Johnny saying, 'McGuigan! Get up!' Out we'd go and catch his breakfast, maybe half a dozen trout. He wore these big waders, and he'd drop the trout down the waders and jump on the bike home.

A couple of days later I had to go to London for a press conference, and the morning I came back poor Johnny died of a massive heart attack. It was very sad, and Blain missed him terribly.

Chapter Twenty-Three

'He was hard work for anybody: one tough, brave man.'
Barry McGuigan on his second world title challenger,
Danilo Cabrera

Barney wanted to put me on again before the end of 1985, against Fernando Sosa of Argentina, but I refused so he put it back to February and booked the Simmonscourt Pavilion at the Royal Dublin Society's showgrounds at Ballsbridge. It meant I couldn't enjoy my Christmas. I actually ran ten miles on Christmas Day, over the mountains, to sicken myself so much that I wouldn't be able to eat Christmas dinner. It screwed it up for Sandra and the family, but I knew that if I ate a big dinner I'd bloat up, and if that happened I'd only have to work the weight off again.

I went into camp in January, staying at Jean Anderson's house in Bangor with two Mexicans Barney had brought in for sparring. They were tough boys, hard as nails. It was a fairly mild January, by our standards, but they were always complaining about being cold. They had a big green anorak apiece, with fur-trimmed hoods, and they wore these things everywhere, even doing roadwork. The two Mexicans were staying up at the top of the house, and one night about ten o'clock I had to go up to their room to tell them about some change in the next day's programme, something like that. The heating was on full blast in the room, but there were the two boys lying in bed, covered in blankets, with the anoraks on them. They even had their workout suits on, ready for the morning, so when they got out of bed they'd only have to put their boots on. I didn't look, but maybe they had them on as well.

I found out as much as I could about Sosa. He was a hard pro, a typical tough Argentinian who did everything well but nothing brilliantly. And then, just seventeen days before the fight, I got a call at the gym in Belfast to say that he'd broken his finger and was out. All the training had been to fight a squat, come-forward guy, but now I had a new opponent with a totally different style, Danilo Cabrera of the Dominican Republic. He had been training to fight for the Dominican title a day or two before the Dublin date, so he was fit and ready to step in.

They sent us a tape of him and I got a bit complacent watching it. I thought, 'I'm going to eat this guy alive.' I'd been sparring really well, and Barney too was satisfied that I'd need no more than six or seven rounds. But what they'd done was to lead us into a false sense of security. The tape was about eighteen months old, and Cabrera looked bad on it, but he'd improved immensely in the meantime. What I'd failed to recognize, too, was that he took a tremendous bang on the chin, and once we were settled in Dublin we started getting reports about Cabrera's sparring. He had a stablemate with him who was a far better boxer, but Cabrera was able to keep coming back at him when the fellow tired.*

We both made the weight comfortably, and I went back to our suite at the Berkeley Court Hotel for a sleep. The hotel is next to Lansdowne Road rugby ground, and this was the day of the Ireland–Wales game. The fans were gathering for the game, and they knew I was staying there, so all I could hear was chants of 'Bar-ee, Bar-ee', and next thing a bloody jazz band turns up playing outside my window. I thought maybe Cabrera had sent them round. It was even worse when the game got underway, because I could hear every cheer. In the end I got Sean McGivern to help me pull the mattress into the bathroom, and I lay on the floor there listening to Phil Coulter on the headset and trying to rest. But I never got a minute's sleep the whole day, between the noise and the nerves that I had before every fight.

During the afternoon I rang room service and ordered baked beans on toast. Half an hour later it hadn't arrived, so I rang again and was assured that it was on the way. My beans finally arrived an hour after I'd ordered them: the Berkeley Court was such an upmarket place that they didn't have a tin of baked beans and they'd had to send somebody out to the corner shop to buy them.

We left for the fight about an hour before it. The nerves had gone, and I felt great. Sean McGivern acted as the decoy for me; he ran into the Rolls with Barney, so that the fans outside the hotel

---

* The stablemate was Antonio Rivera, who six months later won the IBF version of the title.

would think it was me, and while they were distracted I left by a side door and was driven to the RDS.

The dressing-room was a wee Portakabin at the back of the arena. Gregorio Benitez came in to watch me tape, and there was no bother; it was all very friendly. Gregorio's son, Wilfred, had won world titles at three weights, so he'd been through the routine many times before.

Barney had suggested that this time my father shouldn't sing 'Danny Boy'; he wanted a harpist to play instead. But I told him that my father was part of me, and Barney gave way.

Early on in the fight I banged Cabrera hard with the jab, to see what he was like. But he was young [twenty-two], and as I went on in my fighting career I learned that the younger a boy is, the better he can take a shot. Even if he's not experienced, he's more durable. For the first ten minutes or so I was actually moving backwards and outboxing him, moving quickly in and out. I wasn't doing anything perfectly, not doing enough of either boxing or fighting, but everything was working well enough even if I wasn't putting him under any sustained attack. He was there to take my title and he was coming to me, but when he went forward I was boxing neatly on the retreat. No Fancy Dan stuff, just stepping back and drawing him on to good shots.

The referee, Ed Eckert of America, warned me for a low right in the third, and in the fifth Cabrera went down on one knee, claiming he'd been fouled. Eckert walked around the ring, speaking to all three judges, and I thought I'd got a public warning and been docked a point. But in fact he'd been unsighted, and was only asking what they'd seen.

In the eighth round I got cut. Cabrera hit me a right hand and burst open a swelling that had started coming up under the right eye in the second. I could feel the warm blood running down my face and I saw his eyes double in size. He was running at me and making mistakes, and I thought, 'I'm going to get you, you bastard.'

I stepped in and bounced one off his head and he went sprawling into the ropes. I rushed back in, hit him another couple of punches, and he grabbed on to me. He felt strong as a horse, and I couldn't get his hands off me. He wanted to fall, but I couldn't push him away from me. Finally I did, and hit him a couple more. The referee came in, and so did Cabrera's manager, Hector Rivera, and everybody thought the fight had been stopped.

The ring was suddenly full of people. Dermot was there, of course, and Paddy Byrne was working on my eye. He was only getting it presentable enough for the TV interviews, but he quickly realized that the fight wasn't over and that he was instead trying to save my title.

Some of Cabrera's people were protesting to Eckert, but old Benitez came over and congratulated me, accepting that they had lost. But in fact Eckert hadn't hear the bell, nor had anybody else, and after Eckert consulted with the timekeeper he ordered the fight to resume. I'd just been cut and because they'd had to clear the ring Cabrera had been given an extra minute and a half to recover.

They were getting worried in the corner because I'd got a couple more cuts, little ones. There was arguing going on and Barney was nervous as hell. He wasn't happy with the way Paddy was working on the cuts, so he took a lump of Vaseline and stuck it straight into my eye. Eddie took the towel and wiped most of the muck out of the eye, but then the bell went and I had to go out and move around for half a minute until the eye cleared.

At the end of the eleventh I came back to the corner and heard Barney say, 'Hang on, Eddie, I'm going to let Teddy [Atlas] up.' Eddie said, 'Why? Am I not good enough?' I'm sitting on the stool saying, 'Ah Jesus, boys, come on', trying to make peace. So Teddy came up the stairs and he's whispering in my ear while the two boys are arguing, telling me to double up on the left hooks because when I'd been hitting him with one, he was staying there for the second.

It took me until the fourteenth to catch him. He lunged forward with a left hand, and as his left hand came down I moved in with a left hook and a right and down he went. He got up and walked towards his corner, looking up at the sky. Eckert wiped his gloves and waved him on, without even asking if he was OK. I ran over and hit him again on the side of the head, and his legs went. He tried to grab me but went down, and as he fell he spat his gumshield out. He started to get up, holding on to me, and then doubled over, searching around for his gumshield on the canvas – and Eckert said, 'Box on!'

Cabrera was bent over with his back to me, and I didn't know whether I was supposed to hit him or kick his arse. I even thought about slapping him on the arse, which would have been hilarious, but he was so gone that even a tap there would have put him over and probably got me disqualified. So I tapped him in the body instead and put my arms up, and Eckert took the hint and stopped the fight. But it was the worst bit of refereeing I've ever seen.

After the fight my face looked like a butcher's block, cuts and lumps everywhere. I went to the press conference afterwards, feeling very depressed. The press were very critical; they felt I should have got rid of him long before that. But when I watched the fight a few days later I thought I'd boxed quite well; he was just a bit more durable than I'd expected. He subsequently proved himself a good fighter. He went ten rounds with Azumah Nelson at two weeks' notice, when he hadn't been training for any fight, and he gave good fights to champions like Julio Cesar Chavez and Juan Martin Coggi.

I got stick from some reporters, who wrote that I had boxed below my best and made hard work of him. But that's not giving Cabrera credit. He was hard work for anybody: one tough, brave man.

Chapter Twenty-Four

'When over 27,000 people went to Loftus Road, who were they going to see – a guy from Panama named Eusebio Pedroza or me?'

Barry McGuigan, discussing his crowd appeal

In early March, with the Cabrera fight safely if painfully behind him, there was time for McGuigan to have a short holiday before resuming training for his fourth world title fight. He and Sandra went to Portugal for eight days, with Dermot and his girlfriend, Janet Dillon. Eastwood also took to the air, flying off to America on a double mission: to see Mickey Duff's fighter, John Mugabi, challenge Marvin Hagler for the undisputed world middleweight title and, more importantly, to explore the likely options for McGuigan's next fight.

In the middle of his Portuguese interlude, early on the Wednesday morning, McGuigan phoned the Eastwood office in Belfast to enquire if there had been any developments. He left a number at which he could be contacted and within a couple of hours he had received a call from his manager. The contents of that call would become a matter of considerable dispute within a very short time, and would help propel the increasingly rocky five-year-old 'marriage' of McGuigan and Eastwood towards its ultimate divorce.

Eastwood would later maintain that he told McGuigan in the course of that call that his next fight would be against his originally intended opponent for the Dublin bout, Fernando Sosa, in Las Vegas on 23 June, and that the world champion had raised no objection to the proposal. But McGuigan, while acknowledging that Eastwood did inform him of the Las Vegas venture in the course of the telephone conversation, is adamant that it was mentioned only as one of a number of possibilities and not as a specific commitment. Another possibility was one that had been in the air since the previous summer, the long-mooted challenge to Wilfredo Gomez for the WBA junior-lightweight title.

*

After Cabrera, that was the fight I really wanted. It seemed to make perfect sense: I could challenge for a second world title without risking my featherweight one. Gomez was coming up to thirty at that stage. He had had a long and tough career and had struggled in his more recent fights. Although he was a truly great champion in his day (one of the best of modern times), he certainly looked ready for the taking.

When the idea of fighting him came up first, just after I had won the featherweight title from Pedroza, there wasn't much we could do about it then because of the mandatory defence obligations I had to Bernard Taylor. There might have been a chance of making the Gomez fight [the Madison Square Garden bid of John Condon] towards the end of 1986, but it would have been too soon after the Taylor one; and anyway, once the Irish Permanent Building Society came in as our sponsors instead of Smirnoff's, they wanted a fight to go on in Dublin, and Gomez wasn't interested in that.

Then, immediately after the Cabrera fight, Barney started talking about a fight in the King's Hall in April. At first he mentioned a date early in the month, but when I told him I'd never be ready by then he switched it to 25 April. But the whole idea was crazy as far as I was concerned; it was just too soon after Cabrera and I was still all sore and my cuts needed a lot more time. It would have been suicide from my point of view.

So April fell by the board and I went off to Portugal. When Barney phoned me there he did tell me about Bob Arum's offer of the fight with Sosa [as was then the intention] in Las Vegas, but what he said was only that it looked like the one to go for, not that he was committing me to it. I told him again that the fight I fancied at that point was against Gomez in Madison Square Garden. 'It's not as far away as Vegas and there's more Irish in New York,' I said to him, but he said that the Duvas [the father and son team of Lou and Dan Duva] were proving too difficult to deal with. But by the time we came home from Portugal, the fight in Las Vegas with Fernando Sosa had already been announced.

*

That announcement had come in a Dublin paper, the *Sunday Tribune*, on 16 March. Saying that McGuigan would receive a purse of 'some $500,000', the report also stated that four days previously, on the Wednesday, Eastwood had rejected what amounted to a $1.5 million offer from Dan Duva for a McGuigan title challenge to Wilfredo Gomez in, most likely, Madison Square Garden. That night, around ten o'clock, Fight Fan called.

'It is your turn now.'

'For what?'

'To provide information. There is something between the lines in that story and I am sure Barry and McEvoy would like to know what it is. From what I hear, you have understated the purse by $100,000 but I think they would still like to know why a purse of $1.5 million was turned down in favour of one that is only 40 per cent of that; it just does not make sense. The Boss will be back in a couple of days and, seeing as to be forewarned is to be forearmed, no doubt McGuigan and McEvoy would appreciate a little enlightenment. Find out what you can. Duva would seem to be as good a starting point as any.'

Dan Duva maintained, and continues to maintain, that far from being 'too difficult to deal with' he actually went out of his way to accommodate Eastwood in the matter of a McGuigan–Gomez fight. Gomez, he conceded, was nearing the end of his illustrious career and was anxious for 'one last big payday' and knew that by far his best chance of achieving that lay in having McGuigan in the opposite corner, particularly if the bout could be held in New York, where both the Irish and the Puerto Ricans formed such large ethnic groupings. Duva, who held promotional rights to Gomez as a result of the latter's winning of the WBA junior-lightweight title from Rocky Lockridge, claimed that he had long been in favour of getting McGuigan and Gomez into the same ring.

And Eastwood himself had apparently been of a similiar mind. As long ago as the previous January Mickey Duff had sounded out each of the three major American television networks about what financial interest they might be prepared to express in a possible McGuigan–Gomez bout. Duff – and, presumably, Eastwood – put a $1 million asking price on the fight but received a mixed response from the networks. CBS, because of prior commitments, was unable to become involved until July at the earliest and therefore did not even bother to quote a figure; NBC was only willing to go to 'not much more than $400,000'; and ABC, while suggesting that it 'might be prepared to offer in the region of half as much again', was still falling a long way short of Duff's seven-figure target.

There had been more success with another potential obstacle to a McGuigan–Gomez fight: the reluctance of the WBA to permit the Puerto Rican champion to postpone any longer his mandatory defence against his number one challenger, Alfredo Layne of Panama. Layne had been the WBA's official challenger since late 1984 – he was paid a reputed $50,000 in 'step-aside money' to allow Gomez to challenge Rocky Lockridge for the title in May 1985 – and by March 1986 the WBA was reluctant to let Gomez, who had been inactive since the Lockridge bout, to leave Layne waiting any longer.

But a unique solution to the impasse was reached: the WBA decided that it would permit Gomez and McGuigan to fight for the junior-lightweight championship provided that the title would be declared vacant regardless of who won the bout. McGuigan's part in the agreement was of little consequence to the WBA, but the Panama-based organization was adamant that if Gomez wanted to circumvent Layne yet again he would have to meet this condition – and do it in writing. The WBA's patience with Gomez was wearing thin, and while understandably reluctant to stand in the way of a lucrative McGuigan–Gomez fight (not least because of the sizeable sanctioning fee the WBA would receive from it), it was anxious to ensure that Gomez would not get his 'one last big payday' and then, if successful, continue to avoid Layne.

Thus, despite Gomez's long-standing mandatory defence commitment, the only real obstacle to a high-profile clash between the triple world champion from Puerto Rico and McGuigan was the obvious one: money. But Dan Duva, despite the failure of his late 1985 attempt to secure a Gomez–McGuigan match, was convinced that now, a mere four months later, he had at last managed to overcome that hurdle. The deal Duva states he offered Eastwood was for around $1.5 million. In precise terms, he offered McGuigan's manager a flat purse for his fighter of $1 million plus the complete British and Irish TV rights, a concession that promised to bring in a combined total of a further $500,000 or certainly something very close to that sum. The offer was put to Eastwood when he met Duva in New York on 10 March, the Monday of the week McGuigan was in Portugal and while Eastwood was en route to the Hagler–Mugabi fight in Las Vegas.

'My understanding,' said Duva, 'was that we had a deal. Sure, we still had to dot a few i's and cross a few t's, but we certainly seemed to have an agreement in principle. That, at least, was my clear impression of how the meeting had gone and I can hardly have been alone in taking that view, because when we broke up it was on the basis that Barney would return in a couple of days and then we would sort out the remaining details.

'Barney, though, never returned. Instead, on the Wednesday morning I was told that the Arum offer had come in in the meantime and that they were going to take that. I wasn't told exactly how much they were getting, but it had to be in the order of something like $1.6 million, otherwise they would hardly turn down my bid, would they?'

McGuigan's manager never sought to deny or even dispute the $1.5 million assessment of Dan Duva's proposal, either at the time of the original *Tribune* story or when, less than a month later, the fighter himself cited it in a letter to Eastwood. Had Duva's offer been accepted and a fight with Gomez resulted, McGuigan would have fared considerably better financially, win or lose, than he did from the subsequent Las Vegas deal.

For one thing Eastwood would have been involved only as McGuigan's manager and not as the fight promoter. As such he would have been entitled only to his $33\frac{1}{3}$ per cent manager's commission, leaving McGuigan with the remaining $66\frac{2}{3}$ per cent. (Under the standard BBBC contract a manager is entitled to take $33\frac{1}{3}$ per cent for overseas engagements, and 25 per cent for domestic matches.)

All expenses, of course, would come off the top, but as these would entail only training camp costs and the like, and no promotional expenditure, a figure of up to $100,000 would represent a more than adequate allowance. That would leave $1.4 million to be split between boxer and manager, giving McGuigan over $900,000 for challenging for the junior-lightweight title compared to the $600,000 he received for *defending* his featherweight title in Las Vegas.

McGuigan knew for three months before the Las Vegas bout what his financial return from it would be. What he did not know then was what financial harvest his manager would reap from the Nevada venture. That information would have to be wrung out of Eastwood bit by bit over the next year.

*

When Barney first told me about the Las Vegas deal he said that the purse was $400,000. Then, when I said I wasn't interested, he came back and said that he'd got it up to $600,000. At that stage I thought that the fight was going to be held inside, in Caesars Palace, in the Pavilion, but even at that I said, 'The heat will kill me.' 'No, it won't,' he said. 'The heat's not going to be any harder than in the King's Hall.' I never liked the idea of Vegas from the start.

The minute I came back from Portugal I went to see Eamonn to talk to him about it. It was by far the biggest purse of my career, so obviously, in one sense at least, I was delighted with it. But I still wasn't sure about either the fight or the money. Things were never the same between us after the Cabrera fight. We'd had our differences in the past – and, I suppose, more and more of them as time went on – but after the Dublin fight everything seemed to be gone. I was beginning to realize that I just had to be worth more than he was paying me.

I kept being told about how well I was being paid, about how the likes of Azumah Nelson had to defend his title for maybe $200,000 and sometimes even less, and how I should be grateful for what I was being paid. Well, Azumah Nelson wasn't drawing in the money that I was. Do you know that when Nelson defended his title in San Juan against Danilo Cabrera the day before I fought Steve Cruz in Vegas, he drew a crowd of just over 400 people? Just over 400! I was fighting in front of crowds of 6,000 and 7,000 people and would surely have been able to pull in a lot more if we'd had a bigger venue. When over 27,000 people went to Loftus Road, who were they going to see – a guy from Panama named Eusebio Pedroza or me?

And every one of my major fights, as well as having full houses, also had both television and sponsorship money. I just knew, given the money that was involved in my fights, that a comparison with the likes of Nelson wasn't fair.

*

Eamonn McEvoy's advice to McGuigan was that he ask his manager to let him see a copy of the Las Vegas fight contract. Eastwood was returning to Belfast the following day and he and McGuigan were to meet to discuss what had already been announced as the latter's next fight.

That meeting took place in the Manor House Hotel in Enniskillen in the middle of the week following McGuigan's return from Portugal. It was, McGuigan admits, decidedly strained. And for a third reason: besides his dissatisfaction with both the venue and purse for his next title defence, he had since discovered that, by the terms of the deal Eastwood had struck with Bob Arum, he was also committed to a major pre-fight publicity tour that would take ten days and would involve flying to up to a dozen US cities.

McGuigan opposed the publicity tour first because he felt it to be an unnecessary diversion in the immediate run-up to a defence of his world championship, and, second, because he resented the fact that his manager had neglected to mention it to him in any of their telephone conversations while he was in Portugal. The first he heard about the tour, he maintains, was when he read about it in the papers a couple of days after the original Las Vegas fight story.

Ten days after the Las Vegas fight was first disclosed, Eastwood called a press conference at the Berkeley Court Hotel in Dublin to reveal further details about the bout and about the controversial pre-fight publicity tour. Bob Arum, in a telephone link-up with the conference, publicly stated that the fight would share top billing in a triple-bout extravaganza that 'could gross up to $10 million' and added that both the fight itself and the publicity tour represented the ideal opportunity for McGuigan to establish himself in a big way in America.

McGuigan, however, was not present to hear the glowing appraisals of the golden opportunities that awaited him. He had, his manager explained to the gathered media, been struck down with 'a gastric upset' and had therefore been unable to attend. Most of those in attendance accepted Eastwood's explanation, but a few thought the world champion's non-appearance 'not insignificant'.

Five days after the Dublin press conference, on 31 March 1986, Eastwood sent a letter to McGuigan. It turned out to be the opening chapter in a lengthy series of correspondence that would eventually be taken over by their respective solicitors and would culminate in a total and highly acrimonious dissolution of their once famous 'partnership'.

After noting the success of the Berkeley Court function and remarking that he had explained McGuigan's non-appearance at the reception as being due to a gastric upset, Eastwood got down to the nitty-gritty. The plans for the Las Vegas fight, he assured McGuigan, were 'as we agreed when I phoned you from New York', to which he added that he had since signed contracts with Top Rank. McGuigan's manager also raised yet again the subject of multi-bout agreements by advising the fighter that he had Antonio Esparragoza (the WBA's number one challenger, against whom McGuigan would have to make a mandatory defence in the event of his retaining his title in Las Vegas) already 'signed up'. Eastwood ventured the opinion that he doubted if it would be financially viable to stage this bout in Ireland, but assured McGuigan that they could discuss the matter while on the publicity tour of America.

The following day, on receipt of the letter, McGuigan drove the forty-six miles from his home in Kilroosky to Eamonn McEvoy's office in Lurgan. He told his solicitor he wanted to give a full response to the Eastwood letter. That, he felt, was seemingly the only chance he might have of getting his current feelings on the developing controversy across to his manager. After discussing the matter with McEvoy, McGuigan returned home and, with a little additional help from his father, sent his own letter to Eastwood later that same evening.

*

I was just so confused about the whole situation. No matter how often I tried to tell him how unhappy I was about the whole thing or how uncertain I felt, he either didn't seem to know or else was simply incapable of taking it in. The situation by then seemed so hopeless that, after that first meeting in Enniskillen after he'd come back from America, I never bothered even asking him for the contract again. There just wasn't any point in pursuing the matter because I knew it would end up like those sort of things always had in the past – with me not getting the information I was looking for and then becoming even angrier and more frustrated with him because of it.

*

McGuigan wrote:

Dear Mr Eastwood,

I was very surprised to receive your letter today and particularly your statement that the plans are 'as we agreed when I phoned you from New York'. I have absolutely no doubt that nothing was agreed when you phoned me from New York. During that telephone conversation you said that a lot of people were offering me things but that the best prospect seemed to be Arum.

(You told me that it was not possible to arrange a fight with Gomez. You knew that this was the best prospect and the fight which I wanted. It gave me an opportunity of becoming a double world champion, and I understand that Duva would have paid a million dollars plus the TV rights for the British Isles for this fight in Madison Square Garden.)

When you told me during the telephone conversation that Gomez was not available, I said for you to see what else you could get and let me know. You mentioned a number of possibilities in Las Vegas, including Sosa. I specifically said to you the figure which I would have to get to fight Sosa in Las Vegas. That is not the figure which you mentioned to me during our recent telephone conversation, and I am certainly not prepared to fight for less than the figure which I specifically said to you that I would not accept during the telephone conversation from New York. I made it plain that the figure mentioned was of course the net amount to be paid to me.

Insofar as the proposed tour is concerned, it was never mentioned during the telephone conversation and I never heard of it until it was published in the press. From what details I know of the tour it would be detrimental to my training, and certainly I do not intend to have years of hard preparation go by the board for some publicity stunt.

However, the first matter which has to be dealt with before anything is agreed is the purse for the Sosa fight. You are aware of the figure which I said I required and which I made plain was a net figure to me.

Finally, I should say that I want to deal with one fight at a time and after the Sosa fight I will discuss with you Esparragoza. I want to make it absolutely clear that I will not be tied up in any multi-fight package deal with any promoter. My view at the present time is that I should have my compulsory defence in Ireland in accordance with our previous discussion.

PS – I am not mentioning the figure in this letter in case it is read by someone else. However, you know exactly the figure that I am talking about.

The correspondence course in relationship disintegration was now in full swing. Already it appeared to be developing a momentum of its own. The two had still not had any personal contact since their inconclusive Manor House Hotel meeting almost three weeks previously and, on 7 April, Eastwood began round two of the letters battle.

Describing the tone and content of McGuigan's letter as 'perverse', Eastwood outlined the difficulties inherent in big fight negotiations and, after telling McGuigan that he had signed a binding contract with Top Rank on his behalf, he listed what he said were the two main points of that contract: that McGuigan was obliged to begin the publicity tour in New York on 21 April, and that he was also under contract to arrive in Palm Springs for training on 19 May and then report to Caesars Palace in Las Vegas on 13 June to complete his training in public.

He went on to warn the world champion of the likely consequences of a refusal to fulfil any of the conditions of the contract, adding that while he regretted the form the letters between the two were taking, he had developed the feeling from McGuigan's letter that 'I may not be enjoying your full confidence and goodwill'.

He closed by suggesting an early meeting in Belfast, in the presence of a third party acceptable to both, to remove the 'misunderstandings and suspicion' which he saw developing.

Chapter Twenty-Five

'I do not require your written consent or signature to commit you to fight, and if I did, it would belittle me and leave me in an almost impossible position to act on your behalf.'

Barney Eastwood, in a letter to Barry McGuigan in the spring of 1986

From McGuigan's perspective it could be said, rightly or wrongly, that Eastwood's second letter marked the beginning of the end of their relationship, as there were a number of comments in it which the fighter felt unfair. Not least of these was his manager's assertion that his, McGuigan's, own letter did not seem to be the type 'that should be exchanged between two people with as much as we have got riding on a harmonious relationship'.

A harmonious relationship, McGuigan felt, was only possible when each party had complete confidence and trust in the other and when the basic format of that relationship was one of mutual frankness and an absence of secrecy. He did not then know what he would later learn about the Las Vegas fight, and the financial arrangements relating to it, but he did know that he was not being brought into the full picture – and that in itself was worrying. It did not, to his way of thinking, help towards the formation of 'a harmonious relationship'.

In one area, though, he appeared to be making a degree of progress in getting through to his manager. Eastwood had written that it seemed to him that McGuigan saw himself 'as negotiating with me and not me with Top Rank on your behalf', which suggested that Eastwood had at least a glimmer of understanding of McGuigan's feelings. The problem was that the boxer had felt that way for over three years, and had Eastwood appreciated that earlier and given McGuigan some degree of involvement in the decision-making process regarding his career, they might not have found themselves in their current predicament. Eastwood's apparent understanding of McGuigan's feelings, though, had come too late in the day to stave off an increasingly inevitable breach.

*

Something else in that letter bothered me: Barney's comment that he 'almost thought that a stranger had written it'. Well, a stranger hadn't written it. Eamonn had helped me sort out my thoughts and the kind of things I wanted to say, but I wrote it myself when I got back home and, in fact, my father contributed as much to it as Eamonn. Besides, and this really did upset me, so what if Eamonn had written the entire letter for me? It was OK for Barney to surround himself with legal advisers, but whenever I tried to get somebody to help me with things I didn't understand or didn't know how to say, that was a different matter.

There was no misunderstanding whatsoever about the pre-fight publicity tour, because that was never mentioned in the entire course of the phone call in Portugal in any way, shape or form, either directly or indirectly.

As for 'confidence and good will', well, who had withheld that from whom? I never at any time in the five years we were together enjoyed Barney's confidence. He never confided in me, certainly not about what concerned me most, the boxing business.

*

Four days later, while McGuigan was still pondering the previous communication from his manager, Eastwood wrote again. This time he included a specific threat, declaring his intention to forward copies of his letters to McGuigan to the BBBC, the WBA and Top Rank unless he received a reply within three days, by 15 April. He did not say whether McGuigan's letters to him would be included in the dispatch.

That letter, however, was never answered, at least not in written form. Two days after it was written, on Sunday 13 April, McGuigan and Eastwood had their first face-to-face meeting for over three weeks. Once again the chosen venue was the Manor House Hotel in Enniskillen and, as was the case at the previous get-together at the same establishment, the atmosphere was decidedly strained. The pair, in short, made no headway whatsoever and the meeting finally broke up with a request from McGuigan that Eastwood refrain from signing any further contracts on his behalf without first consulting him.

The following Friday (18 April), in the wake of the unsatisfactory session in Enniskillen, Eastwood wrote again. This time he reproduced in full their obligations to each other under the BBBC contract they had signed in March 1981, which had been subsequently extended by Eastwood under its automatic provisions when McGuigan became British champion. The clauses which Eastwood felt it necessary to spell out in detail were:

2. OBLIGATIONS OF MANAGER:
The Manager agrees and undertakes during the continuance of this Agreement:
(i) to act as Manager for the Boxer;
(ii) to arrange and supervise a suitable training programme for the Boxer;
(iii) to use his best endeavours to arrange for the Boxer a proper programme of boxing contests, matches and exhibitions, and other professional engagements and events (hereinafter together called 'the Events') which may include but shall in no way be limited to:
   (a) engagements as sparring assistants to other boxers in training;
   (b) music hall, theatrical or cinema film appearances;
   (c) literary contributions or authorizations for literary contributions to any suitable publications;
   (d) radio, television or other broadcasting; and
   (e) suitable product, preparation or commodity recommendations and advertisements, acceptable to and honestly subscribed to by the Boxer, and complying in each jurisdiction in which such recommendations and advertisements are to be used or appear with the relevant laws and standards (whether statutory or not) from time to time applicable thereto;
(iv) to arrange the Boxer's professional affairs with a view to the Boxer securing due and proper profit and reward therefrom, to negotiate in every transaction terms and conditions as advantageous as possible to the Boxer, regularly to render to the Boxer a full account of all monies received and all expenses incurred, and promptly to pay to the Boxer the monies to which he is entitled pursuant to Article 5 of this Agreement in connection with any Event, or which have otherwise been received on the Boxer's behalf;
(v) to take reasonable steps to supervise the health and safety of the Boxer in the pursuance and context of his profession;
(vi) not to contract the services of the Boxer for any Event arranged to

take place after any date on which this Agreement may reasonably be expected to terminate; and

(vii) to observe all regulations and conditions of the BBB of C applicable to Managers, and to observe and ensure that the Boxer observes all regulations and conditions of the BBB of C applicable to Full Professional Boxers.

3. AUTHORIZATION OF MANAGER:

The Boxer hereby irrevocably authorizes the Manager during the continuance of this Agreement to act as the Boxer's Agent for the specific and sole purpose of fulfilling the Manager's obligations set out in Article 2 above.

4. OBLIGATIONS OF BOXER:

The Boxer agrees and undertakes:

(i) during the continuance of this Agreement to be managed and directed exclusively by the Manager and not to enter into any agreement or arrangement with any other Manager or person for any of the above mentioned purposes without obtaining the prior written consent of the Manager;

(ii) to accept and fulfil to the best of his ability all Events reasonably negotiated on the Boxer's behalf by the Manager;

(iii) throughout the continuance of this Agreement to use his best endeavours to keep himself in the fittest possible physical condition for the purposes of his profession;

(iv) during the continuance of this Agreement to observe all Regulations of the BBB of C applicable to Full Professional Boxers.

The problem with that letter, to McGuigan's mind, was obvious: his manager, while at pains to point out the various responsibilities that their BBBC contract placed on each of them, had repeatedly ignored one of *his* primary responsibilities under the contract: 'regularly to render to the Boxer a full account of all monies received and all expenses incurred' as required within Clause iv of the Obligations of Manager. Further, reasoned McGuigan, his obligation 'to accept ... all Events reasonably negotiated' by his manager was surely somewhat redundant when he himself had contended from mid-March – in excess of three months before the Las Vegas fight – that the disputed contract had not been 'reasonably negotiated on the Boxer's behalf'.

On Sunday 20 April, McGuigan reluctantly departed with Eastwood for what had already become their highly controversial prefight publicity tour of America. Eastwood flew down from Belfast in his private plane to collect McGuigan at Enniskillen, from where the two continued on to Shannon Airport. There they boarded an Aer Lingus flight to New York, the first stop on their multi-city crisscrossing of the United States.

*

We spent almost the entire time in the plane from Enniskillen to Shannon arguing. It was mostly about the letters, but the whole Las Vegas thing – and the publicity tour – also came into it. But by the time we got to Shannon it had sort of fizzled out, probably because we were both just so tired of the whole thing. We called a sort of truce.

Barney told me on the way over that the tour would not take much out of me. Not take much out of me? It nearly killed me. We did New York, Boston, Miami, Chicago, St Louis, San Francisco, San Diego, Las Vegas and Los Angeles in nine days. I'm not saying that it wasn't enjoyable enough in itself, but it was a really gruelling schedule and even before I went on it I was worried about how I'd feel when I came back and what sort of effect it might have on my training.

*

On 14 May, less than two weeks after they had returned to Ireland from the trans-America publicity tour, the correspondence between fighter and manager was resumed when the former wrote the most revealing letter in the series, the one that showed clearly just how far the breakdown in the relationship had advanced. It also clearly laid out McGuigan's opposition to the Las Vegas project.

> In view of the terms set out in your correspondence I wish to make the following points:
> 1. My previous letter was not perverse, unless it is perverse of me to want to prepare properly for my fights. Really, you should not have committed me to the punishing schedule of the tour such a short time before my next fight.
> 2. I also believe that you should not have committed me to fight in Las Vegas at 6 o'clock in the month of June without having checked the temperature with the Met Office in Las Vegas, and the average for the last fifteen years is 95 degrees. With the kind of heat they have in Las Vegas this certainly puts me under a lot of pressure.

3. You know my views about the money I was to receive. It is very disheartening to find that I am to be paid less and have all these other commitments under a contract signed by you on my behalf. Please let me have a copy of the contract in order that I can see exactly what you have signed for. Having done the tour – which was a day longer than we agreed – I now expect to receive the $150,000 bonus plus the $20,000 as promised in your letter of 7 April 1986.

4. Finally, to avoid any misunderstandings in the future, I do not wish to be committed to any fight without my previous written consent. I am sure you will agree this is the best solution in order to avoid any problems or misunderstandings which cause such unpleasantness.

Within three days, on 17 May, Eastwood replied. He categorically dismissed McGuigan's request for 'previous written consent', and in doing so completed a remarkable about-face. In November 1984, in the first personal letter between the two (and the only one prior to the Las Vegas controversy), Eastwood had assured McGuigan that he would 'only negotiate on your behalf with your prior written agreement'. Now, however, he maintained it would 'belittle' him to implement his own proposal, made just eighteen months earlier. Even before they departed for America and McGuigan's third defence of the world title, boxer and manager were on a collision course.

Chapter Twenty-Six

> *'In twenty years of covering boxing, I've never heard of any manager making such a magnanimous gesture.'*
> Colin Hart, writing in the *Sun* about Barney Eastwood's $250,000 promise to Barry McGuigan

On 21 May, three weeks after their return from the publicity tour, McGuigan and Eastwood were once again heading west across the Atlantic. This time they were en route to the WBA featherweight champion's third title defence, scheduled against Fernando Sosa at the outdoor arena at the Caesars Palace complex on Monday, 23 June. By the terms of their Top Rank contract the two were obliged to 'present themselves' in Las Vegas ten days before the bout, but before that they and the rest of their entourage would stay at the Americana Canyon Hotel in Palm Springs, where the serious phase of McGuigan's training would be completed.

The journey was an intensely unpleasant one, though not for quite the same reasons that had marred McGuigan and Eastwood's previous flight together to America. They flew direct, first class, to Los Angeles from London, an eleven-hour marathon during which McGuigan fell victim to altitude sickness. But that was far from the end of their travel problems. The trip by limousine from Los Angeles to Palm Springs, being just under 130 miles, should have taken little more than two hours. Instead it took exactly five, as the Irishmen found themselves ensnared in freeway traffic, the likes of which neither of them had ever seen.

*

The heat was just incredible; it was out of this world compared to what we were used to. The limo was air-conditioned so there wasn't any problem during the drive down from Los Angeles, but it almost burned through you once you opened the car door. The instant you stepped out of the car you could feel how unbelievably intense it was, and it seemed to get hotter and hotter each day.

After we checked into the hotel I went for a short run, as much just to get a look at the place as anything else – and the very first person I saw when I came out of the front door of the hotel, standing against an old lime-green 300 Mercedes, was Cameron Mitchell, the guy who plays Buck in *The High Chaparral*. I didn't do any training the next day, apart from a bit of a run with Ross [Mealiff, Sandra McGuigan's brother], but we did go for a ramble to see where the gym was.

I started training the following day, our second full one in Palm Springs. Luis Spada [the Panamanian promoter with whom Eastwood first linked up while negotiating the Pedroza fight and with whom he was subsequently to form a promotional partnership] brought a couple of sparring partners from Panama – including one whose name, by coincidence, was Sosa – and about a week after we went out Paul Hodkinson arrived. The training went fine for the first few days but then, all of a sudden, I hit a bad patch towards the end of the first week or so.

That in itself wasn't unusual because it often happens when you're in training camp, and things normally right themselves after a day or two. But this one was different, this was dragging on and on and on. I felt so incredibly sluggish and I just couldn't figure out what was happening. Gyms are always hot places but I'd still always been able to handle the heat in any gym I was ever in, but not in this one. Several times during training I would shrug my shoulders and gesticulate with my hands about the heat to Eastwood but he'd just look the other way and say nothing.

*

Fernando Sosa was having problems of his own at the same time that McGuigan was suffering in the California heat. Just after seven o'clock on the morning of Monday 26 May (McGuigan's fifth day in Palm Springs), the twenty-eight-year-old native of Rio Hondo awoke in his Mar Del Plata training camp and immediately complained of having 'a problem' with his eyes. A local doctor was summoned to the camp and the unfortunate Sosa's trouble was quickly diagnosed as 'probable detached retinas in both eyes, with the right one being by far the more severely threatened'.

Tito Lectoure, Sosa's manager, promoter and general mentor,

was then contacted. He ordered that the ill-fated Sosa be rushed to Buenos Aires, where a second opinion was sought. That second opinion served only to underline the earlier one. The original diagnosis was confirmed around noon on the Tuesday morning and within minutes of being informed of the result, Tito Lectoure had made contact with the fight promoter, Bob Arum. For the second time in less than four months, Fernando Sosa was compelled to pull out of a scheduled world title fight with Barry McGuigan.

The search for a new opponent for McGuigan began immediately. But this time, in contrast to when Sosa had been forced to withdraw from the Dublin bout the previous February, a replacement was near to hand.

Within eight hours of being told by Lectoure that he would have to find a new challenger for McGuigan's world title, Bob Arum had drawn up a list of four possible replacements: Antonio Esparragoza of Venezuela, José Marmolejo of Panama, Antonio Rivera of Puerto Rico, and a twenty-two-year-old Texan, Steve Cruz. Realistically, though, the choice was between just three: Esparragoza was the number one contender for the WBA championship and as a result was guaranteed a mandatory shot at the winner; with this in mind, Eastwood, as he had informed McGuigan when initiating the pre-Las Vegas letters exchange, had Esparragoza signed up, while McGuigan for his part had told his manager that he was anxious to have his compulsory defence in Ireland 'in accordance with our previous discussion'.

*

Barney came into my hotel room and told me, 'Sosa has done his eye in and has pulled out of the fight.' Bloody brilliant, I said to him, maybe now I can go home out of this place. With the way I had been feeling and the way my form had been going, all I wanted was a chance to get out of there. But Barney wouldn't hear of it. 'Don't worry,' he said. 'They'll find someone else for you.'

Later that day there was a press conference about Sosa pulling out and Arum and Eastwood said they were following up on a number of possible substitute opponents. I rang Eamonn and my father at home that night and they both said the same thing: 'Get out.' So I went to Barney and said, 'Look, nothing feels right about any of this. Let's just go home.' But he wasn't the least bit interested.

'We're contracted to a fight and that's it,' was all he'd say. The next day, the Wednesday, we got videos of Marmolejo, Rivera and Cruz.

Marmolejo I didn't like at all, because he'd done some sparring with me before the Pedroza fight and I thought he was a dirty fighter, so we more or less concentrated on Cruz and Rivera. Barney has since said that I was the one that picked Cruz, but that's not strictly true. I didn't want to fight anybody at that stage, but Barney kept telling me that I had no option but to go through with the fight and that Cruz looked the safest. I only went along with it when it seemed that there really was no way I was going to get out of it.

We were walking up and down beside the hotel pool, and I begged him over and over again to let me go home. I even said to him, 'Look, I'm not trying to walk out on a contract but, please, why can't we just go home now and come back in three or six months when I'm feeling better? Other boxers have been able to pull out of fights. It's crazy to go through with this – just look at the way I've been performing.'

He really read me the riot act on the Thursday. He told me that if I didn't go through with the fight then the WBA would strip me of my title, the BBC and our sponsors would have nothing more to do with me, American TV would lose all interest in me, and that Bob Arum would make sure that I could never fight in America again. I said, 'Please, I'm going to lose my title; look at the state I'm in. I can't fight in this heat.'

He said: 'You're not going to lose your title, I know it. In fact, I'm so sure you'll beat this guy Cruz that I'll give you $250,000 if you lose – and I'll give you that in writing.' For the previous two days he had been threatening me with all sorts of consequences if I pulled out, but now he was offering me more money to stay. But in exchange, I had to give a written undertaking to go through with the fight no matter what. And that was when I knew, really knew, that there was something wrong.

*

Luis Spada was present throughout that heated Thursday session in Eastwood's hotel room, and it was he who witnessed the promissory note that Eastwood wrote out there and then. Written on Americana Canyon Hotel notepaper and headed 'To Barry McGuigan, 29 May 1986', it reads: 'I, B J Eastwood, agree to give you 250,000 dollars if you, Barry McGuigan, lose your title (WBA) against Steve Cruz in Las Vegas on 23 June 1986. Signed, B J Eastwood.'

Ten days after the Las Vegas fight, when the existence of what McGuigan and Eamonn McEvoy would come to refer to as 'the marker' first came to light, Eastwood talked expansively about it to Colin Hart of the *Sun*. 'As the Cruz fight approached,' he said, 'I suddenly had this gut feeling that something might go wrong. After all, Barry was far from home in strange surroundings, with the heat at 100-plus every day. I just thought the little fella should have extra insurance in case he lost his title.' Hart added that, 'In twenty years of covering boxing, I've never heard of any manager making such a magnanimous gesture', and Eastwood said not a word to disabuse him.

The marker was to have an eventful history. McGuigan's brother-in-law Ross Mealiff had been present for the early stages of the Thursday meeting in Eastwood's suite but had departed when it became clear to him that his presence was not welcomed by Eastwood. As soon as the meeting ended, McGuigan joined his brother-in-law in the suite they shared.

Mealiff recalls: 'He handed me a single sheet of doubled-over paper and said "Here, take that and guard it with your life. Never let it out of your sight." And I didn't. Barry suggested locking it in the hotel safe but I wouldn't even trust that, so I took it everywhere with me. I carried it with me when we went on our runs every morning, and it was under my pillow when I went to bed every night. Even when we got back home to Clones I had it with me day and night for about two weeks, then Barry collected it off me and, presumably, brought it to Eamonn McEvoy.'

Steve Cruz had also had a hectic time of it on Wednesday 28 May. The winner of the Golden Gloves bantamweight title in 1981 and of all but five of his 'about two hundred' amateur fights, Cruz had a record of twenty-five wins to one defeat since making his professional debut in October 1981, just five months after McGuigan, and had broken into the world rankings with a ninth-round stoppage of rated Tommy Cordova the previous December. Cruz's only defeat had come in his twentieth fight when he had been floored for the very first time and stopped inside the opening round by a hard-hitting Mexican, Lenny Valdez.

'He caught me cold,' said Cruz. 'Training hadn't been going too well in the build-up to the fight either. It was just one of those things.'

But while McGuigan had been preparing to defend his world title against Fernando Sosa, Cruz had also been training for a very important fight of his own in Las Vegas: a return bout with Valdez, scheduled for the Showboat Hotel the evening following McGuigan's world title defence at Caesars Palace. But when Cruz, a native of Fort Worth, turned up for training at manager Dave Gorman's gym on the last Wednesday in May, he had a major surprise waiting for him.

'I knew there was something going on the instant I arrived at the gym, because every single guy I met on the way in told me that Dave wanted to see me in his office straight away. It was clear that something big was happening, but I never dreamed that it was what it turned out to be.'

Cruz had, in fact, already been considered as an opponent for McGuigan. When Sosa had pulled out of the Dublin title fight four months earlier, Cruz's manager had been sounded out about the possibility of his charge stepping into the breach. 'Thanks, but no thanks,' was Gorman's reply. 'Steve isn't ready for such a fight yet.' Now, however, he evidently was. And even though Cruz had not fought since outpointing Rocky García eight days before McGuigan's win over Danilo Cabrera, Gorman had two valid reasons for revising his opinion of his protégé's state of readiness to do battle for a world title: Steve Cruz was not only a Texan of Mexican ancestry but he had also fought in Las Vegas half a dozen times – he should thus be eminently more at home in the heat of Nevada than the man whose title he would be trying to take.

'A world title shot was what I was aiming for since the very day I turned professional but I never, ever, expected to get the chance so soon. It's only since the Cordova fight that I've had a top ten ranking, and I thought that I'd have to wait maybe another year for a title fight.' It may indeed have been a dream come true for the challenger, but for the defending champion it was but another sequence in what was rapidly turning into an American nightmare. And two more setbacks were to take place in quick succession.

Two days after Steve Cruz had been named as his new challenger, McGuigan suffered the first of two injuries. While sparring with Umberto Sosa, McGuigan caught his right foot in a one-inch gap that had somehow worked its way into the padding underneath the ring canvas. The training session was aborted shortly afterwards when an obvious swelling of his ankle was noticed and the world champion was taken first to Palm Springs Hospital and then to Dr Tony Daly in Los Angeles.

*

The first doctor, the guy in Palm Springs Hospital, told me that I would have to take six weeks' rest. He said that I'd have to have plaster of Paris put on the ankle and not to attempt even to walk on it. I went to Barney and told him this and he nearly had a heart attack. I said to him, 'Look, you can see for yourself how things are going. Why can't we just tear up those pieces of paper and go home?' But he wouldn't hear of it. He got in touch with Bob Arum, and the end result was that what the Palm Springs doctor had told me was ignored and I was sent off to Los Angeles to some sports injuries guy that Arum knew there.

The guy from Los Angeles, Tony Daly, sent Mike Chemiliski from the Los Angeles Clippers basketball team back to Vegas with me. Chemiliski told me in the beginning that I wasn't to do anything on the ankle for at least six days, but then after three days he said it was OK to do a bit of light work. He did tell me just to walk on the ankle and not to run, but I had no choice about running because I still had to get my weight down. So I had to get up an hour earlier every morning for Chemiliski to strap up the ankle so I could get a bit of roadwork in.

After I'd lost the fight, Barney said that things hadn't gone well in training and that he'd known I was in serious trouble when he'd seen me getting floored in training. Well, I worked harder for the Las Vegas fight than I've ever worked before in my life. I worked so damned hard it was unbelievable, but the heat out there was just killing me and I knew the training wasn't coming together the way it should. Then on, I think, my second day back in the gym after the ankle injury, I had a sparring session with Jeff Franklin. He pushed me backwards and then came after me with a right and I instinctively turned to my right to slip out of reach of his punch. I had been favouring the injured ankle by trying to keep all my weight and movement on the left one, but I turned on the injured ankle and went over; that's what Barney calls a knockdown and what he has since used as his justification for saying that he knew things weren't going well in training. Of course things weren't going well in training – I had been telling him that almost from the day we went out there.

I knew from the very beginning that things were wrong. When I was back in the gym in Belfast everybody used to tell me that I was dynamite. In Belfast I could handle anybody in the gym, including full welterweights and even light-middleweights, but in America I was having trouble with guys that I would have eaten alive back in Belfast, ordinary ten-round fighters like Sosa and Azael Moran and even Franklin. The one thing I always had going for me was perfect balance – that's how I was able to take those two big right hands from Juan Laporte – but that vanished when I did in my ankle and then had to try to keep all my weight on the left side of my body. And then, when my eardrum went in sparring later on, the balance was gone to hell altogether.

Busted eardrums are a bit of an occupational hazard for a fighter; Seamus McGuinness had done it to me before in the gym in Belfast and it had even happened to me when sparring with Dermot at home in our own gym in Clones. It's actually the headguards themselves that cause it: if you get a punch smack on the ear-protector part it can shoot a pocket of air right into the ear – and bingo, your eardrum is burst! It's a horrible feeling, and you keep trying to yawn in the hope that that'll clear it. They gave me cortisone injections and I carried on as best I could, but my confidence was at an all-time low and I just knew that my training was pure crap. I was never so underconfident in my entire life, let alone in my boxing career. And Barney knew it too, but he still wouldn't let me go home. I knew in my heart that something was going on but I just couldn't put my finger on what it was.

*

Others too knew that 'something was going on', in the sense that all was not well between McGuigan and Eastwood. Hints, and in some cases extremely strong hints, to that effect made their way across the Atlantic and surfaced in a number of papers, including the *Sunday Tribune* and the *Sun*. Even between the two protagonists, the rules of the game changed.

If McGuigan was, to use his own words, 'never so underconfident in my entire life', his substitute opponent was having no such crisis of belief. Steve Cruz, as he told an Irish journalist two weeks before the biggest fight of his young life, was approaching the bout in a totally positive frame of mind.

'Barry's a very talented fighter, a champion who deserves to be treated with respect,' he said. 'But respect and awe are two different things. I think McGuigan usually gets more freedom to dictate things the way he wants them to be because his continuous pressurizing tends to force the person he's fighting to panic. That won't happen with me: my best weapon is probably my ability to keep cool – and it's a weapon I plan to rely on heavily against McGuigan.

'The similarity in styles between McGuigan and Cordova is not lost on me, although Cordova cannot hit as hard as McGuigan. Cordova doesn't throw half as many punches when he's not allowed to come straight in at you; my pre-fight plan against him was to keep jabbing and moving from side to side, and it worked perfectly.

'I know I'm very lucky to be getting this shot at McGuigan and the WBA title and I intend to make the most of it. I have never gone in for predictions about my fights – that can make you look either a loudmouth beforehand or just plain silly afterwards – but I know what I am capable of and I have only one promise to make: I will make a real fight of it.'

Chapter Twenty-Seven

*'I never reached the point where I didn't care any more.
I was going down, but I was determined to go down like
a warrior.'*

Barry McGuigan, describing his mental attitude on the
lead-in to the Steve Cruz fight

We flew into Las Vegas from Palm Springs about six days before the fight. The temperature there was not a lot hotter, but it was a different kind of heat: Palm Springs had been humid, but this was a dry desert heat, nothing like what I'd been experiencing.

There was a gym set up inside Caesars Palace, in the auditorium, and I sparred there for a couple of days with a Panamanian called Moran. It wasn't any indication of what it would be like fighting in the open air, but we couldn't do anything about it. Obviously, I didn't want to show how bad I was, so I had to be very cagey about who I sparred with. Cruz trained at Johnny Tocco's gym downtown, but he had people in to watch me. The Caesars Palace workouts were public, anyway.

My weight was OK, although it was always a struggle the last couple of days. I didn't run; my running had been pathetic anyway, because of the ankle. It was more like walking; I was just trying to bounce on my toes to get a bit of confidence in it. There was no need to run in that heat anyway, a walk outside in the morning with the sweat gear on would have done, so I'd just move my body, shadow-box, and hope to break sweat.

My mental attitude was crap, really terrible. I said to Ken Gorman of the *Daily Star* three days before the fight: 'I don't know what the hell I'm doing here, but I know I'm going to lose my title.' I was convinced of that. I just wasn't ready for the fight. I always had a lull in training, but usually it would only last a few days. This time it had lasted three weeks, and I'd never snapped out of it, not even once. I'd never shown a day when I was sharp. My condition was the worst ever. It went on and on, the bad sparring.

I wasn't right physically, and because of that it screwed me up mentally. But I never reached the point where I didn't care any more. I was going down, but I was determined to go down like a warrior. I kept trying to tell myself, 'You're going to win, you're going to win.' Probably only Dermot and my brother-in-law Ross knew how negative I was feeling at this time. They were the only ones I would let my feelings show through to. Eastwood knew how bad I was, physically; that's what made me so resentful, because he knew me better than anyone except Dermot and Ross. Dermot knew me inside out, and did his best to make me think positive.

The day before the fight I did about twenty minutes' shadow-boxing and skipping at the back of the pool at Caesars, and then jogged a while with big Tom McNeeley, the old Boston heavyweight. He'd been looking after me in Vegas. I went to bed for a while, and ordered a light meal of fish. Later on I walked around the hotel corridors with Ross and Dermot. I didn't want to be near food, so we couldn't go down into the casino area.

Next morning I got up early, before seven, and went to the scales for a test weigh. The security men had to open the back of the auditorium to let me in. They weren't going to open up at all, until they found out who I was. I was twelve ounces under the weight. I went back up to the room, had two mouthfuls of lemon tea and went back to bed before heading off again for the official weigh-in. This time, the scales showed me a quarter-pound over. I argued about it, but Jay Edson, Bob Arum's man in charge, wasn't having it. I went outside, raging. The Panamanian guy Barney had brought in told me to piss, but I said, 'I can't bloody piss – I'm so dry I can't even spit.'

In the meantime Cruz had got on the scales, and was three-quarters of a pound over the weight. He wasn't happy either: he'd weighed two hours earlier, and was under. I tried again, and they still showed me a quarter-pound over. I insisted that they reset the scales to zero again, and this time Edson had to accept that the scales were faulty. There was nobody there who could fix them. Las Vegas, the world centre of boxing, and there's nobody who can fix the scales! So we both got back on the scales again, and this time they called us both at 126 pounds – nine stone. I'm not saying that I was over or under the weight, nor him either; all I can say is that officially we had both made it, according to the scales. I know this much, though, that I was never over the weight in any of my title fights.

Later on we had Mass, with Father Salvian Maguire and Father Brian D'Arcy. I had a light meal, walked around for a while, and went back to bed until it was time to leave for the fight. When I'd been taped and had the ankle bandaged we strolled around the back of the arena, which was sparsely filled. It was too hot for people to sit out there in it. Some Irish boys I met later told me they were so sweltered that the only way they could cool down was to buy tins of ice-cold Coke and pour them all over each other.

The heat was as bad as I'd expected, but the sun was so bright that it nearly blinded me. As champion I had the choice of corners, so I made him sit in the corner with the sun shining into it. But Dave Gorman [Cruz's manager] was smart enough: he got this big fat Mexican second to stand in front of Steve and block the sun out.

*

By the time McGuigan and Cruz entered the ring, the odds against the challenger had fallen dramatically to five to two. The previous day he had been quoted at nine to one. A senior member of Caesars Palace staff said: 'It's not our policy to disclose exactly how much it would take to shift the odds a point, but you can take it that for the Cruz odds to move so spectacularly, we are talking about a very substantial amount of money indeed. Not all the bets would have been placed with us, of course, but quite a few of the other casino sports books would take their lead from us, particularly for a fight which we were hosting.

'When Barry boxed here, he brought a lot of Irish fans with him, and you might have expected their money to cancel out the bets on Cruz. After all, the Irish were unlikely to have been betting against their own man. Of course, the sudden fall in the odds could have been simply because the Hispanic fans didn't arrive in town until the day before the fight. We find that's the pattern, for example, with Thomas Hearns fights. There might not be much betting action on a Hearns fight until the Detroit fans arrive, but once they're here they love a bet.'

McGuigan's newly acquired stablemate Herol Graham, then European middleweight champion, also appeared on the Las Vegas bill. Going in two fights before McGuigan, Graham made a successful American debut by stopping Ernie Rabotte in the opening round. Back in the dressing-room after Graham's win, Eastwood was heard to remark, 'That's the worst corner I've ever been in; you can't even get water through to it.'

While Eastwood, Graham and Brendan Ingle (Graham's trainer and former manager) were in the ring for the brief bout, Dermot McGuigan was in the dressing-room with his brother. The older McGuigan was far from happy with the way the conversation went. 'Barry said to me, "I don't feel right. I feel like shit." I told him, "Don't worry, you'll be all right." What else was I supposed to say? But he said, "I don't *feel* all right – I feel terrible." He certainly didn't look too good, but it wasn't that that worried me; he'd looked pretty bad before a couple of other fights and had come through OK in the end. But what was different this time was that, unlike the other times when he might not have looked the best, he was saying it himself. I had been with him for all his fights, amateur and pro, and he had never once said anything like that to me. And that frightened the life out of me, even while we were still in the dressing-room.'

*

The doubts had been there even before I hurt my ankle in Palm Springs. I had tried to explain to Barney how I felt, but he's a very persuasive man and it was just like pissing in the wind: I couldn't get through to him. When I got in the ring I said to him, 'My arms are heavy. I don't feel right.' It was the first time I had ever felt physically unwell in the ring, but he just said, 'Go on, you'll be all right.' The heat was unbearable. The temperature was around 110 degrees Fahrenheit, but with the ring lights and TV lights it was a good ten degrees hotter inside the ropes.

I tried to snap myself into the fight in the first, banging out the jab and giving him lots of movement, slipping and sliding from side to side. I noticed in the second that he wasn't particularly good coming forward, although he was trying to back me up. Obviously he'd been well briefed on me. I let him throw a few punches at me, to see what he was like. He was quick, neat, and compact, kept his hands up and didn't give me a lot of target.

I was never a fighter who burned out, and punches rarely had any effect on me. I would give a guy a target and then pull out of the way, and sometimes I wouldn't punch, just make him miss and let him know that there was a gap there for me to come through when I wanted to. But I couldn't snap into it this time. It felt as if I was punching through water, and I couldn't get any speed going. He was hitting me with jabs, and my punches wouldn't flow. All the time I was running like hell on a treadmill, and getting nowhere.

The third and fourth were better rounds, and I started to think that maybe Eastwood was right and I would come through it, but Cruz boxed smartly in the fifth and sixth. He boxed beyond his years: it looked as if he was more experienced than he actually was, although of course he was a lot more used to the heat and could cope with the conditions so much better than me.

He wobbled me twice in the sixth with rights. I wasn't feeling his punches, but my legs were going. Jesus Christ, I thought, what the hell's going on here? He wasn't a puncher. You feel a guy's power, you feel his strength, and you know if he's a puncher. When I fought Laporte, I could hear the whoosh! when his punches went past me and I knew if one of those hit me it would take my head off. I didn't have a lot of respect for Cruz's punches, because they didn't feel hard, yet my legs were going. I was completely *compos mentis*, in total control all the time. There were none of the effects you feel from a really bad punch. I couldn't understand it.

It was an uphill struggle for me. It wasn't just a struggle to beat Cruz: I felt as if I was battling through a bad day in the gym. Some days you can be tremendous in the gym, but next time you come in you're a bit sore and the work is rough and hard. Your punches don't feel like anything when you hit the bag, and that's how it was for me. Cruz boxed a very intelligent fight, and I kept saying to myself, 'Come on, Barry, get yourself going.'

Cruz kept coming in the seventh, and hurt me with two rights and a left hook. I was warned for two low lefts. Already I was tired, and yet in all my years of training I had never, ever known fatigue in the ring before. I kept missing with punches. He could see them coming, and I kept banging his arms and his gloves. In the eighth he seemed to be tiring, and his arms started coming down. But even then, when I was able to hit him I was empty. There was no power in the punches. I was hitting him, but they weren't doing him any harm. I'm sure he felt them, but they were having no effect.

I started the ninth well, and then he hit me very low with a left hook and was warned. It was a difficult fight, and I'd thrown a few borderline body punches that landed on the top of the cup but never hurt him. But he hit me deliberately so low that he actually lifted my cup up. He was so neat and accurate with his punches that he knew exactly what he was doing, whereas mine weren't intentionally low. I was trying to bully him, to get close to him and push him back: what the old American manager Lou Duva calls 'bulldog tactics'.

I had a good round. I was able to smother his counters and force him back, but at the end of the round I said to them in the corner, 'Say a prayer for me – I'm gone.' That's how tired I was: I was running on an empty tank. It was like when you're on the M25 and you've gone past one service station and there's ninety-seven miles to the next; you know you're not going to make it, but you still keep driving anyway. My feet felt as if they were on fire, and I couldn't dance about. All I could do was keep coming forward, tuck up and throw punches that didn't have the usual snap and speed.

My punches had been slow all night, and every time I threw a right hand he'd step in with a left hook. But I'd been doing fairly well in the tenth, pushing him back, until I gave him a little bit of space between punches. I tried to throw a right hook to the body, right hook to the head, and just as I was turning to throw the second he hit me with his left hook, right on the money. I went down on my knees, but the punch didn't have the same effect as when I was hit by Laporte. I didn't panic – I turned to my corner, and signalled that I was OK, but I was thinking, 'What the hell am I doing down here?' I took the full nine count on one knee, and when he came in to finish me I managed to box him off and get through the round.

I came in close to him in the eleventh, trying the same tactics that had worked in the ninth. I knew the Americans liked aggression, so if I could just keep throwing punches I had a chance. When I got tired I would move back and box for a bit, stay out of trouble. But I got a public warning in the twelfth, which cost me a point, even though I'd done enough to win the round.

I tried the same tactics in the thirteenth, in and out quick, but every time I moved away, Jesus! My feet were burning. I knew I had to win the last couple of rounds, because although I had landed a lot of punches I didn't have any power in them. He was landing the better quality punches. They were neat and compact. I leaned on him to smother the punches, and then let my own punches go, to make it look like I was still there and working, keeping busy. But it just didn't happen: I just didn't have it. I could hear Barney shouting from the corner, 'Box him! Box him!' and I thought, 'What's this guy talking about?'

The corner was very amateurish throughout. It wasn't until the tenth round that they told me to swallow some water between rounds instead of spitting it out, while all the time I was dehydrating. They should have been cooling me down, but they were only confusing me. I needed a calm old pro like Paddy Byrne there, but Paddy had been relegated to handing up the water bucket while Barney, Eddie and the Panamanian were doing the talking.

Those sixty seconds are vitally important. You can be making mistakes and not know that you're making them, yet all you need is one little piece of sensible advice. Dermot could have been such a help to me if he'd been sitting ringside instead of ten rows back. I could always hear Dermot's voice above the rest, but I couldn't this time, when I needed it most.

There's a famous photo of me in the corner before the last round, staring out of dead man's eyes while the Panamanian tugs at my ears. I believe it won the Sports Photograph of the Year award. I look as if I'm on another planet, but in fact I was still rational. I was thinking to myself, 'You've performed pathetically here.' What really upset me was that I'd boxed like a weakling, and that was never me. That gutted me; I'd never been a weak person, but I was weak then. I was angry with myself for being weak, and I didn't want anybody having any sympathy for me. I didn't want to end up with people feeling sorry for me; I wanted to win.

Coming out for the fifteenth round I was exhausted. I'd won the last few rounds, but it was a desperate effort. It was working, and I was hoping that it would still work in the fifteenth, but I had been so badly weakened by the effort I'd put in that there was nothing left. I hoped that if I could stay out of trouble for the next three minutes I might hang on to my title. I didn't know at that stage how they were scoring it, but I was determined to do the best I could anyway and then we'd hear the result. No matter how aware you are, or how well you think you've done, you don't know until the judges say yea or nay.

But then he put me down, and after that it was just a case of trying to survive the round. The first knockdown in the fifteenth was the only time in the fight when he hurt me, *really* hurt me. He caught me with a couple of rights and, when I tried to move back, the ankle I'd hurt in Palm Springs let me down. I'd favoured the left foot all night, and when I started going backwards my legs were all over the place. I was off-balance and spent, exhausted, and two more rights and a left hook knocked me down. They were the only punches I had truly felt in the whole fifteen rounds, and it was the fatigue that did it.

I tried to keep out of the way when I got up, but my feet were so sore; they were on fire. I was down again late in the round, but it was more that he bundled me over rather than knocked me down. When the bell went I moved in to grab Cruz, and the crowd booed! I thought we'd given them enough entertainment for fifteen rounds.

The verdict was unanimous for Cruz. Medardo Villalobos of Colombia scored it 143–139, but there was only a point between us on the other two cards. Guy Jutras of Canada scored 142–141, and Angel Tovar of Venezuela 143–142. If I'd gone down once instead of twice in the last round I'd have saved the title, but to be honest I wouldn't have wanted to retain my title after finishing like that. I didn't want to win that way. I finished like a weakling, not a champion. If I couldn't do it right then I didn't deserve to win.

I could hardly walk back to the dressing-room. The last forty feet or so were awful.

It was only when I was at the door of the dressing-room that I realized I had actually lost my title. I started to cry. I lay on a couch drinking ice cold water and minerals, gulping down anything I could get as quickly as I could get it. I was shivering with the cold and was incredibly thirsty and dizzy and had stinging pains in my head. I didn't feel well at all and at one stage I vaguely heard Dermot saying to my father that I looked 'funny'. One of the ring doctors was with me and he ordered that I be taken to hospital. Barney, Paddy, Eddie, Dermot, Sandra, my father and a few other people were there, and the doctor asked for somebody to go with me. Barney and Eddie didn't volunteer, so Paddy said he would, and Sandra did too. Daddy had to play at the Dunes that night, which can't have been easy for him.

They wrapped me in foil to keep me warm while I was wheeled to the ambulance at the side of the stadium. People were cheering me, and I was in tears by that stage. I spent the night on a drip at the hospital. Sandra had to go and pick up an award I was supposed to get, and I kept asking, 'Is Eastwood here yet? Has Eastwood arrived?' But Barney was at a party instead, quaffing champagne. He came down next morning at about 9.45, because he'd arranged a press conference for 10.45, and he wanted to tell me what to say.

I had to make my own way from the hospital to Caesars for the conference, and get my own taxi back there to have an MRI brain scan done that cost me a thousand dollars. Months later, I was still getting bills from the hospital. I had thought that the Nevada State Athletic Commission or the WBA might have taken care of them. The Commission paid some, but in the end I paid the rest. They weren't even going to let us out of the hospital to begin with, because when Sandra went to pay the bill her credit card was refused: she'd loaned Jean Anderson $450 to buy a suit, and it had put her over her limit. So I had to go off and get my card before they'd let us leave.

I was happy to pay it: I couldn't get out of Vegas fast enough, and the reception we got at home in Clones was fabulous, just the way it was when I won the title. They had banners saying things like 'You're still our champ' and 'We still love you, Barry'. It meant an awful lot to me, because I'd thought that I had let everybody down. But they showed me that I hadn't let them down, and that I'd done more than enough for the town.

I was glad to be out of Vegas; it's a horrible plastic city. Three months later we were back there, myself and Eamonn McEvoy, but that's another story.

Chapter Twenty-Eight

'I hope he's going to be all OK... I didn't want anything like this to happen. I'm used to the heat; I walk around in it the whole time. Barry doesn't.'

Steve Cruz, an hour after the fight

Dermot McGuigan had had trouble seeing the fight, at least in the manner and from the kind of vantage point from which he had been accustomed to watching his brother box. Dermot was seated not in his usual position directly under the ring apron, but what he estimated as some sixty feet away from the ropes.

'Barry himself always said that the one voice he could always pick out was mine. It didn't matter how many thousands of people might be shouting at the one time and creating the most almighty racket, he could always pick out my voice and hear exactly whatever I was saying to him.

'But from back where I was, sitting with my father and Sandra, he couldn't pick me up at all. I was no use to him whatsoever there. I knew that even before the fight, as soon as I discovered where I was to be seated. I pleaded with Barney and with a Top Rank official to let me in nearer the ring, near enough for Barry to hear me, but I got nowhere with either of them.

'Then, while the fight was actually going on and I was sitting in my seat, there were four big security men – each well over six feet – guarding the two corners of the ring nearest me. And two of them, one in each corner, spent virtually the entire fight making sure I didn't leave my seat. Three times during the fight I tried to get into the official area around the ring, but each time the two heavies stopped me.

'I was doing my usual shouting at Barry, trying to tell him to do this and do that, but it was obvious he hadn't a chance in hell of hearing me, so I tried to get closer to him. The first time I made a move to leave my seat the two guys just stepped in front of me and told me to get back where I was. The second time they were a bit more aggressive and said that I wasn't to move or they would throw me out. And the third time they told me flatly that if I was to even get up off my seat again they "would fuck me out on my head". But the really curious part came when the fight was over. The instant the last bell went, even before the official decision was announced – the very time when the security guys should have been doing their jobs by making sure nobody could get near the ring – I scrambled over some seats in front of me, tore down the aisle and climbed straight into the ring. All four of the heavies just stood looking at me.'

Father Brian D'Arcy still describes 23 June 1986 as 'the saddest night of my life'. Father D'Arcy had walked as far as the ambulance with the dethroned champion (and would follow him to the hospital later) and retains 'very vivid pictures' of the unfolding drama.

'He was lapsing into a kind of unconsciousness by this stage, but as we got to the ambulance he grabbed my hand and said, over and over, "Don't let me go to sleep, don't let me go to sleep. I don't want to be like Young Ali." As the ambulance pulled away – they wouldn't let me go in it – I turned round to walk back towards the dressing-rooms. There was an ITV camera and crew behind me, and one of the team asked me, "How bad is he?" I thought of Katie back in Clones, and what she must have felt seeing the picture of her son being carried away in an ambulance, so I said, "He's fine; he's just dehydrated and he needs plenty of water, but he's going to be all right." Katie told me afterwards that hearing that was what helped her most that night, but I just wish I could have been half as confident as I sounded when I said it.

'The whole concept was a disaster. When you think of the build-up to that fight, all the top people who were there, all the fans who had travelled so far to see it and what a proud day it was for the Irish, the opportunities that were lost then were unbelievable – and the real tragedy was that none of it need ever have happened. It just should not have taken place at that time of the day. All they had to do was put it on an hour later. After the ambulance had left, I hung around for a while looking at a few rounds of the Tommy Hearns fight [Hearns stopped Mark Medal in eight rounds to retain his light-middleweight title] and the place was practically dark and really rather cold – and nearly empty, because most of the fans had come to see Barry. Had Barry been fighting then he would have been fine, and he certainly would not have ended up in hospital.'

After leaving Caesars Palace, Father D'Arcy walked to the Dunes Hotel with Pat McGuigan, who was committed to accepting an award on behalf of his boxer son at an Irish-American function. 'Pat and I made little speeches,' said Father D'Arcy. 'There was a band there and people tried to act normally, but it didn't work. The place was like a morgue. We stayed for about an hour and then went down to the hospital.'

At the Valley Hospital McGuigan was given two and a half gallons of water intravenously to replace the twelve pounds of body fluid he had lost along with his world title. Semi-delirious at times, he asked repeatedly for Sandra even though she was sitting by his bedside. Kate McGuigan phoned the hospital two hours after her son was admitted but was unable to speak to him because he was still in the intensive care unit, but by one o'clock on the Tuesday morning he had been removed to a private room.

Paddy Byrne, a man for whom McGuigan has retained a special affinity, was the only member of the ex-champion's boxing 'family' to present himself at the hospital. Duane Ford, chairman of the Nevada State Athletic Commission, called in person to check on McGuigan's post-fight condition.

Ross Mealiff did not go to the hospital at all that Monday night, having been detailed by Dermot McGuigan to stay at Caesars Palace to be on hand for enquiring friends. But by ten o'clock, having drifted into an acute depression, he had had enough and decided to go to bed.

'After coming out of the lift, I had to pass Barney's suite to get to my own room. As I walked along the corridor I could hear loud laughing and joking somewhere. Somebody was obviously having a party, but it wasn't until I turned round a corner that I realized where it was coming from – Barney's room. There were maybe a dozen or more empty champagne bottles in the corridor outside the room and the door was open. Barney came to the door with a champagne bottle in his hand just as I was passing it. We both stopped for a second or two and looked at each other without saying a word. Then he closed the door slowly and I walked on towards my own room.'

Among the visitors to Eastwood's suite that evening was an Irish journalist who was covering the fight. He tape-recorded an interview with Eastwood, which is reproduced here verbatim.

'It was a great fight,' Eastwood said. 'Barry looked like winning it until the tenth round, when he got caught with a sucker punch himself and down he went. From that point on his legs were never the same, and it was hard to motivate him. He never got back into the fight, although he won a couple of rounds after that. The other factor was that he lost a point for a low blow.

'In the final round, all he had to do was stand on his feet and hold his own and he'd get the decision, despite the fact that he'd been down and lost the point, but that punch in the tenth had taken all the sap out of him. The heat had nothing to do with it, I don't think. What did you think, Eddie, about the heat?'

Shaw: 'I'll tell you about the heat. We've worked seven, eight, nine four-minute rounds at 125 degrees in Palm Springs, and McGuigan was doing them handy, as Herol can tell you. No problem. I wouldn't take nothing away from Steve Cruz, with the heat.'

Eastwood: 'I thought McGuigan was having a field day, up to the tenth round. He hit him in the tenth and the guy's legs went. Barry went in to finish it but he dropped his hands, got hit with two shots, and down he went. Now, after that, that was the first time we saw Barry's legs going. I told him "Box and move" for the next two rounds, and we sort of half got him back into the fight a wee bit, but, as I say, the main factors were (1) he lost a point for a low blow and (2) he got hit on the chin, when he almost had the fight won, and he never was the same fighter after that.

'In the last five rounds, when he normally finishes strong, he couldn't; that punch had taken a lot out of him. In the last round, if he'd gone out and just jabbed with the one hand, been able to move, and shared the round, he was the winner. Remember the judges' scoring in the last round were 10–7 – three points, boy, that's unbelievable – 10–7, and 10–8, so there it is.

'The preparations went great. He hurt his ankle, but it never did him any harm. He was back in the gym and Herol Graham or any of them can tell you that his ankle was perfect. He was able to spar six, seven, eight rounds in the heat. Everything went well. That probably was a blessing in disguise, because you know he kills himself in the gym.

'How can anybody say that he's been having too many fights?

He's like Marvin Hagler – Hagler only fights three times a year, but the way Barry trains he should fight six times a year, otherwise the training's all lost. He's a glutton. Other fighters, like Herol [Graham] here, he'll take four weeks off after a fight and then he'll start to work again, but two days after a fight Barry is back in doing fifteen rounds.

'As Shaw here says, you can train them and you can tell them, but you can't live with them.

'When Barry McGuigan turned professional I said to him, "I think you have a great future", and I told him he could become champion of the world. But I told him, "Always remember, you'll have great nights and you'll have disappointing nights, and that sorts the men from the boys. You have to be a man in defeat. It's easy to be a man in the good times."

'It's sad the way the thing went. It's very disappointing for Barry. There's nothing wrong with him, in my opinion. I'm not a doctor, but I'd like to bet all sorts of money that he's perfect. His heart's broken, and he's depressed, but in a couple of days it'll be nothing.

'And he has nothing to be ashamed of. So he has to take a good rest, and then we'll talk about it and see what he wants to do. It's all entirely up to him after that.

'Tonight, I'll be staying here. I'll probably have a few oul drinks, and I might have a song and I might have a dance – you never know where we'll end up.

'But anyway ... they're all talking about who's going to fight Hagler next. I've got the man here – Herol Graham. He's the man.

'What a fighter he is! We're going to throw out a challenge [to Hagler] very, very shortly; tomorrow, it could be. I don't want to mess about with this guy. I want him to get his chance, because this guy ...'

Father Brian D'Arcy had had an unexpected encounter of his own a little earlier that evening. On his way back into the Caesars Palace arena, after seeing the beaten champion off on his ambulance ride to the Valley Hospital, Father D'Arcy encountered a solitary figure standing just inside the entrance to the barn-like dressing-room area. The new featherweight champion of the world, still in his shorts and with only a short robe draped over his shoulders, was standing alone with not a single member of the fight media even remotely interested in him.

'Will he live?' said Cruz to the priest he had earlier seen coming out of the McGuigan dressing-room.

'I think so,' replied Father D'Arcy.

'I hope he's going to be OK,' said Cruz. 'I didn't want anything like this to happen. I'm used to the heat; I walk around in it the whole time. Barry doesn't.'

'I'm sure he'll be fine. What are you going to do now?'

'About what?'

'The title you've just won. You're the world champion now.'

'I don't feel like a world champion.'

'Why not? Because you didn't expect to win it?'

'Because I didn't expect to get the fight, never mind the win.'

'Have you thought yet about defending it?'

'No.'

'Would you fight Barry again?'

'Sure.'

'Would you be prepared to go to Belfast?'

'Sure.'

'Really?'

'Sure. Barry's a name, I'm not. I won't get any money unless I go to him.'

Cruz's wife, Terri Ann, then appeared round the corner and joined her husband. For another few minutes the three talked on, mostly about the baby Terri Ann was expecting, before the new champion, almost reluctantly, retreated to his empty dressing-room. Several hours later, not much before midnight and as he was on his way back from the Valley Hospital, Father D'Arcy met Cruz again, this time walking with his wife around the garden that lay at the rear of the Caesars Palace Hotel. Once again not a single newspaperman was in sight.

The following morning, Dermot McGuigan, having returned from the Valley Hospital in the middle of the night, received a telephone call in his hotel room a little after nine o'clock. It came from Joy Williams, head of the Sports Department of BBC Northern Ireland and a close associate of Eastwood, who asked, 'Is Barry out of the hospital yet?' When told that he was not, she told Dermot McGuigan, 'Barney wants to go there.' Dermot agreed to accompany Eastwood and so, half an hour later, they and Paddy Byrne arrived at the Valley Hospital by taxi.

Inside Eastwood's gym in Chapel Street, Belfast: Dermot and my father keep a close eye on the sparring.

Country boy . . . me in my element, walking the dog near our house in Kilroosky.

Bernard Taylor looked brilliant for five rounds, until my body punches started to get to him.

Danilo Cabrera claims a foul in the fifth round, but this tough little Dominican is no quitter.

Cabrera left his mark on me, but Sandra and Daddy were just happy that I'd won.

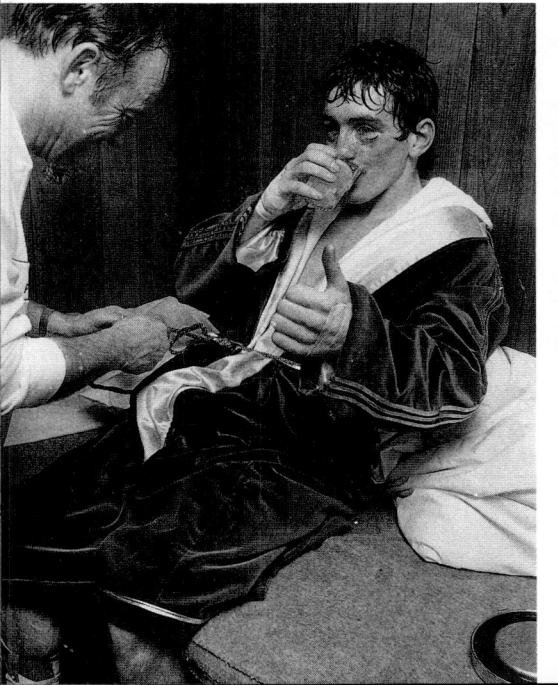

Working up a sweat . . . I was an obsessive trainer, often back in the gym the day after a fight.

Barney outside his house in Cultra, where I used to stay before my early pro fights.

At Mass with Barney in St Patrick's Cathedral, New York during the pre-Las Vegas publicity tour.

Another Irish-American fight fan signs on . . . New York's Cardinal O'Connor obliges with an autograph, watched by Top Rank publicity man Irving Rudd.

Nightmare in the desert . . . note how flat-footed and off-balance I am as Cruz comes at me again.

This final knockdown in the fifteenth round cost me the championship; without it, I would have snatched a draw.

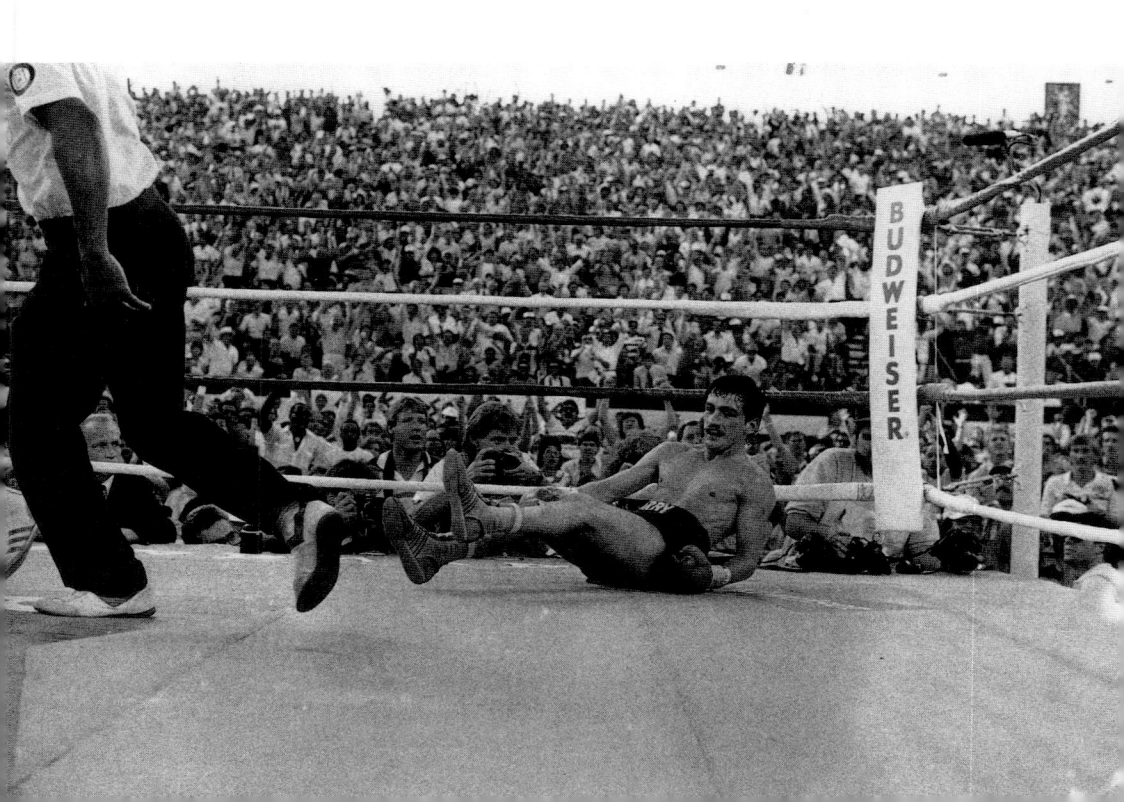

'Staring out of dead man's eyes . . .': Chris Smith's famous study of me preparing to come out for the final round.

Barney came to the hospital around 10.00 the next morning. I thought he had come to see how I was, but he seemed more concerned about what I was going to say at the press conference which had been arranged for 10.45. He left the room as soon as he had finished telling me the sort of things he wanted me to say at the press conference. He wanted me, for instance, to tell the press that my losing was nothing to do with the heat. OK, Steve Cruz beat me fair and square on the night, I've never denied that, but who in their right mind can claim that the heat wasn't a factor? He didn't even wait for me to get dressed or go with him. He just barged out of the room and left me to get up and make my own way to the conference by taxi. I made up my mind there and then that while I wasn't going to blame him publicly at the press conference, I certainly was not going to go out of my way to defend him either.

*

The poolside press conference back at Caesars Palace was, to put it tactfully, a decidedly strained affair. Few captured the mood as graphically as Hugh McIlvanney:

> When he coped with the cameras and notebooks next morning at the Caesars poolside, pouring generosity over everybody from the conqueror he called 'a class guy' to the supporters who received apologies for a non-existent let-down, he was so movingly eloquent that a few unlikely cases found themselves in need of a little surreptitious dabbing of the eye. All those who delight in parodying his niceness should try out their turn after being battered about by Steve Cruz at 110 degrees Fahrenheit.
>
> Once we knew he was all right, perhaps the most persistent sadness was not the loss of the title, or even the thought that we might have seen the last of his exhilarating talent for conflict, but the unmistakable cloud of suspicion and resentment that these days hangs over his relationship with Barney Eastwood.

There had been no direct dialogue between the two throughout the entire conference. McGuigan had sat alongside his wife while his manager had stood behind the couple. Still, uncomfortable or not, McGuigan resolved to give the media their sought-after interviews. Irving Rudd, the Top Rank public relations officer assigned to the ex-champion, attempted to rescue him from the ordeal. 'No,' McGuigan insisted, 'I've come to talk to these guys and I'll stay as long as they have questions to ask.'

Almost immediately after the press conference ended, Eastwood left to return to Ireland. But before departing the Caesars Palace poolside he spoke to the McGuigan brothers. 'I feel bad about this and I'm going to get torn apart by the press,' he said to Dermot. And to Barry, he said, 'I'm very disappointed that you've lost your title. We'll have to keep these press guys away from us. Do you need any money?' Apart from brief momentary glimpses of each other at their two subsequent court cases, a related meeting at a Northern Ireland hotel, and a mumbled handshake at the settlement of their first court case, McGuigan and Eastwood have never met since they walked away from that Las Vegas press conference.

Chapter Twenty-Nine

*'I cannot go on being a manager in name only. I must
have complete control according to our agreement.'*
Barney Eastwood, writing to Barry McGuigan in July 1986

There was, though, one further conversation between boxer and manager. On the morning of Wednesday, 2 July, nine days after the Caesars Palace press conference, Eastwood telephoned McGuigan at his home in Kilroosky. The reason for the call, however, was not quite what McGuigan might have expected. Eastwood phoned not to enquire about the former world champion's well-being, or even to ask if he had thought any further about whether or not he intended fighting again – he phoned for an entirely different reason altogether.

McGuigan, at the time his manager phoned, was preparing to leave his house to drive to Belfast, from where he was to catch a flight to London. He was due to appear on the 'Wogan' programme on BBC1 that same evening, and it was about this that Eastwood wished to talk.

*

His only reason for calling was my appearance on the 'Wogan' show – he wanted to know what I was going to say. And his tone was different to what it had been for the poolside press conference in Las Vegas. There he had been asking me to say this and say that, and not to say this and not to say that, but at least he had been asking me.

For the 'Wogan' programme, though, he was different. This time he just wasn't *asking* me to tell things in a way that would make him look good – it was an order. The call really got my back up, the fact that he was phoning me and giving orders about what I could and could not say. I might not have said anything at all if he hadn't been so quick to boss me around, but once I got the call from him I made my mind up to make one or two implied criticisms, but I still didn't really say anything other than that I thought the decision to take the fight in Las Vegas had been 'a mistake'.

*

Eight days after McGuigan's appearance on the 'Wogan' programme, on 10 July, Eastwood reopened the exchange of letters that he had initiated four months earlier. This, though, was the first written communication between the two since over a month before the fight in which McGuigan lost his world title.

After repeating his version of the events that led up to the signing of the Las Vegas fight contract with Top Rank (and the rejection of the proposed fight against Wilfredo Gomez), Eastwood went on to tell McGuigan that while any decision about whether or not he would fight again would be 'entirely' left to the boxer himself a 'comprehensive understanding' would be needed if that decision were in the affirmative.

In particular, Eastwood insisted on 'complete control' over all aspects of McGuigan's career, ranging from supervision of the training camp to total authority over the dressing-room, the corner and 'the actual fight itself'. Eastwood then acknowledged that the British Boxing Board of Control's official observer at the Las Vegas fight, Ray Clarke, had submitted 'an adverse report' on these issues, a report, McGuigan's manager conceded, 'that affects my standing as a licensed agent to manage fighters under their rules'.

Exactly two weeks later, on 24 July, after the appearance of two newspaper interviews with Eastwood of the precise nature that he (Eastwood) had suggested should not be given, McGuigan wrote to Eastwood for the first time in almost three months:

I have received your letter of 10 July which, in common with two articles in the Irish Sunday papers, seeks to transfer the responsibility for the Las Vegas fight to me.

The reality, of course, is very different.

It is true that after the Cabrera fight which took place on 15 February 1986 you did suggest to me that I fight in April. At that time I was not over the effect of the injuries sustained in the February fight and totally unfit to accept an April commitment. Had you been taking even a casual interest in my well-being at that time you would have been aware that, among other things, the scar tissue had not healed and I was not physically prepared for an April commitment.

Subsequently when you phoned me from America I explained again that the fight which I preferred was with Gomez. You told me that was not possible. I asked that you find out what the possibilities were and let me know. During the course of our telephone conversation a number of possibilities were mentioned, including Las Vegas. In the event I was subsequently told by you that you had signed a contract for me to fight Sosa in Las Vegas on 23 June.

Only bit by bit did the full horror of what you had committed me to emerge.

Firstly I was amazed to learn from the press that I was committed to a long punishing publicity tour of America which would interrupt my training and physically weaken me, and then the real disaster emerged that I had been committed to fight in the car park of Caesars Palace on 23 June in conditions in which people from this part of the world should not even stand out in, let alone fight in. Not surprisingly, the more I learned of the Las Vegas trip the less I wanted to do with it. I made my position as clear to you as you would allow me to do. Your response was that you had signed a binding contract for me and I was committed to it. Both at our meeting in Enniskillen on 13 April and in your correspondence you stressed that I was committed to the contract and indeed threatened to report me to the BBB of C and the WBA.

I was so concerned about the absolutely gross folly on your part in committing me to this fight that I wrote to you on 14 May asking that you never again commit me to a fight without my previous written consent. (This information was leaked to the press by 'sources close to the Eastwood organization' and became the subject of an article in the London *Times* which I found quite insulting.) In my letter of 14 May I complained that I should not have been committed to the trip nor to fighting in the heat in Las Vegas. In your reply of 17 May my objections were brushed aside and you stated, 'you will agree that I have always acted wisely on your behalf and I think that my judgement to date in all matters speaks for itself'. It certainly speaks for itself now.

Worse still was to follow.

When Sosa pulled out I was, as is well known, determined to come home. Your attitude was very different. You told me that under the contract which, despite having requested earlier, I was not permitted to see, I would be sued by Top Rank for at least $500,000, that I would never fight in America again, that the TV networks, including the BBC, would not want to know me, etc., etc. My determination to come home was only exceeded by your determination that I should fight in Las Vegas on 23 June and you agreed to pay me an additional $250,000 in the event of me being beaten if I would go through with the fight against the substitute opponent. I was not given the time or opportunity to seek independent advice on my rights under the contract. In the light of all this I naturally feel pretty let down that a campaign is now being waged publicly and privately to transfer the blame for the Las Vegas venture to me and by public statements made by you about me since the fight.

These include:
1. That the heat was not a factor. I do not know where you would have to go to find somebody to agree with you on that point.
2. I was spending too much time at out-of-the-ring activities. Your normal complaint is that I train too much.
3. I have not been the same since the Laporte fight. This is very much at variance with your private and public statements.
4. That you did not want me to fight Cruz and that my brother Dermot and I picked him. Dermot was 3,000-odd miles away at the time.
5. Most hurtful of all, that it was really all Sandra's fault.
6. That I refused to fight Gomez and instead picked Sosa in Las Vegas for the money. You *now* tell me that you have a signed contract for the Gomez fight still in your possession. It is a pity you did not tell me this earlier as I had made it clear both in correspondence and discussion with you that Gomez was the option I preferred. When it came to light that Gomez had been agreeable to fight me your defence was that Dan Duva was playing cat and mouse and was only prepared to come to terms after you were already committed to the Sosa fight in Las Vegas but that then it was too late.

Why or how you came to sign me up for the Las Vegas affair in those conditions I suppose I will probably never know.

As for the future, obviously I shall require a lot of time and thought before deciding finally what to do. It is clear, however, that I am so physically drained and weak after the dehydration that it will be several months before I could even start light training, if that is what I decide.

Finally, I would just say that I have not dealt with everything in your letter but have replied to the more controversial points raised in your letter; there are, of course, many other issues of concern, not least the absence of Paddy Byrne from my corner, substituted at two days' notice by a Panamanian who could not speak English, the corner work and instructions and the scant account taken of the injuries I sustained in Palm Springs.

On the final day of that same month, 31 July, McGuigan wrote to Eastwood seeking payment of the balance of the money due to him for the Las Vegas fight:

As you will understand I am disappointed that only part of the monies due to me were paid to my accountant at the meeting last week. Leaving aside the question of the $150,000 bonus from Top Rank, I am due a further $269,000 from you. I have been quite patient in waiting for payment of the monies due to me and am disappointed to find that the entire amount due by you has not been paid.

The next day, apparently before receipt of McGuigan's letter about the outstanding money due to him, Eastwood wrote a reply to the fighter's letter of a week previously. Beginning by chiding the former world champion for a lack of any 'response in kind' to his manager's 'benign sentiments', Eastwood then rejected what he termed 'this nonsense' about an Eastwood-orchestrated public campaign to 'saddle' McGuigan with the responsibility for the decision to fight in Las Vegas, after which he dismissed the fighter's six-point criticism of his manager's public statements as 'tittle-tattle'. After alleging that he had on one occasion been compelled to pay McGuigan '£2,000 out of my own pocket' to get him to attend a press conference announcing a European title fight in London, Eastwood concluded by denying that he had not kept the fighter fully informed about the possibility of a bout with Wilfredo Gomez.

The correspondence between fighter and manager came to an end on 13 August, when, in an apparently partial response to McGuigan's written query about payment of the money outstanding to him, Eastwood enclosed a cheque for $18,200 which, he explained, was comprised of $19,000 incorrectly withheld by Top Rank, less the sum of $800 which he himself had advanced to McGuigan in America.

Regarding the $250,000 marker, Eastwood claimed that (although he would have to check the point) his statements had no effect in law – but in the interests of 'a sound business basis in good faith', he expressed a willingness to deal with the issue when straightening out their overall affairs. He closed by suggesting a meeting between their respective lawyers.

*

The bit about him having to pay me £2,000 'out of his own pocket' just isn't right. I know the incident he's referring to; it concerns the Esteban Eguia fight at the Albert Hall. We had had a press conference in Belfast for the fight, but then Mickey Duff [who was promoting the show along with Mike Barrett] said he wanted another one in London. None of us, myself or the Eastwoods, wanted to have to travel to London just to go over exactly the same ground, so at first we all said, 'No.' We wouldn't go.

I had the feeling that none of the Eastwoods ever liked Duff, so when Mickey insisted that we should go to London it was decided that we should make him pay. It was Brian Eastwood's idea that we would tell Duff that unless I was paid £2,000 there'd be no press conference in London. That letter was the first I ever heard about Barney paying the money himself, because it was his own son's idea that we ask Duff for it.

*

The exchange of letters in the post-fight period made one thing clear: the relationship between the two, as was evident from their earlier correspondence prior to departing for Palm Springs and Las Vegas, had by now grown strained almost beyond salvation. Both McGuigan and Eastwood were by this time already firmly rooted to opposite sides of a chasm that was widening daily. Each, indeed, appears to have been so overtaken by the intensity of their respective feelings on the developing controversy that they themselves became somewhat confused on a number of points.

Take the question, for instance, of whether or not Paddy Byrne was in McGuigan's corner during the Cruz fight. The answer, in reality, is a matter of interpretation: what, precisely, constitutes being 'in the corner'? Paddy Byrne himself is not too sure on that one.

'I was standing down under the ring apron, handing up anything that was required. Barney only told me on the day of the fight that I wouldn't be in the corner; instead there was a Panamanian and another guy, who I think is a South American but who lives in Las Vegas. I was not in the McGuigan corner. Things were hot that night in more ways than one.'

McGuigan was less than pleased that Eastwood had seen fit to dismiss his six-point criticism of his manager's public comments as 'tittle-tattle'. Point number five, 'that it was really all Sandra's fault', may not have been correct in the full literal sense, but it was valid as regards Eastwood's stated objections to Sandra's presence in Palm Springs.

Those objections, however, were in themselves puzzling, not least to Sandra herself. Even at the time they were first voiced, in an Eastwood interview in the *Daily Mirror* a month before the bout in Las Vegas, they did not ring true as far as either of the McGuigans were concerned. To them, and others, it appeared as if Eastwood was seeking both to establish his excuses and put the blame firmly on McGuigan – in advance of the fight. It looked, as one journalist noted at the time, like a good old-fashioned case of covering one's ass.

'Why else should Barney object to me doing something that I had *always* done?' asks Sandra McGuigan. 'I had always gone to see Barry when he was in training. Barney had never once objected to it in the past, so what grounds did he suddenly have for doing it in America?

'Every time Barry had gone to Bangor to train before a fight and had stayed in Jean Anderson's house, I had gone there too. I didn't, of course, stay with him in the house, but I did stay in a little room at the back of the house with Blain, and we never once interfered with Barry's training. We kept away from Barry the whole time; all we'd ever see of him was an hour or so around teatime. That certainly did not constitute interfering with the training, and not even Barney Eastwood himself ever suggested that it did. But then, just because Barry was fighting in America, it was suddenly very wrong for us to do what we had always done.'

Another question that was to figure prominently in the whole McGuigan–Eastwood furore was that of a possible challenge by the WBA featherweight champion to Wilfredo Gomez for the same body's junior-lightweight title. Here, too, both fighter and manager appear somewhat confused. More precisely, they were both confused over exactly which of the several Gomez fight offers they were referring to.

Eastwood maintains to this day that he has in his possession a fight contract signed by Gomez's original manager, Pepe Cordero. He may well have but, as Dan Duva maintains, even if that is the case, the contract is not worth the paper it is written on.

'If Barney Eastwood has such a contract,' says Duva, 'it is a totally useless and unenforceable one. I hold the exclusive promotional rights to Wilfredo Gomez, and unless my signature is on that – or any other – contract, then, in the real and legal sense, it is not a contract at all.'

The only McGuigan–Gomez fight contract that could have had

any validity was the one Duva himself had offered Eastwood in early March 1986, and which, after initially indicating his apparent acceptance of the offer, Eastwood then rejected in favour of the Las Vegas deal proposed by Bob Arum. The Gomez fight deal that Eastwood has often referred to was, in fact, doomed on two separate counts: apart from being negotiated without Dan Duva, it was intended to stage the fight before Christmas 1985 – and this McGuigan, who had defended his own title againt Bernard Taylor on 28 September, considered impossible and unfair.

All in all, Eastwood's final letter to McGuigan struck the boxer as a near-perfect example of what Eastwood himself, in his opening paragraph, effectively accused McGuigan's own earlier letter of being: 'written for someone else's eyes more than mine: almost as if it is not a reply to my letter but written to make a separate set of points to someone in another context'.

The dispute had by now prompted others besides the two principals to put pen to paper. In mid-August Hugh Russell, the retired former British flyweight and bantamweight champion, wrote in support of his former manager. Russell sent his letter to *all* the Sunday papers in Ireland as well as to *Boxing News*.

I have deliberately held back until now from commenting on the recent unfair criticism levelled at B J Eastwood in the wake of the Barry McGuigan fight in Los Angeles [*sic*]. B J was my manager throughout my career. He led me to winning both the British bantamweight title and a Lonsdale Belt outright when I moved down to the flyweight division: I feel compelled in the light of these personal experiences to speak in his defence.

B J is as fallible as any other manager. But I reckon that he takes more care of his boxers, puts more of his personal resources than any other manager into a boxer's preparation, like the use of a well-equipped high grade gym and an excellent back-up arrangement under the control of the invaluable Eddie Shaw; and he regularly over-compensates boxers in a number of ways to offset his promotional interests in them.

I have found B J honourable in all his dealings with me and with others who travelled to Belfast to box on his promotions. Any of those boxers and sparring partners for his main boxers will tell you of how well they are treated in the best hotels – treatment rarely extended by other promoters outside Belfast.

If I were to take up boxing again I would ask B J Eastwood to manage me. I think Herol Graham, contender for the world middleweight title, made a wise move in getting into the Eastwood camp in his pursuit of a crack at Marvin Hagler's title. Without B J, Barry McGuigan, regardless of his skills, would never have been in the same ring with Pedroza for a title fight last summer.

The Russell letter was received with some scepticism. Aside from the fact that he was to prove himself well wide of the mark on Herol Graham's association with Eastwood (a development that, in fairness, only a handful could have anticipated at the time), the letter struck many as being less than totally spontaneous. Of the many replies forwarded to the several papers that published the letter, one from the *Sunday Press* of a week later indicates the general reaction.

So now Hughie Russell is being trotted out to bolster up the sagging Eastwood image. He's surely right about one thing – B J is fallible all right! Even that description flatters a manager who sent the best sporting hero Ireland ever had out in the sweltering heat of Las Vegas.

Whatever Eastwood's contribution to McGuigan winning the world title, he certainly is entitled to full credit for the loss of it. It is a pity he has not even got the good grace yet to admit it.

One other reference in the letters exchange was to play a major role in the subsequent developments that would see McGuigan and Eastwood move towards their acrimonious parting of the ways: the $250,000 'promissory note' offered in exchange for McGuigan's written undertaking to go through with the Las Vegas fight 'no matter what happens'.

On Monday 21 July, exactly twenty-eight days after the Las Vegas fight, Leo Rooney – christened 'The Bag Man' by Fight Fan – travelled to Dublin for an arranged meeting with Eastwood. The sole purpose of the meeting was for Eastwood to hand over to McGuigan's accountant uncle the monies owed to the fighter from the Nevada fight.

'It was a very cool meeting,' explained Rooney. 'We met in the Berkeley Court Hotel, and for the first time ever in all my dealings with him, Barney had his accountant – Eddie McLoughlin – with him. I drove down to Dublin while Barney and McLoughlin flew down. We met around lunchtime and although we had a couple of drinks, it was not what you could call a particularly convivial meeting.

'It was all very strained and formal, and even a bit unreal. Barney never once offered any kind of explanation or even a bit of commiseration for the defeat. He was very stand-offish for the entire duration of the meeting. He had the money broken up all over the place and he handed me over four different cheques – but the one for the "marker" was not among them.'

Eastwood, with the fight over and McGuigan's title gone, was clearly having second thoughts about his $250,000 written promise to McGuigan. This he made quite clear in his letter of 13 August, when he informed McGuigan, 'I believe (but I would have to check this) that my statements have no effect in law'. Eastwood, obviously, was unaware of the care that McGuigan and Ross Mealiff had taken of the 29 May marker.

A written suggestion from McGuigan's manager that the two should meet with their respective lawyers was an implied acceptance by him of how far the relationship had deteriorated. In the past he had always resented McGuigan receiving outside advice; now he apparently recognized that things had become so bad that perhaps the presence of lawyers might even help the situation.

The proposed meeting, however, was never to take place, at least not in the form envisaged by Eastwood. The respective legal representatives would indeed get together again a little over a month later, but by then the agenda as originally perceived by Eastwood would have been overtaken by other developments.

Chapter Thirty

'The Defendant does not admit that the Plaintiff lost the contest on 23 June 1986, or that he lost the World Boxing Association title.'

Extract from Barney Eastwood's defence to Barry McGuigan's writ

Early in the morning of Tuesday 2 September, McGuigan boarded a plane at Aldergrove Airport in Belfast to begin a journey that, as far as his relationship with Eastwood was concerned, was to be a one-way flight.

He had learned, via the Danish manager-promoter Mogens Palle, rather more of the complex financial arrangements for the Cruz fight. The informaton was sufficiently startling for McGuigan and his solicitor, Eamonn McEvoy, to return to Las Vegas, less than ten weeks after he had left there minus his world championship, for a meeting with Bob Arum which Palle had arranged. (Palle was in Las Vegas that week because his heavyweight, Steffan Tangstad, was challenging Mike Spinks for the American's IBF title at the Hilton Hotel on 7 September.)

Palle had no wish to interfere with McGuigan's contract with Eastwood, but hoped to secure an agency agreement should McGuigan succeed in gaining his release. Given the nature of the information which the Dane had unearthed, that was a real possibility. By the time the pair returned to Belfast in the afternoon of the following Friday, the McGuigan–Eastwood partnership would be history.

Just before seven p.m. local time on 2 September, McGuigan and McEvoy were met at McCarron Airport, Las Vegas, by Bob Arum's representative and driven to the Sahara Hotel, where they checked into rooms 2323 and 2324. Having travelled from Belfast via London and Dallas and spent, in all, some twenty hours in transit, they were happy to agree to Arum's suggestion of an early night before the next morning's meeting, which was set for half past ten.

It took place in McEvoy's room; Palle was also present. When the meeting began it soon became clear to all concerned that they were gathered for different reasons.

Arum was clearly of the opinion that McGuigan was contemplating a return to the ring and that the former champion, with the strain in his relations with Eastwood one of the fight game's worst-kept secrets by this stage, was seemingly prepared to discuss coming in under the Top Rank umbrella. But McGuigan and McEvoy were in Las Vegas for an entirely different reason: they were concerned only with the past, not the future. The two visitors from Ireland were interested in discovering further details of the financial arrangements surrounding the Cruz bout, and obtaining confirmation of what they had already been told. McGuigan, at that time, was still highly uncertain about his boxing future; indeed, he was largely of the opinion that he simply didn't have one. Cruz and the Valley Hospital, after all, were still only a matter of weeks behind him, and he felt there was plenty of time before any final decision about fighting again would have to be made. All that McGuigan and McEvoy were looking for from Bob Arum was information, not a future fight offer.

Eastwood, though, was unaware of the true motive behind McGuigan's return to the scene of his traumatic championship defeat just over two months earlier. When word of McGuigan's meeting with Arum and Palle reached him (through Paddy Byrne, who was in Las Vegas as cuts man for Steffan Tangstad and who spotted McGuigan in the lobby of the Sahara Hotel), he said, 'Maybe he [McGuigan] has ideas about going his own way', and promised that he [Eastwood] would 'take whatever steps I need to protect my interests' if either Arum or Palle attempted to 'interfere' again.

'I understand that he met the two boxing managers. They have been interfering with my contract to Barry and I will not accept that. They are not entitled to approach Barry while he is still under contract to me.'

Eastwood, in common with the bulk of the British and Irish media when word of the fleeting return to Las Vegas emerged, assumed that McGuigan had made the journey with the intention of getting his boxing career moving again, albeit from within a rival promotional camp. Within a week, though, that would change.

On 9 September, exactly seven days after his departure to Nevada in company with McGuigan, Eamonn McEvoy, after lengthy consultations with Michael Lavery, QC, and Donnell Deeny, now QC but then a member of the junior bar, wrote to Eastwood for the first time. In the wake of their trip to Las Vegas and the information they had uncovered while there, McEvoy and McGuigan both felt that the situation had reached such a critical point that it was essential that they consult counsel and consider whether litigation was necessary. The factors that led them to this conclusion were threefold. First, in view of all that had transpired before, around, and after the Las Vegas fight, McGuigan really did not want to be managed any further by Eastwood. Second, there was a strong suspicion – although at that stage no more than that – that Eastwood had not disclosed the full details of the Las Vegas deal, and had thus perhaps denied McGuigan money which was rightfully his. Third, Eastwood had not paid the $250,000 marker which he had promised to pay.

McEvoy's letter, sent to Eastwood's home in Holywood, left little doubt that McGuigan had made his second trip to Las Vegas to discuss something other than a possible resumption of his boxing career.

Dear Sir,
We have been instructed by Mr Barry McGuigan to act on his behalf. As you know from your correspondence with him, Mr McGuigan has been deeply concerned about your conduct of his affairs. Since your letter of 13 August we have obtained cogent evidence that has greatly increased that concern, not only about the financial arrangements for the Las Vegas fight but in regard to your dealings with our Client in connection with previous fights.

We have consulted with Counsel at length and their advice is that proceedings should be issued against you. We note in your letter of 13 August you suggested a meeting with our Client at which lawyers should be present. Our Client, with some hesitation, is willing to attend such a meeting, on a without prejudice basis, in response to your request provided that you will attend with the bona fide intention of satisfying our Client's grievances. The form of such meeting would need to be discussed and agreed in advance.

It is for that reason that we are not as explicit in this letter in setting out the causes of action against you as we would be in normal circumstances. If you wish such a meeting to take place on that understanding, you should instruct your Solicitors to communicate with us forthwith. If we do not hear from you or them within seven days we shall assume you no longer wish to pursue your suggestion and proceedings will be issued without further notice.

Three days later, on Friday 12 September, Eamonn McEvoy received a telephone call from Mr Oscar Beuselinck of Wright Webb Syrett, the London firm of solicitors retained by Eastwood. The two discussed the dispute on a preliminary and without prejudice basis and, after a meeting had been provisionally arranged to take place in Belfast on the Saturday week (20 September), McEvoy sent a short letter to Beuselinck.

Dear Sir,
Given the frank way in which you have approached this matter, I would wish to make our views plain.
The intended action will involve very serious allegations against your Client. We consider that once these allegations become public it will make any settlement of the dispute extremely difficult. Therefore it is likely that, if the case can be settled at all, the best opportunity is before the issue of proceedings. We take the gravest view of your Client's conduct, which has occasioned enormous loss to our Client, and would require very substantial compensation. We think it best that you and your Client should appreciate this or else our meeting will be futile.

Because of what Beuselinck described as 'circumstances, both of my client and myself', the agreed meeting did not in fact take place until the following Monday. The chosen location was the Dunadry Inn, fifteen miles north-west of Belfast and, apart from a brief glimpse of each other in the reception area as they arrived for the meeting, there was no contact whatsoever between McGuigan and Eastwood. The meeting, indeed, had been so arranged that the two principal players, their initial accidental sightings apart, would not even set eyes on each other throughout its entire duration. Three adjoining rooms had been reserved: one for the McGuigan party, which, in addition to the fighter himself and his wife, comprised McEvoy, Lavery and Deeny; one for Eastwood, who was accompanied only by Beuselinck; and the third – the middle room of the three – for the respective legal representatives to meet in in their efforts to work out a mutually agreeable solution.

Thus, for over two hours, the doors to all three rooms opened and closed on countless occasions as the lawyers met each other in the middle room or made brief returns to an adjoining one to clarify or query particular points of progress or contention with their respective clients. And, on the day at least, considerable progress appeared to have been made, but no final settlement was reached. Beuselinck had to return to London that same evening to attend a Royal Gala performance, so the meeting broke up with an agreement by both sides that they should meet again at the Dunadry Inn the following Friday afternoon.

On the Wednesday, however, Michael Lavery had a brief, unarranged discussion in the Law Library that was the first intimation to the McGuigan team that the position had changed drastically since the meeting two days earlier, and that the prospects of settling the dispute without court action had apparently vanished forever. Robert McCartney QC approached Lavery and informed him that Oscar Beuselinck would no longer be handling the case and that he, McCartney, would be taking over. He added that he would need about six weeks to study the relevant papers.

In the eyes of the McGuigan legal team, that seemed to indicate that whatever progress had apparently been achieved at the Dunadry meeting was now being cast aside.

On the Thursday evening, McEvoy organized what developed into a marathon four-hour session at Michael Lavery's house in the Malone Road area of Belfast. As well as Lavery himself and McEvoy, McGuigan and Donnell Deeny were also present. The atmosphere at the meeting was a strange mixture of confidence and dejection: confidence in the merit and justice of the group's case, and dejection that the final settlement that had appeared so close to being reached only three days previously now seemed as far away as it had ever been. Eastwood's replacement of Oscar Beuselinck by Robert McCartney and the latter's insistence that he would require at least six weeks to acquaint himself with the intricacies of the case meant that, in the eyes of both McGuigan and his entire legal team, they were back to square one in terms of the reaching of any satisfactory out of court settlement.

*

I didn't want to meet Barney at the Dunadry Inn because it didn't seem as if we could have much to say to each other at that point, so we all operated out of different rooms. Eamonn and Sandra and I and our senior and junior counsel – Michael Lavery and Donnell Deeny – were in one room, Barney and Oscar Beuselinck were in another, and in between was a third room in which Eamonn, Michael Lavery and Donnell Deeny would have their talks with Beuselinck. It was like a game of revolving doors, with the four legal guys going in and out of the middle room every couple of minutes to keep Barney and me, in our separate rooms, up to date on how the discussions were going.

It was then agreed by everybody involved that we would all get together again a couple of days later to finalize the agreement – but then Eamonn got a phone call from Oscar Beuselinck telling him that Barney had replaced him. We certainly had no desire to get bogged down for God knows how long in a court case and all that would involve, but once Barney went back on the progress that had been made at the Dunadry Inn, we just didn't feel that we had any alternative but to go ahead with the action.

Eamonn and Michael Lavery and Donnell Deeny were all convinced that we had a particularly good and strong case. But Barney's refusal to listen to it left us with no alternative. Barney, it was obvious, was trying to call our bluff – and the only way we had of showing him that we were not bluffing was to go ahead with the issuing of the writ.

*

Barney Eastwood, meanwhile, was seemingly unaware that his relationship with the most famous member of his boxing stable had reached such a critical stage. That, certainly, was the clear impression conveyed by his public comments. On the Monday after McGuigan's return from Las Vegas with Eamonn McEvoy, for instance, Eastwood was quoted in the majority of the Irish morning papers as being 'unaware' that McGuigan was planning a million-dollar lawsuit against him.

And, in the *Irish Independent* of Monday 21 September, the very day of the original Dunadry Inn meeting, he not only dismissed any hint of court action as sensationalist but hinted strongly that his understanding of McGuigan's second visit to Las Vegas was that his estranged charge was endeavouring to reactivate his fighting career.

'I know nothing about intended litigation at this stage. I think this kind of stuff makes good headlines. I am still Barry's manager and he is under contract to me. He cannot enter into a contract to fight without me. He told me after the Cruz fight that he was taking a long rest and that he would come back to me when he wanted to fight again. So far he has not come back. He is entitled to go to Las Vegas if he wants to.'

Eastwood's ignorance of 'intended litigation' was short-lived; soon after four o'clock on the evening of Friday 26 September, a courier made the twenty-three-mile journey from the Lurgan office of McGuigan's solicitor to the High Court in Belfast to lodge a writ of summons and a statement of claim on behalf of Finbar Patrick McGuigan against Bernard J Eastwood. The pairing that, five and a half years earlier, had set out to conquer the boxing world – and had succeeded – was about to disintegrate under the weight of just twelve pages of legal documents.

Not yet knowing the identity of the firm of solicitors who would be representing Eastwood following Oscar Beuselinck's replacement (Robert McCartney was, and is, a senior counsel), McEvoy wrote directly to Eastwood at his Holywood home upon the lodging of the litigation papers with the Queen's Bench of the High Court:

Dear Sir,

As you know, we act for Mr McGuigan. We regret that you have not seen fit to honour the arrangement made on Monday 22 September 1986 adjourning the meeting which had been called on that date at your request to today's date. You will by now realize the full extent of our Client's very serious complaints against you and we regret that it is impossible to delay any further the issue of proceedings.

Accordingly, we enclose herewith by pre-paid First Class Post a copy of the Writ of Summons and Statement of Claim in the above action by way of service pursuant to Order 10 Rule 1 (2) of the Rules of the Supreme Court (Northern Ireland) 1980. As we are unaware of the identity of the Solicitors in Northern Ireland who are acting for you in this matter, we are sending a copy of this letter to Mr Beuselinck.

The accompanying statement of claim spelled out McGuigan's charges about Eastwood's management in greater detail. The statement, in addition to general damages, also sought payment of the by now infamous marker, the $250,000 promised in writing to McGuigan by Eastwood on 29 May 1986, the day Steve Cruz was drafted in as Fernando Sosa's replacement. However, inconspicuously tucked away in Paragraph 15 of the document's twenty-two paragraphs, was McGuigan's 'Exocet': that a further $1m had been paid by the promoter, far more than McGuigan had received or than he had been made aware of.

*

The moment I first heard of the million dollars [in August 1986] any chance of a reconciliation with Barney disappeared. Later, he tried to dress it up as selling promotional rights in me to a Panamanian company called Panaprom SA, but who the hell were they? As far as I was concerned, the total on offer for me to fight in Las Vegas was $1,600,000, and all I'd seen of it, or been told about, was $600,000.

When Barney came back from America in April 1986, that's what he told me I'd get for fighting Fernando Sosa. But in fact, Bob Arum's company Top Rank Inc. paid $1,200,000 to Panaprom, and $260,000 direct to Barney as being the amount shown on the actual fight contract lodged with the Nevada State Athletic Commission on 1 June. There was another $140,000 in sponsorship from the Irish Permanent Building Society. That's $1,600,000, however you add it up, and I found it staggering that I'd only been told about $600,000 of it. We'd spent seven years together, and I'd believed I was more than just another business to him: now I knew differently.

Why should a Panamanian company of which I'd never heard get a million dollars? I had no contract with them. It is nonsense to say that the money went to Panaprom in payment for promotional rights. Nobody held any promotional rights in me; not Panaprom, not Eastwood Promotions, and not Barney Eastwood himself. The only contract between Barney and me was a managerial one, and if anybody was entitled to a million-dollar fee for Barry McGuigan's appearance in Las Vegas, it was me, and nobody else. Once I found out about it, everything was finished between us: the trust was dead.

This was what our High Court action was all about. As far as I was concerned Barney had committed me, without prior consultation, to a fight I didn't want and in conditions which I couldn't believe, and he had not told me of either the true nature or the full extent of the deal he had made. In my view, that meant that he had broken our contract. I felt I was entitled to two-thirds of that extra million dollars, and I was prepared to go to law and fight for my money – my blood money.

*

The total monies paid by Top Rank and the Irish Permanent Building Society in connection with the bout did indeed come to $1,600,000. And McGuigan himself was indeed paid a purse of $600,000 (less US taxes). That, though, was the end of the road as far as simplicity or straightforwardness was concerned. The money, regardless of in which direction it was travelling, moved in a bewildering array of detours and tangents. McGuigan, for example, was paid by four different cheques (and two cash sums totalling $1,200) with money that reached Eastwood by three different routes.

The boxer's 'official' purse, the $260,000 as stated on the revised fight contract lodged with the Nevada State Athletic Commission on 1 June (three days after Steve Cruz had been drafted in to replace Fernando Sosa), was paid direct to Eastwood by Bob Arum's company, Top Rank, minus $52,000 in US taxes. The $140,000 sponsorship fee paid by the Irish Permanent Building Society also went direct to McGuigan's manager, but the remaining $1.2 million was paid by Top Rank, via three separate cheques drawn on the Chemical Bank of New York, into the account of Panaprom SA in Panama City.

Three days after issuing the writ, McEvoy was informed that the Belfast firm of John Johnson and Son would be representing Eastwood within the Northern Ireland jurisdiction. Wright Webb Syrett, however, continued to assist McGuigan's manager on the other side of the Irish Sea and it was through his London solicitors that Eastwood, on 3 October, wrote to the British Boxing Board of Control, seeking to have the dispute dealt with under the Board's own arbitration procedures and informing the Board of his intention to apply for a stay in McGuigan's High Court proceedings in view of the proposed arbitration.

Clause 9 in the standard BBBC contract as signed by both Eastwood and McGuigan on 23 March 1981 and lodged with the Board two days later is headed 'Disputes' and decrees that:

> In the event of any disputes in respect of any matter arising under, out

of or pursuant to this Agreement, the parties shall refer such dispute for arbitration by way of a complaint to the applicable BBB of C Area Council or to the Board in accordance with the provisions of the BBB of C Regulation 15a entitled 'Complaints', and such arbitration shall be subject to the provisions of the BBB of C Regulation 16 entitled 'Appeal'. The procedures contained in the said Regulation shall be exhausted and an order, decision or award made in accordance with the said Regulations by the aforesaid Area Council or Board or, in the case of an appeal, by the BBB of C Stewards of Appeal, before any application may be made to the Courts of Law by any of the parties hereto.

That, particularly the latter sentence, was not acceptable to McGuigan and his legal representatives. They held that a ban on the right to have redress to the courts was both dictatorial and an infringement of McGuigan's civil liberties and further, that 'fraud, deceit . . . negligence and conspiracy' as cited in the writ of summons were matters of such gravity that they simply had to be dealt with by the courts and not by internal BBBC procedures.

On 9 October, after having received his courtesy copy of Wright Webb Syrett's letter to the BBBC, McEvoy wrote to both London offices. To Wright Webb Syrett he expressed surprise 'at your Client's evident reluctance to answer the charges of fraud against him in open Court' and added: 'We consider the attempted reference to arbitration to be merely an attempt on your Client's part to delay the Trial of the Action, which is of course in keeping with your Client's publicly stated attitude. The application to stay the Action and refer to arbitration will be opposed and your Client's efforts to delay Trial will be vigorously resisted.'

And, to the Board itself, he wrote: 'If any arbitration provision had ever any validity then it has been rendered inoperable by the conduct of Mr Eastwood. As you have been told, we have issued proceedings in the High Court of Justice in Northern Ireland on behalf of Mr McGuigan against Mr Eastwood. In the circumstances, we do not consent to and will oppose any purported arbitration by the Board into the matters in dispute between the parties to that Action. Please confirm, therefore, that you will take no steps in this matter in the light of the proceedings in the High Court.' Wright Webb Syrett responded by saying that it would 'be up to the Court to determine how best this matter should be resolved', while John Morris, successor to Ray Clarke as General

Secretary of the BBBC, answered by enclosing a copy of his response to Wright Webb Syrett's letter of 3 October and added: 'You will note that this makes it clear we would only be prepared to attempt to arbitrate in this matter either with full agreement of all parties or following a stay of proceedings in the High Court.'

Dear Sirs,
    I acknowledge receipt of your letter of 3 October, and the matter you raised has now been discussed by the Board at their Meeting this week.
    Under the terms of Clause 9 of the Board's Articles of Agreement, either party to the Agreement is entitled to apply for a dispute to be considered by the Board. The capacity of the Board to implement its arbitration procedure in this case has been pre-empted, however, by virtue of the fact that Mr McGuigan has instituted proceedings against Mr Eastwood in the High Court in Belfast.
    Until the Court has determined whether or not those proceedings should be stayed or until the parties agree that the proceedings should be stayed pending the dispute or disputes being submitted to the Board for arbitration, we feel it would be inappropriate for the Board to attempt to arbitrate.
    If the disputes between Mr McGuigan and Mr Eastwood arise out of matters over which the Board legitimately can assume jurisdiction and the parties either agree jointly to submit to arbitration by the Board, or the Court stay the proceedings pending the outcome of arbitration by the Board, then at that stage the Board would make its proceedings available to the parties and hear disputes in accordance with the manner laid down in the Board's Regulations.

    The British Boxing Board of Control, in short, was declining to become embroiled in the dispute. Barney Eastwood, whose public response to the news of the issuing of the writ by McGuigan was to say, 'As far as I'm concerned this is going to be a marathon – I will fight it to the bitter end', while saying nothing of his bid to have the matter settled internally by the Board, was being left to fight his battle with Barry McGuigan on his own. In the High Court in Belfast.

On 23 October, four weeks after the McGuigan writ was issued, a defence and counterclaim by Eastwood was lodged by John Johnson and Son. In it, Eastwood denied that 'at any time material to this action he failed to disclose the full terms or conditions' of the Las

Vegas fight agreement with Top Rank, and also insisted that he had never 'agreed to pay the Plaintiff the sum of US $250,000' and also denied that McGuigan 'provided any consideration to support the alleged agreement [regarding the $250,000] or that there was any intention to enter into a legal contract'.

McGuigan's manager went on to charge that he had never taken from the boxer the 25 per cent commission to which he was entitled under their BBBC contract and that, as part of his counterclaim, he was therefore seeking the payment of 'monies due and owing' to him from the former world champion, as well as 'a declaration that the Plaintiff has agreed to be managed and directed exclusively by the Defendant'. In addition, the Eastwood defence contended that he was 'entitled to act as promoter of *all* [italics added] the Plaintiff's contests' and that, as a direct consequence, he was equally entitled to receive additional monies 'in consideration of forgoing his right to promote the contest in Las Vegas'.

One of his denials was decidedly curious: Paragraph 28 says, in its entirety: 'The Defendant does not admit that the Plaintiff lost the contest on 23 June 1986, or that he lost the World Boxing Association Title.'

Chapter Thirty-One

'I didn't take any commission off him. Managers are entitled to twenty-five per cent, but I've never taken any commission off McGuigan – ever.'

Barney Eastwood in an interview with the *Guardian*, 20 September 1986

The battle, meanwhile, was also being fought on another, somewhat more public, front. The media, which had played such a significant role in the rise of the whole Eastwood–McGuigan 'father and son' perception, were now also to have a part to play in the downfall of that relationship. On Saturday 20 September 1986, exactly two weeks after the Spinks–Tangstad fight in Las Vegas and six days before the issuing of the High Court writ by McGuigan, the *Guardian* published an interview with Eastwood by Geoffrey Beattie. Beginning with how Eastwood had first spotted McGuigan, it included the following quotes from McGuigan's by now estranged manager:

> I spotted Barry McGuigan on television. He was fighting Ian McLeod from Scotland. I said to my wife: 'There's a good kid there'.
>
> There wasn't much in it. I thought the referee could have given the decision to McGuigan but he didn't, he gave it to McLeod. [It was an amateur contest and therefore was scored by three judges, not the referee.] I said to my wife: 'It's not three rounds that kid needs, it's thirty-three.' I thought he was a kid who was strong, with plenty of stamina.
>
> Later on I had a talk with him, and he turned professional. He was a raw fighter when he turned. He'd nothing except strength and stamina. There was only one way he could go – and that was up.
>
> People say the heat, the heat, the heat. In my opinion the heat had nothing to do with it. Nobody mentioned the heat before the

fight. But there's something else that people forget – McGuigan won the twelfth, thirteenth and fourteenth rounds, not bad for a fella suffering from the heat. All he had to do was to stand on his feet in the last round. Even if he got knocked down once in the last round, he'd still have won the fight. But he got knocked down twice.

If you get knocked down twice your opponent gets awarded the round with double points. [Eastwood meant that the judges can score a knockdown round 10–8 instead of the customary 10–9, or a double-knockdown round 10–7.] That's what did it. In the fifteenth round, McGuigan got hit on the chin and he wobbled and put his arms around the other guy's neck and held on grimly. If the other guy had had any strength, he just had to push him off and hit him and McGuigan was gone. But he hadn't the strength. They were both drained. It was all down to who wanted to win the fight most in the fifteenth round. It was down to who was the hungriest, and that's the way it ended.

I've been saddened by all the criticism from the press and the public. By McGuigan's own admission it was him who wanted to go to America. He wanted to exploit the American market. He was tempted by all the endorsements. Why would I want him to go to America?* I wasn't promoting the fight and I didn't take any commission off him. Managers are entitled to twenty-five per cent, but I've never taken any commission off McGuigan – ever.

I wasn't keen for him to go to America. As a bookie, I've had to follow my gut feeling all the way. I had a gut feeling that we would not have control of the conditions under Top Rank promoters in Las Vegas, like we would in Ireland or even in London. I thought things would not go our way. But I still

---

*The question of precisely who wanted to cross the Atlantic and who did not was another matter of serious contention. 'I wasn't keen for him to go', Eastwood said in the *Guardian* interview, adding, 'He wanted to exploit the American market.' But, to another publication, McGuigan's manager told a rather different story.

In an interview with the then editor of *Ring*, Nigel Collins, and published in the June 1986 issue of the magazine as a preview article on the Las Vegas fight, Eastwood claimed the credit for 'persuading' McGuigan – whom he himself called 'a wee country lad' to travel to the New World and then told Collins: 'I told him it was for his own good. I explained to him that he could be a very big star in America. I have a lot of things in mind for Barry and this is a good step forward. It will be good for his image and we're also hoping to pick up some spin-off endorsements.'

thought his opponent was very ordinary and the McGuigan of a year ago would have walked through him in a couple of rounds. The way things had gone in the training camp had certainly caused me some concern. But I still had the feeling that Barry had the extra capacity to beat Cruz.

Don't forget, I jumped the queue with McGuigan to get him a shot at the world title. To do that I had to go to Panama, the headquarters of the WBA, and practically live there for a month to get everything arranged. The champion was Eusebio Pedroza, from Panama. He was thirty-two and a hero in his own country but, in my view, on the way down. The time was right.

I also watched Nelson, the WBC champion, fighting and realized that he was on the way up. I could have got Nelson to fight at the QPR ground for a quarter of a million dollars but I didn't. I went for Pedroza. He cost a million. I wasn't just promoting to make money – how could I be? I was giving McGuigan a real chance to win the title. It cost me an extra three-quarters of a million dollars to do that. And don't forget, if McGuigan had lost at QPR, I'd have lost a lot of money, but I backed a winner. Pedroza had only one fight since he lost to McGuigan, against a guy who wasn't rated. He had his jaw broken.

The future? McGuigan has still got eight months to go on the present contract and he's got an agreement with me for a further three years, but I don't know whether he'll fight again. I'd be delighted for him if he decided to retire. It's up to him to make up his own mind. Nobody can do it for him. He's very comfortably off now and he didn't have anything when I met him – except a kind of hunger.

From the McGuigan standpoint, the article was highly objectionable on several counts, not least its opening and closing claims that 'there was only one way he could go – and that was up' and that he 'didn't have anything when I met him – except a kind of hunger'.

That McGuigan had a talent far above the average even as a teenage amateur was a matter of fact, not merely opinion. He certainly had a lot more than just strength and stamina, and while nobody, himself included, ever sought – or should be permitted – to discount or minimize the significant part played in his subsequent professional career by Eastwood, the latter's comments to Geoffrey

Beattie clearly seek to do precisely the reverse: Eastwood, according to Eastwood, created McGuigan out of nothing, and the boxer himself contributed absolutely nothing.

Had that truly been the case, then would such experienced and successful managers as Mickey Duff, Terry Lawless and Eddie Thomas all have been so keen to acquire the then twenty-year-old McGuigan's signature on a professional contract? While Eastwood very definitely had a central role to play in what would subsequently become the McGuigan success story, Duff, Lawless and Thomas had all themselves helped mould highly promising amateurs such as Howard Winstone, Charlie Magri, John Stracey, Maurice Hope, Alan Minter, John Conteh and Ken Buchanan into world champions. Who is to say that each of the three could not have achieved everything with McGuigan that Eastwood did?

Eastwood's remarks concerning the Cruz fight itself were equally contentious. His comment that all McGuigan 'had to do was to stand on his feet in the last round' was easily uttered from outside the ropes. Eastwood was not the one who had had to endure the cumulative effect of fighting fourteen previous rounds of what *Ring* magazine designated its 'Fight of the Year' in a totally alien environment and, most crucial of all, in an inside-the-ring temperature of something around 120 degrees Fahrenheit.

And Eastwood, as has already been shown, was most certainly wrong about the heat. His contention that 'nobody mentioned the heat before the fight' ignored the fact that at least three papers, the *Sunday Tribune*, the *Times* and *Ireland's Saturday Night*, had all raised the question before the event, and that McGuigan himself had protested about the temperatures in Las Vegas in his letter of 14 May to Eastwood, five weeks before the fight. Eastwood's claim that 'the heat had nothing to do with it' was a total and public contradiction of his own comment in Las Vegas a matter of minutes after the fight: 'The heat was terrible. I don't think I'd bring a fighter to this place again. Barry gave everything and it just wasn't enough.'

Steve Cruz himself, speaking a week after his victory, described the early evening timing of the fight as 'absolutely ridiculous' and insisted that he would never even consider defending his newly won title under similar climatic conditions. 'We were both lucky we did not get seriously injured. The heat probably took more out of Barry but I can tell you I was pretty drained, too. I could feel the heat through my boots from the sun on the ring.

'A world title fight is difficult enough without having to take on the heat too. I said all along that I had great respect for Barry and it increased after our fight. I am glad to hear he is OK, because I know the heat took an awful lot out of him. It was a tragedy that the fight took place in such conditions.'

That McGuigan managed a late rally to win the twelfth, thirteenth and fourteenth rounds is apparently proof in Eastwood's eyes that the about-to-be deposed champion was not suffering in the heat and should, had he 'wanted to win the fight most', have been able to survive the last three minutes to hang on to his title. That, however, is a rather conveniently simplistic analysis, one that neglects the fact that it was precisely the effort required to win those three late rounds that left McGuigan so completely drained that physical survival alone was all he could aim for during those frantic final three minutes.

'They were both drained,' Eastwood had said, and indeed they were. But if Steve Cruz, Texas-born and with Mexican blood in his veins (as well as the benefit of six previous appearances in Las Vegas rings, even though they were at more appropriate times of the day), had felt the effects of the heat to the extent that he himself later acknowledged, then what must McGuigan have suffered in that same heat?

The fact that he could do no more than simply last out that traumatic fifteenth round was, given all the circumstances at the time, surely more of a testament to McGuigan's courage than some sort of obscure verification of his manager's assertion that he, McGuigan, somehow was not as hungry for victory as was Steve Cruz.

There were other points in the interview to which ready responses could have been made. They, however, would wait.

Eight days after the *Guardian* article, Pat McGuigan entered the fray in defence of his son by publicly challenging the Eastwood version of the events surrounding the defeat in Las Vegas in an interview with the *Sunday Tribune*. Eastwood, said McGuigan senior, was 'either a fool or a member of the Flat Earth Society' to insist that it had been the boxer's idea to take the fight in Las Vegas.

Barry never wanted to go to Las Vegas, ever. He even wrote to Barney and told him that he – Barney – had no right whatsoever to sign him up for the fight without first consulting him, but Barney sent a letter back saying, in effect, that as the fight was already signed for the point was academic. So Barry wrote another letter asking Barney to ensure that it would never happen again.

Eastwood also said that 'by McGuigan's own admission it was him [sic] who wanted to go to America' and offers this as the reason for taking the fight in Las Vegas, which just wasn't so. Yes, Barry wanted to go to America, of course he did, but the American fight he wanted was against Wilfredo Gomez in Madison Square Garden in New York for the junior-lightweight title, which was an entirely different proposition from risking his own featherweight title in the heat of Las Vegas in June.'

And, acknowledging that the *Tribune*, *Times* and *Ireland's Saturday Night* had all queried the wisdom of fighting in the Nevada desert prior to the event, Pat McGuigan also took issue with the Eastwood contention that 'nobody mentioned the heat before the fight'. In addition to his son's objections as initially voiced at his 13 April meeting with Eastwood in Enniskillen and then laid out in written form in his 14 May letter, said Pat McGuigan, he himself had complained to Eastwood in early May, following the McGuigan family's receipt of the statistics supplied by the State of Nevada Weather Bureau.

My complaint was verbal, but Barry's was in writing. I actually helped him write the letter in which he outlined his various objections to the fight – and very high up on that list was his concern over the temperature, based on the figures we had obtained from the Nevada Weather Bureau. Yet Eastwood publicly claimed that 'nobody mentioned the weather'!

The fighter's father admitted that he took particular exception to Eastwood's closing remark in the *Guardian* interview, that 'Barry didn't have anything when I met him – except a kind of hunger'.

That is a slight on everybody who has ever been associated with Barry McGuigan, be they the members of his own family or the people involved with him during his amateur days in the Smithboro club. Barney Eastwood is trying to make out that he –

and he alone – took Barry from nothing to a world championship. As an amateur, Barry not only had above-average resources at his disposal – how many amateurs have had their very own fully equipped gym or were full-time fighters before their sixteenth birthdays? – but above-average talent as well, a fact recognized by the great Lazlo Papp, among others.*

Barney Eastwood, give him his due, must be credited with having done a lot for Barry and with having spotted exactly what Barry had, but it is important to remember who approached who: Barney Eastwood approached Barry through first Charlie Gray and then Gerry Storey and he did it not because Barry 'had nothing', but because he was fully aware of precisely what Barry did have – a very special talent.

Then, the following Thursday, trainer Eddie Shaw claimed, in a first-person article in the *Sun* for which he received, according to one *Sun* source, £5,000, that McGuigan 'would do anything for money' and additionally hit out with the following quotes:

> 'He's one of the meanest people I have ever met. He has never even bought me a Coca-Cola. I'm fairly sure that he hasn't put his hand in his pocket for Barney Eastwood, either. And to think we were the people who made him rich.
>
> 'There were many days that I didn't feel like going to the gym. I simply couldn't face the prospect of McGuigan complaining about everything. He was upsetting the other boxers. It is a great weight off my mind knowing that I will never have to work with him again.'
>
> 'If he crawled into my gym on his hands and knees asking me to train him again, I would tell him: "Get lost. I've been a mug once – but never again."
>
> 'If I saw him coming down the street, I'd walk right past him without saying a word. He is not the chirpy fellow that he would like everybody to think he is. He seems a nice chap to many people because he rarely, if ever, criticizes anybody else. Other people do it for him.'
>
> 'His act was a sham . . . he has been rumbled.'

*After a 1978 amateur international between Ireland and Hungary at the National Stadium in Dublin, Papp, a triple Olympic champion but then the coach to the Hungarian team, described McGuigan as 'the best seventeen-year-old I've ever seen'.

McGuigan responded to this outburst personally six days later when signing his name to another first-person piece – for which he was not paid specifically but which was part of an on-going exclusive contract – in the *Daily Star*, in which he described Shaw's attack as a 'stab in the back'. Venturing the opinion that Shaw's article may have come about because his former trainer might have been in need of financial assistance ('Maybe he's skint and needs the money. He's had financial problems in the past.'), he claimed that whenever he'd had a monetary dispute with Eastwood in the past, he had been told by Shaw to 'fight for every penny you can get'.

And, in a reference to the 'hands and knees' comment, he closed the piece with a personal message to Shaw: 'Eddie, if I ever see you down on your hands and knees, I'll help pick you up. I can't accept that even you believe the rubbish that's been printed under your name.'

*

Eddie depended on Eastwood for his wages, and I tried to use that to colour out what he said about me in the *Sun*. It was a very shabby and silly interview, mind you, but the fact that he had written it and said I was ungrateful was very hurtful.

The standard deduction for a trainer is ten per cent. Eddie was always hard up, although if he'd got ten per cent of what I earned in my career he should have been OK. I had done nothing but good for Eddie, and he often said he'd never forget that, yet when I split with Eastwood he did the dirty.

I never fell out with Eddie himself, only with Eastwood. I rang Eddie after the fight in Las Vegas, but he was very cool, and then a couple of weeks later he'd done the piece in the paper. That was it for me: we never spoke again after that.

Shortly before the piece appeared in the paper, I saw his brother Mo one day when he was out running. I waved at him, but he ignored me, so I turned the car round and I followed him for about half a mile. Finally I slowed alongside him, rolled the window down and shouted, 'Hey, Mo!' But he just raised his hand and carried on running, and I knew then that I was being cold-shouldered.

Eddie died while this book was being written, and I'm sorry I never got the chance to make peace with him. We had some good times together, and it's a shame we didn't part friends.

*

Within a matter of hours of McGuigan's answering article appearing in the *Daily Star*, Shaw was contacted by journalist Liam Kelly on behalf of the Dublin *Evening Herald*. Shaw's response to McGuigan's reply to his own (Shaw's) article was:

> You can understand there's nothing I can add to it. I've been advised by B J Eastwood not to say anything more because of the court proceedings, and I respect his wishes. I said a few months ago that there was no point in engaging in a slanging match, and it would be better that all this be thrashed out around a table instead of in the newspapers.

Eddie Shaw's reluctance to discuss the matter was understandable. But it was also a classic example of locking the stable door after the horse had not so much bolted as been urged to run free.

The following day the *Daily Star* ran another McGuigan-related story in which Pat McGuigan repeated, and in some areas expanded on, his earlier *Sunday Tribune* interview. Boxed within the article was an official comment from Eastwood himself: 'I feel very saddened and very hurt by what has been said. After some of the greatest nights in British boxing history, it's sad that all this had to happen. But I've already stated that I am not going to comment on anything that's been said. There is a time and place for all that, and that will be dealt with in a court of law.' McGuigan, unusually at this stage of the chronology, was in full agreement with Eastwood. But, as in the case of Shaw's apparent reticence, Eastwood's exhibition of discretion came somewhat late in the day; almost three weeks after his *Guardian* interview, to be precise.

Almost six months later, on Thursday 26 March 1987, just six weeks before the scheduled start of the court case, an interview with Mickey Duff, conducted by Kevin Moseley, appeared in the *Daily Express*.

Entitled 'McGreedy', the story quoted Duff as saying, 'The problem was that McGuigan became influenced by greed. He made money, on a short-term basis, the overwhelming factor. And he paid a terrible price.' The article continued, 'Duff believes that

McGuigan's insistence on a higher purse persuaded Eastwood to accept the Las Vegas fight in unfavourable conditions.'

'I feel that McGuigan,' said Duff in the same article, 'may be suffering from listening to people who are happy to cause problems. I saw the way it was going. Of the fighters I have known, I would probably rate McGuigan among the most difficult to handle – but then he wasn't my responsibility.'

Perhaps not, but then Mickey Duff neglected to mention a particularly salient point. Two days before the *Daily Express* article appeared, Duff had been served with a subpoena by Eamonn McEvoy. The man who said McGuigan 'wasn't my responsibility' was to be asked to explain to the High Court in Belfast how he came to receive six-figure sums from each of McGuigan's world title fights.

Chapter Thirty-Two

'I didn't have to fight this fight. I wanted to come back to prove something. I was trying to get back something [the championship] someone took away from me. I don't need the money. Everyone knows I'm rich.'

Former heavyweight champion Larry Holmes, justifying his decision to return to the ring to face Mike Tyson

By the final month of 1986, the old appetite for fighting was starting to stir within McGuigan once more. He had, in fact, gone back into his own Clones gym as early as 4 August, six weeks to the day after the Cruz bout, but that had been more to satisfy his obsession with physical fitness than a deliberate step on the road to a resumption of his ring career. After four months of working out on a daily basis, however, something more than just a feeling of physical well-being was required: McGuigan, as always, needed a definite goal to work towards.

The one he settled on was redemption. He always disliked the term 'comeback' being applied in his case, insisting that he was never officially retired or away, merely resting and recharging his physical and psychological batteries. A return to the ring would offer him the chance to show that were it not for what he was convinced had been the folly of the Las Vegas fight, he might still be the featherweight champion of the world. There was, though, a major problem to be overcome before any plan of campaign could actually be implemented: his relationship with Barney Eastwood.

On 10 December, two days after McGuigan admitted at a function in London that he could foresee himself at some point wanting to box again, John Johnson and Son wrote to Eamonn McEvoy with a two-fight proposal for McGuigan from Eastwood. The first, which was to take place in mid-January 1987, would be against 'a suitable opponent selected from the top twenty in the world rankings'. If McGuigan won, Eastwood's solicitors promised him that 'our client would then be able to arrange a world championship bout against the winner of the Cruz–Esparragoza fight'. The letter concluded by pointing out that if McGuigan won his two fights he would be restored as world champion, while if he was not prepared to end what the letter described as his 'self-imposed break in his career', that would be his choice and not Eastwood's fault.

The reference to the 'self-imposed break' made the McGuigan camp doubt the letter's sincerity. True, nobody was physically preventing him from boxing again, but given his relationship with Eastwood, even the most casual observer could see how unworkable any proposal of co-operation would be just then. Also, Eastwood had not always regarded McGuigan's exile as being a self-imposed one. In the *Belfast Telegraph* of 10 September – over two weeks before the issuing of the writ – he was quoted as saying: 'He was washed out before Vegas, and with nobody but himself to blame. Clearly, the training he has been doing in Clones has burned a valve or two. That's why I ordered him six months' rest from the game.'

Accordingly, McEvoy responded to the two-fight 'offer' a day after receiving it by pointing out much of the above. Plus one or two other points.

We refer to your letter of the 8th inst. and must confess to finding the suggestion contained therein, to say the least, unrealistic while the present litigation is pending. Indeed, it is difficult to believe that the proposals contained therein are put forward in a serious vein in view of the background to this matter and indeed also in view of the press campaign of vilification of the Plaintiff in which the Defendant and his associates have engaged. In addition, it is noted that the Defendant saw fit to release the proposal contained in your letter in an interview with the *Evening Herald* which was published in that paper on 9 December, the day before your letter was received.

If your Client is serious in not wishing to prevent the Plaintiff from pursuing his career as a boxer perhaps you would confirm that he is agreeable to the Plaintiff, if he so desires, having discussions with bona fide promoters on the understanding that 25 per cent of the Plaintiff's net earnings from any fights would be lodged on joint deposit pending the outcome of the present proceedings.

Frank Warren, around this time, was stepping up his campaign to tempt McGuigan into launching phase two of his ring career from his London stable. And he seemed to be making progress, particularly as McGuigan had decided against an association with Mogens Palle on the grounds that he needed guidance from closer to home. A week before Christmas, McGuigan had announced that he hoped to get back into the ring some time around the following March, but of a likely promoter would only say 'he has hair'. Warren, through his usual Irish-based intermediary, had continued to express his eagerness to work with McGuigan whenever the former champion was ready and able to begin official talks. By early 1987 McGuigan was ready, if not formally to do business, at least to hear suggestions about what might lie down the road for him.

Thus, by 7 January, Warren felt in a position to lay out at least semi-formal proposals to McGuigan. Increasing his verbal offers of the previous few months, he sent the following telex to be relayed to McGuigan:

PLEASE FORWARD THE FOLLOWING TO OUR FRIEND.
10-ROUND 'WARM-UP' CONTEST IN LONDON 25 MARCH. A MUTUALLY ACCEPT-ABLE OPPONENT AT 9ST 4LB. PURSE (US) 120,000. I WOULD ARRANGE TRAINING FACILITIES AND ACCOMMODATION IN LONDON IF REQUIRED.

I WOULD ALSO WANT 2 OPTIONS ON BARRY, 1ST OPTION AGAINST CRUZ OR ESPARRAGOZA. (I CAN GET OVER E'S [EASTWOOD'S] SO-CALLED OPTIONS ON CRUZ – REMEMBER I PRE-EMPTED THE PEDROZA SITUATION AFTER I AGREED TERMS WITH HIS PEOPLE – IT WAS ONLY THAT E WOULD NOT AGREE TERMS WITH ME.)

THE 1ST OPTION PURSE WOULD BE GUARANTEED (US) 400,000 AGAINST A PERCENTAGE OF THE PROMOTION, OR A 50/50 SPLIT ON ALL PROFITS. I WOULD OBVIOUSLY ENSURE THAT ALL ACCOUNTS WOULD BE MADE AVAILABLE TO BARRY OR HIS REPRESENTATIVE FOR INSPECTION.

ON THE SECOND OPTION – I THINK WE SHOULD BOTH SHOW AN AMOUNT OF TRUST AND NEGOTIATE THE FINANCIAL TERMS AFTER THE FIRST OPTION – I FEEL THIS IS BOTH FAIR AND SENSIBLE.

WITH REGARD TO THE WARM-UP, I DO NOT HAVE ANY US TV AND DO NOT ANTICIPATE SEEING ANY, PRIMARILY BECAUSE TIME IS AGAINST ME. I AM THEREFORE PUTTING MYSELF ON THE LINE AS FAR AS THE FIRST CONTEST IS CONCERNED. FOR THE FIRST OPTION, I HAVE BEEN GIVEN TWO DATES BY US TV, 10 OR 24 MAY, AND AGAIN IT IS OF THE UTMOST IMPORTANCE SOME DECISION BE REACHED ON THIS MATTER. I ANTICIPATE THE VENUE AS BEING QPR OR HIGHBURY. I THINK IT IS VERY IMPORTANT THAT THESE CONTESTS TAKE PLACE IN THE UK IN ORDER THAT BARRY'S PROFILE REMAINS IN THE FOREFRONT WITH REGARD TO HIS INTERESTS AND ENDORSEMENT VALUE OUTSIDE OF THE BOXING AREA.

IF ANY FURTHER INFORMATION IS REQUIRED PLEASE CONTACT ME. I MUST STRESS THE POINT THAT A MEETING SHOULD BE SET UP AS SOON AS POSSIBLE IN ORDER THAT WE CAN DISCUSS THE MATTER – TIME IS AGAINST US AS FAR

AS US TV IS CONCERNED. I HAVE JUST HEARD FROM CRUZ'S MANAGER THAT CRUZ WILL BE AVAILABLE TO DEFEND HIS TITLE AFTER 27 FEB.

Although any resumption of his career always appeared likely to involve a move up to the 9 stone 4 pound division (known variously as junior-lightweight or super-featherweight), McGuigan had not totally ruled out the possibility of attempting to regain his old featherweight title. Thus his Las Vegas conqueror, Steve Cruz, continued to loom large on his fighting horizon. Cruz's scheduled defence, referred to by Warren in his telex, was eventually put back by one week to 6 March, when Esparragoza won the title – which he still holds at the time of writing – on a twelfth-round stoppage.

Prior to that fight, though (and, indeed, on a number of occasions subsequent to it), a return with Cruz was a possibility. Eastwood indicated that he had options on the Texan in the wake of the Las Vegas bout and, as the prospects of Warren and Eastwood being able to do business together were extremely remote, Warren was anxious to show McGuigan that either Eastwood did not have any promotional hold on Cruz or, if he did, that this could be circumvented. Therefore, beginning six days after his telexed offer, Warren passed on to McGuigan, on three successive days, three telegrams clarifying Steve Cruz's promotional standing as it then was.

Am very interested in Steve Cruz–Barry McGuigan rematch. I do at this time have obligations with HBA [Houston Boxing Association, the promotional group who had staged many of Cruz's fights]. Please feel free to negotiate with them – David Gorman, manager of Steve Cruz

This is to advise you that HBA currently has promotional rights on Steve Cruz. HBA has permission to pursue negotiations for Steve Cruz–Barry McGuigan rematch. I have no legal promotional obligations to any other promoter. Feel free to call me anytime – David Gorman, manager of Steve Cruz

HBA is looking forward to McGuigan–Cruz 15 rounds WBA title fight in England. HBA has no ties or involvement with Eastwood/Duff/Arum in this venture – Chip Gille, Controller, Houston Boxing Association

During the following week, Warren raised his double purse offer to McGuigan to $125,000 and $450,000, with the latter figure remaining as a guarantee against fifty per cent of all profits. And, once the final date of Cruz's championship defence against Esparragoza was fixed, he also passed on an invitation from ITV – who would be relaying the bout on a delayed-transmission basis – to join their ringside commentary team in Fort Worth. That invitation, though, was not forwarded to McGuigan on the grounds of possibly placing him in a somewhat compromising position.

The suspicion was growing among the members of the McGuigan legal team that all was not proceeding as quickly as it might. Any delay or obstruction in resolving the dispute would hardly affect Barney Eastwood adversely, but it certainly would McGuigan. Professional athletes, after all, regardless of their particular sport, have an extremely limited career in terms of both their ability to compete at the highest level and, as a direct consequence, their earning potential.

On 16 January, the day after the last of the three telegrams about Cruz's promotional situation, McEvoy wrote again to Eastwood's solicitors, John Johnson and Son.

We note whereas we replied in great detail to your Notice for Particulars within the time you specified, you failed to respond in kind. In contrast, we had to obtain an Order from the Court compelling your Client to reply and even then you waited until the last day permitted. We therefore remain of the view that your Client is seeking to delay the trial of this action, whether successfully or not.

You return to the question of our Client fighting again. So long as our client is perceived to be under contract to your Client it is extremely difficult for our Client to conclude any arrangement with anyone with regard to fighting in the near future. We need scarcely emphasize that our Client has had a number of very attractive offers to fight a series of bouts but it is naïve to expect us to disclose these to you.

If your Client were prepared to agree that he was willing to allow our Client to fight three contests under the aegis of other individuals, the Plaintiff would then be able to finalize arrangements. I am sure you will realize that this is an extremely generous offer to your Client. Firstly it may reduce the amount of damages which your Client will ultimately have to pay. Secondly the Defendant could receive 25 per cent of the substantial amounts involved without rendering any services in return.

*

That was a pretty frustrating time, when we were trying to find out things that we all felt I was entitled to know in the first place. The whole process was taking so long that at times I began to wonder if it was ever going to end. And time was obviously very important to me.

It may not have mattered very much to Barney, but then he was never a professional athlete and therefore had no reason to concern himself about how little or how much time the legal wrangling took to sort out. It was totally different for me, however: the active life of a sportsman, any sportsman, covers a relatively short span at the best of times – and every day that the legal in-fighting dragged on was a day out of my life span as a professional fighter.

We did make headway of sorts, but it was slow and painful going. And some of the things I learned really surprised me. It was difficult, for instance, finding out such things as the receipts for my world title fights because Barney – who always liked to highlight his successful businessman image – apparently didn't bother keeping any detailed accounts, either on the fights themselves or on the sponsorship deals surrounding them.

The Eastwood side argued, for instance, that we were not really entitled to know the figures for the Pedroza fight because it was promoted in London by Duff and Barrett – yet the public advertising and posters for it billed it as being promoted by 'Eastwood Promotions in association with Mike Barrett and Mickey Duff'.

And we weren't any more successful when it came to finding out the financial input of either the Irish Permanent Building Society or the BBC. The Irish Permanent enjoyed the prestige and publicity attached to being associated with three of my world title fights, yet they repeatedly declined to tell me how much they had paid for the privilege – and I was the guy who was doing the fighting!

*

On 16 February 1987, however, there had been one instance of the two sides coming together when another Law Library meeting between Michael Lavery and Robert McCartney settled at least one outstanding issue: the date for the court case was agreed as Tuesday 5 May. That, in fact, was the second such date, as in mid-January an unsuccessful attempt had been made by McEvoy to get the case listed for commencement on Monday 23 March. Had that request been granted, an apparently unconscious irony would have been executed; the courtroom battle between McGuigan and Eastwood would have opened six years to the very day after the two had signed their British Boxing Board of Control contract.

Chapter Thirty-Three

'Don't you think it would be better to do it – the whole million-six – up front and you take your end out then?'
From Bob Arum's account of the negotiations with Barney Eastwood for the Cruz fight

Getting as far as the court had been an unusually speedy process; a record-breaking one, in fact. The writ of summons had only been issued at the end of September 1986, and for the case to come up for hearing by the first week in May 1987 constituted (according to court staff in Belfast) a record for a Queen's Bench action within the Northern Ireland jurisdiction. This was all the more remarkable in the light of the case having set another record for the same jurisdiction: that of having the greatest number of interlocutory hearings and applications of any Queen's Bench case.

The latter record had come about through necessity. The former world champion's lawyers were compelled to return to court repeatedly seeking orders to extract from Eastwood documents that directly related to the conduct of McGuigan's affairs – including his world championship fights – which the fighter had never previously been shown. The McGuigan legal team also obtained orders requiring Eastwood to answer on oath a series of questions relating to his conduct of the boxer's affairs. Because of the House of Lords decision in the case of Harriet Harman *vs.* the Home Office, the authors are not at liberty to publish either the documents that were obtained or the answers that Eastwood gave. These will remain known only to a small number of people, unless of course there is a further court action.

Despite its record-breaking progress through the normally slow legal system, the court hearing was very nearly halted a mere four days before it was due to open. In the week prior to the scheduled hearing of the action, the Eastwood side brought an application attacking McGuigan's discovery, alleging that he had not been totally frank and honest in the documents and information he had provided to the court under an order which decreed that both parties should provide such documents. Eastwood and his legal team had, of course, brought discovery applications against McGuigan, although these had been considerably fewer than McGuigan's against him.

The purpose of the last-minute challenge was to prove that the case could not go ahead as scheduled on 5 May. The application was heard on the preceding Friday by Mr Justice Hutton, the judge who was to try the impending action itself. He ruled that McGuigan had indeed fully complied with his duty both to the court and to Eastwood and, accordingly, the application was dismissed.

Tuesday 5 May 1987, at the Queen's Bench Division of the High Court of Justice in Northern Ireland, Chichester Street, Belfast. The opening day of case 5404, between Finbar Patrick McGuigan (plaintiff), of Kilroosky, Newtownbutler, County Fermanagh, and Bernard J Eastwood (defendant), of The Hill, Cultra, Holywood, County Down, a non-jury action scheduled to begin before Mr Justice Hutton at eleven o'clock. McGuigan, accompanied by three family members including his wife, Sandra, arrived at the court less than ten minutes before the appointed starting time and went directly to an anteroom where Eamonn McEvoy, Michael Lavery and Donnell Deeny already awaited him.

Almost half an hour later, and twenty minutes after the hearing had been due to commence, Barney Eastwood arrived in the well of the court, accompanied by his sons, Stephen and Brian, as well as by his close associate and friend, former Belfast city councillor Paddy Devlin. Nobody, however, had missed anything in the interim between the arrival of the two principals in the case. An initial announcement was made that the commencement of the proceedings was to be put back thirty minutes, and it was only when this amended starting time came and went without any sign of activity that the increasingly impatient spectators and media received their first indication that settlement moves might be afoot. And they were, in the network of anterooms and chambers adjoining the courtroom itself.

Professional convention prohibits either side disclosing who made the initial approach, but suffice it to say that Michael Lavery and Robert McCartney, even before the original starting time of eleven o'clock, had begun yet another two-way discussion.

Michael Lavery and Robert McCartney had been courtroom adversaries before, most notably in the controversial Kincora Boys Home case of two years previously, when the latter had represented a number of former students while Lavery had acted on behalf of Northern Ireland's Eastern Health Board, the authority responsible for the administration of the school. Lavery, fifty-two at the time of McGuigan's litigation with Eastwood, was McCartney's senior by two years. A native of Portadown, County Armagh, he had been called to the bar in 1956 after being educated at St Mary's College, Dundalk, Queen's University in Belfast and Trinity College in Dublin, and had taken silk in 1971.

Unlike McCartney, who had previously been an Official Unionist member of the now defunct Stormont Assembly, he had no specific political affiliations. The two, though, did have one thing in common: McCartney, from the Shankill Road in Belfast, had also attended Queen's University. Previously educated at the Grosvenor High School in his native city, he was called to the bar in 1968 and took silk seven years later. The two senior counsel had clashed, often bitterly, in the course of the Kincora Tribunal but, on the morning of 5 May 1987 at least, they seemed at last to be finding common ground.

Shortly after half past eleven, following the completion of an apparently successful preliminary conversation between the two senior counsel, Mr Justice Hutton was formally notified that the two parties were endeavouring to reach an agreement. More or less the same message, that the talks aimed at reaching agreement were continuing, was relayed to him immediately after lunch. Then, at precisely twenty-one minutes past five in the evening and almost six and a half hours after the action had been scheduled to open before him, he was told by Lavery and McCartney that the day-long attempt by the two sides to reach an agreement had been successful and, accordingly, both McGuigan's initial claim and Eastwood's counterclaim were being withdrawn. 'I suspect,' said Mr Justice Hutton, 'we would have been here much longer than one day if the talks had not succeeded.'

*

My father was already in St Vincent's Hospital in Dublin by the time the case came to court, so obviously I had other things on my mind. I was going up and down from Clones to Dublin every day and a long-drawn-out court case was the last thing on earth that I needed just then, but the date we were given for the start of the action came up and that was that. There was nothing I or Eamonn or anybody else could do about it.

We spent the night before the case going through the mill with Michael Lavery and Donnell Deeny in Lavery's house. It would, in fact, be truer to say that we spent the morning of the case itself doing it, because it was something like four a.m. when we packed it in. And then I had to drive home to Clones and leave there again around nine o'clock to get back to Belfast in time for the start of the case.

I drove up with Sandra, Dermot and Ross, and we met Eamonn's wife, Sheila, at the door of the court. Eamonn was already inside, there were pressmen all over the place, and although I was trying to look and act as natural as I could, inside I was really terribly nervous. I had been able to get into a ring on my own and fight four world championship fights, one of them – against Pedroza – before 27,000 or more people, and I'd still been a lot less tense or nervous during them than I was going into that court. But just as we were going up the steps of the court building, a gang of workmen up on some scaffolding directly across the street from the court started cheering and shouting things like, 'Go on, Barry, we're with you', and that, I can tell you, certainly felt good as far as my confidence was concerned.

As soon as we got inside, Eamonn took me into a chamber behind the actual courtroom, where Michael Lavery and Donnell Deeny already were. Once it went beyond about ten past eleven and there was still no sign of the case actually getting started we realized that Barney – whom I'd glimpsed with Brian as they came in – was probably going to settle. At first the case was just put back for half an hour, but the talking had started even before it came to that.

Michael Lavery had left the room at this stage, but after twenty minutes or so he came back and told us that, yes, it definitely looked as if it was going to be settled. It was, he said, by then really just a question of sorting out what the final figure would be, that and a couple of other smaller details.

Eamonn, Michael Lavery and Donnell Deeny all said that it was completely up to me as to whether I wanted to accept the offer or not. With my father in hospital and being as sick as he was, getting bogged down in a court case was something I neither needed nor wanted, so I asked the three of them what their opinion of the offer was. They all said that the figure seemed to be a pretty good one, bearing in mind that if I was to accept it the whole matter would be finished there and then, so I just took out a pen and signed my name on the bottom of the agreement.

*

The document to which McGuigan put his name – as did Eastwood – was headed 'TERMS OF AGREEMENT between BERNARD J EASTWOOD and BARRY McGUIGAN for the resolution of past differences and the conduct of their future relationship' and ran to fewer than eight hundred words. Yet it still managed to encompass even 'the form of words to be used' by not only the two principals in their comments outside the court to the media, but also those of their lawyers to Mr Justice Hutton.

Robert McCartney, for Eastwood: 'I am happy to inform your Lordship that the parties, through the medium of their Counsel, have amicably resolved their differences and the present action and counterclaim are to be withdrawn with no further order.'

Michael Lavery, for McGuigan: 'I agree, and I too am happy that the parties have been able to resolve their differences.'

Eastwood: 'I am very pleased that the differences between myself and Barry McGuigan have been amicably resolved. I have expressed my high regard for Barry on many occasions. I am happy at the prospect of Barry McGuigan boxing again. It is my hope that world championship boxing can be brought again to Northern Ireland.

'The support and good wishes of Northern Ireland's boxing fans played no small part in the resolution of our differences. It is our hope that their loyalty will be rewarded in the near future.'

McGuigan: 'I am happy that the differences with Mr B J Eastwood, with whom I shared so many great times, have been resolved. He is a man of great ability, and I look forward to a happy and successful relationship with him in the future.'

The actual terms that had given rise to this outbreak of mutual optimism were contained in seven points, some of which would later prove to be less clear-cut than appeared at the time of drafting – at least to some of those involved:

1. The present proceedings between the parties under Record No. 5404 Queen's Bench Division of 1986 [when the writ of summons was initiated] shall be withdrawn with no further order, but so that these terms of agreement will be in full and final discharge of all claims of any description by Barry McGuigan against Bernard J Eastwood and of any counterclaim by the said Bernard J Eastwood.
2. R L McCartney, QC shall announce that the above action and counterclaim have been withdrawn with no further order, and C M Lavery, QC will agree as herein set out. The form of words to be used . . . [as quoted above].
3. It is agreed that the lodgement in the present action shall be paid out to the Defendant upon the written consent of the Plaintiff's solicitor, such consent to be given immediately Bernard J Eastwood or his solicitor presents to the Plaintiff's solicitor a Banker's Draft for £650,000.00 payable to him. It is further agreed that such a conditional order for payment out shall be made prior to withdrawal of this action.
4. Bernard J Eastwood will pay to the Plaintiff's solicitor the sum of £650,000 within three weeks from the date hereof in consideration of the following: (a) Barry McGuigan will give to Bernard J Eastwood the option to promote his next two boxing contests; (b) The first contest to be promoted within six months from the date hereof and to be against an opponent agreeable to the Plaintiff currently ranked at the date of signing of the contract with the boxer in the first 15 of the world ratings. In addition to the payment of £650,000 as agreed, Barry McGuigan will receive £125,000 guaranteed plus 50 per cent of the net profit including gate receipts, sponsorship and Radio and TV payments. The expense of independent vouching or checking all receipts and disbursements of that promotion shall be borne by Barry McGuigan; (c) The second contest to be promoted within 15 months of the date hereof shall be for a world championship, and in addition to the sum of £650,000 paid in accordance with these terms Barry McGuigan will receive 50 per cent of the net profit of the title promotion including gate receipts, sponsorship and TV and Radio payments. The expense of independent vouching or checking of all receipts and disbursements of that promotion shall be borne by Barry McGuigan.
5. It is agreed between the parties that neither of them by

themselves, their servants or agents will disclose by direct or indirect means the terms upon which their differences have been resolved, but each of them will use their best endeavour to promote a beneficial public image of their relationship for their mutual benefit. [Although the settlement terms were confidential, they were subsequently read out in open court by Paul Girvan, QC.]
6. Any press statements to be issued will be in the form attached hereto, signed copies of such mutual statements to be handed to each other and agreed [subsequently agreed, as quoted above].
7. If the said sum of £650,000 or any part thereof is not paid within three weeks of the date hereof interest on the said sum or any part thereof then outstanding shall be payable at judgment rate.

Because of the confidentiality clause the press at the time failed to grasp the full significance of the settlement. The boxer himself, though, had no such difficulty.

*

It was only when it was over that what I'd done really began to sink in. Other fighters had tried to challenge their managers in the courts but, as far as I was aware, none of them had ever succeeded, certainly not to the extent that I did. Maybe some of them didn't have the guts to go all the way with it like I did, or maybe they were just not as lucky as I was in finding out some of the things Eamonn and I were able to discover.

The biggest difference between me and all the other fighters who had been trapped in managerial problems, though, was that they didn't have the most important factor of all in my case: they didn't have Eamonn McEvoy. He worked so hard for me. When we went back to Las Vegas, for instance, I spent most of the whole two days that we were there in bed because I was badly jetlagged. But Eamonn didn't: every time I woke up and looked across the room, regardless of what time of the day or night it was, Eamonn was sitting at the table going through dozens of documents and writing pages and pages of notes.

*

Outside the court, McGuigan and Eastwood both furnished their previously agreed statements to the waiting media. But both also added a little extra. 'We are going to be friends again,' said the former world champion, adding, with more significance than those listening realized, 'Now this is over, we are going to be partners.'

'It is not a question of winners or losers,' said Eastwood. 'The matter has been resolved and we shook hands. The marker or promissory note which I gave him has been honoured. There has never been any question about that.' Later he added that, 'The money which I promised him if he was beaten will be paid', and the following day he repeated this, saying, 'It was never my intention to welch on any outstanding monies', thereby furthering the general feeling that not only was the amount of money involved in settling the case little or nothing above the $250,000 he had promised McGuigan in the Americana Canyon Hotel in Palm Springs on 29 May, but that that, essentially, had been what all the legal fighting had been about.

'Eastwood Promotions will promote his next fight,' he said of his new and revised relationship with McGuigan, 'if he decides to return to boxing. That decision is entirely up to Barry. I will not be managing him. I will be in touch with him in due course to discuss future plans, but I stress that I will only be involved as a promoter. I understand that he will have his own advisers and that he may, in fact, manage himself. Barry is making a fresh start. I wish him the very best and I will help him in every way as his promoter. As for immediate plans, it is far too early to make any predictions.'

One person who was prepared to make a prediction was Fight Fan. Hardly had McGuigan, McEvoy, Lavery, Deeny *et al.* headed off for a celebratory meal at Restaurant 44 than he was on the phone voicing his disbelief. Normally laid back virtually to the point of indifference, Fight Fan was bordering on apoplectic.

'In the public relations sense, Barney is the clear winner: the general perception is going to be that McGuigan was just crying because he lost his title and, now that the marker is going to be paid, maybe the row with Barney was not quite so serious after all.'

'Hell. I was feeling pretty good about it until you called.'

'Well, I have more bad news for you: it will never work. The whole agreement, or at least the two more fights aspect of it, is based on a totally false premise: that there is a sufficent residue of goodwill left between Barry and Barney to enable them to get back to working together again – and that just is not so. This is not a

Battered but unbowed ... in Las Vegas with Dermot, the day after the Cruz fight.

Ernie Fossey (centre) and Jimmy Tibbs: the corner team for the comeback.

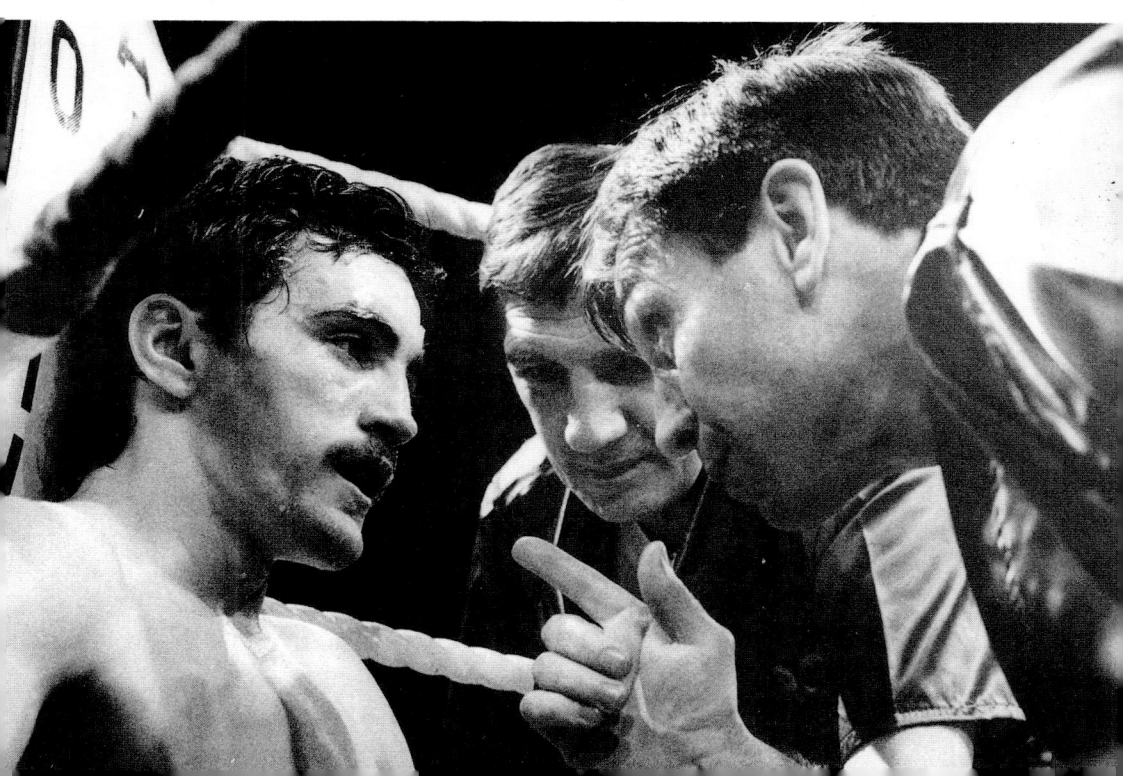

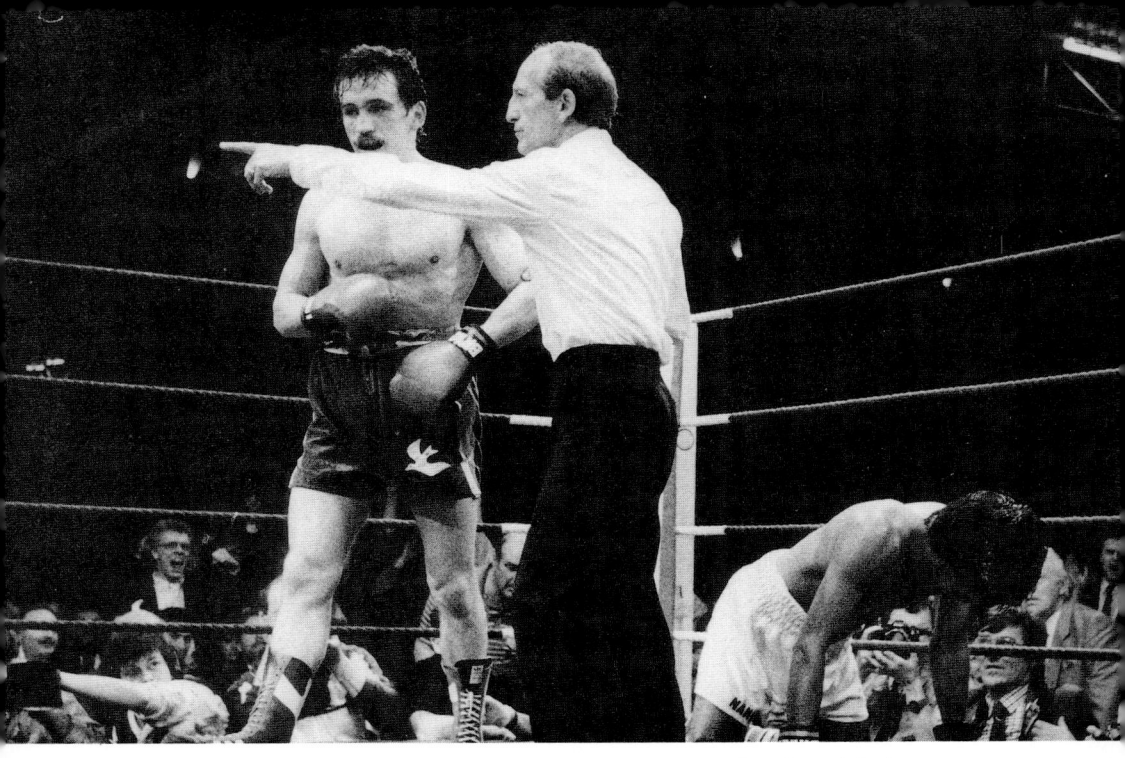

Great to be back... Nicky Perez goes over in the third as part two of the McGuigan story gets underway.

The last of the good nights, as Tomas Da Cruz is pounded to fourth-round defeat at Luton.

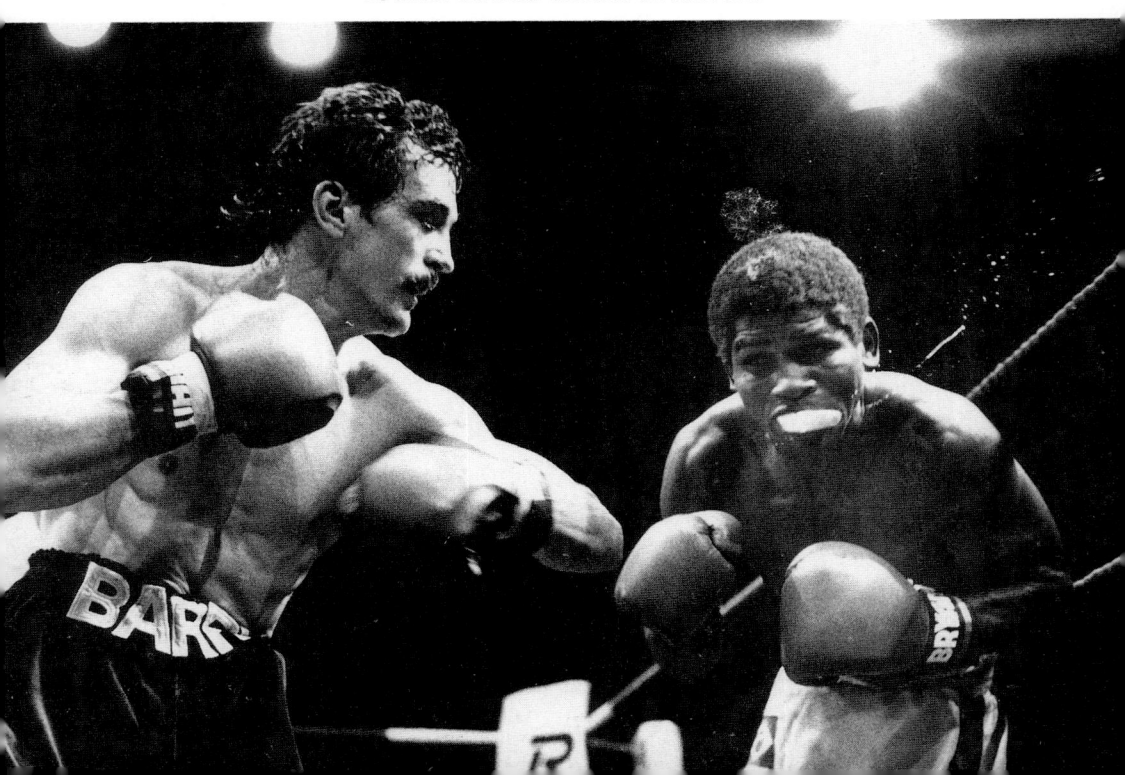

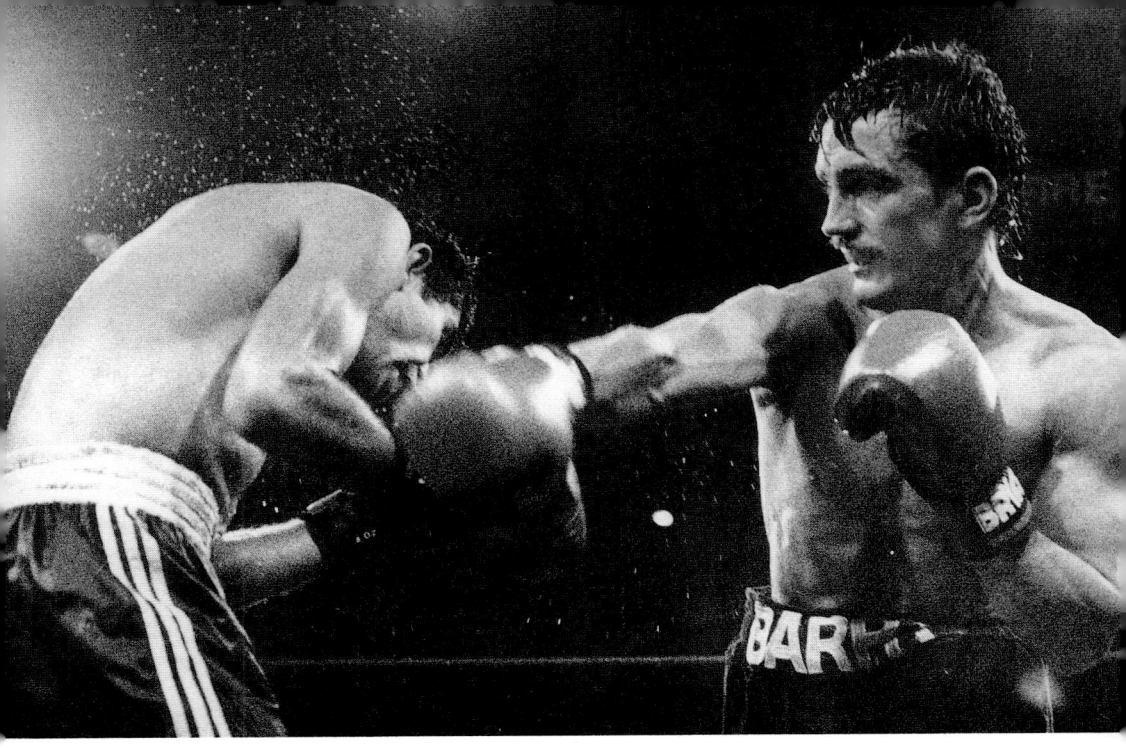

My final victory, but Julio Miranda proved tougher opposition than anyone expected.

End of the line . . . Jim McDonnell on the way to the cut-eye stoppage which finished my career.

Good reasons for a man to fight: the McGuigans at home, with family friend Olive Faux.

reconciliation in the marriage, only a coming together to sort out the furniture.'

*

I suppose I lost the public relations battle at that time, because I was seen in some quarters as being ungrateful to the man who'd brought me all the way to the world title and made me the highest-earning featherweight champion in history. But everything is relative. A wage of £200 a week can sound a lot to an unemployed man, but if the true rate for the job is £500 then the worker is still not getting a fair deal.

The total income for my three world title fights against Pedroza, Taylor and Cabrera was over £3,500,000, of which a shade more than a million was profit. I later learned that an awful lot of people were earning far more than I was from my fights, and that entitles me to feel aggrieved. For example, 'Agents' fees' for the Pedroza fight totalled over £300,000, which was three times more than I was paid for winning the title and drawing a £1 million gate. Even after paying that out, there was still a profit left of nearly £450,000, all of it generated by me.

Mickey Duff was a co-promoter of that show, so he was entitled to his £75,000 share of the profits. But I don't know what his role was in the Bernard Taylor show – which was a mandatory defence, not needing the services of a matchmaker or agent – or in the Cabrera fight. Yet if the figures supplied to me are right, he got £113,442 from the Taylor fight and £119,430.64 from the Cabrera promotion, which means that his overall take from my three world title fights on this side of the Atlantic was over £300,000, or 60 per cent of the total I earned myself from the same fights.

*

Bob Arum maintains that the initial impetus for his getting McGuigan to fight in America came from Barney Eastwood himself – and, more seriously, that the complicated financial arrangements surrounding McGuigan's world championship defence in Las Vegas came about at the behest, nay insistence, of the fighter's manager. In March 1986, Arum claims, Eastwood was in Las Vegas to see Mickey Duff's fighter John Mugabi challenge Marvin Hagler for the world middleweight title, and called to see Arum at Caesars

Palace. Eastwood asked Arum if he would be interested in putting McGuigan on a pay-per-view show in the States.

'I said "yeah" so we came up with the concept of a show for that June, on which McGuigan would defend his title against Fernando Sosa, Roberto Duran would fight Hagler's half-brother Robbie Sims, and Donald Curry would challenge Mike McCallum for the WBA light-middleweight title. Curry then went squirrelly on me because he was having fights with his manager [Dave Gorman] and he pulled out of the bout with McCallum, so instead I got Tommy Hearns to fight Mark Medal as the third part of the triple-header.

'Barney told me that: "The boy will take $600,000, that's enough for him. But I have to have a percentage of the promotion – and you've got to guarantee it ..."'

Arum acknowledged in a taped interview with one of the authors that it was 'very unusual to have a guaranteed profit before you go into a promotion', but then alleged that in his experience 'the British always made arrangements where the fighter would get x and they would get y as a promoter'. By way of an example, Arum cited the case of a British-managed world title challenger. He himself, Arum said, had wanted to pay the fighter a million dollars, 'but they [the boxer's management team] said, "No, seven-fifty and a percentage of the promotion for us." That was the way you always did business with the English guys, so Barney was just continuing it as far as I was concerned.'

Arum, a Harvard-trained lawyer before he got into fight promotion, also alleges that he mentioned the possibility of a 'conflict of interest' to Eastwood and that he asked McGuigan's manager, 'Don't you think it would be better to do it – the whole million-six – up front and you take your end out then?' but that he abandoned his objections when Eastwood again insisted that he was entitled to something out of the promotion.

'Apparently it was OK because there was no rule in England that a manager couldn't be a promoter, even though it *per se* caused a conflict. So I was not violating any English rule or any other law by it; I just felt it was wrong. But no, I never said, you know, "You've got my feet to the fire so I've got to go along with it", or anything like that. I just said, "Hey, is that the right thing to do, really?" and he said, "Yes, it is", so there was no arguing. Panaprom was his idea and he used it as a promotional vehicle, probably because [Luis] Spada was in on all those meetings.'

Did he indicate that he did not want McGuigan informed of it?

'That was always implicit. The one thing they all know about me as a promoter is that I never, ever, deal directly with fighters; I preserve the manager's relationship. I have a business to run and I think it would be improper for me to deal directly with a fighter when that fighter has a manager. Barney didn't make a big point about my not letting McGuigan know about it, but he didn't have to. He could assume, correctly, that it was between me as the promoter and him as the manager.

'He never, in fact, was very fond of McGuigan. Whenever he talked to me about McGuigan, even early on, he always depicted him as this greedy, spoiled person that was very, very difficult to handle. He never professed to me that there was any great love between him and McGuigan. In fact, he invariably did the opposite, he'd say "you gotta watch the kid" and all that sort of stuff.'

Chapter Thirty-Four

'Talent is only part of the requirement; a lot of fighters can have talent, but too many of them don't have enough dedication. And none of them has as much as Barry has.'

Frank Warren

Fight Fan's prediction, seemingly, was beginning to come true rather earlier than even he could have anticipated. By the Monday week after the court settlement, it was suggested by Paul Tweed of John Johnson and Son, the firm of solicitors representing Eastwood, that a joint statement was required to reassure the boxing public that all was still well on the Belfast front. Accordingly, after a telephone conversation between Tweed and Eamonn McEvoy, it was agreed that a joint communiqué be released to the press on behalf of both manager and fighter.

> The boxing partnership of B J Eastwood and Barry McGuigan represented a uniquely successful phenomenon in British and world boxing. The unhappy differences which arose between them were a source of sadness to many people beyond the boxing fraternity and to genuine sporting journalists all over the world. The support of both fans and writers and their desire to see both men settle their differences played a large part in an honourable resolution of those differences.
> In these circumstances, both B J Eastwood and Barry McGuigan view with concern the efforts of a minority of the media who, in printing rumour and inaccurate facts and figures out of their true context, are doing no justice to the past and offering prejudice to the future. Both Barry and B J wish to express their joint hope that truly sporting journalists will concentrate on the future and, in boxing terms, leave old cuts to heal.

On Sunday, 31 May, McGuigan and Eamonn McEvoy were back

at the Dunadry Inn for yet another meeting, this time with Frank Warren. The London manager/promoter flew in on the 12.30 shuttle from Heathrow, was collected at Belfast Airport by McEvoy and then driven to Dunadry for his first-ever meeting with the fighter he had been pursuing for over three years. Also present at the meeting, at McGuigan's request, were his two co-authors.

'It's true,' said Warren, 'we had never met before. Clearly we had been in occasional touch over the previous months, but that had been done through a number of mutual acquaintances. Our only previous direct contact had been a single phone conversation – and even that was only a brief talk about ten days earlier. I simply put some proposals to him; he found them acceptable and that was that. The Dunadry Inn meeting was more of a getting to know each other session than anything else.'

Warren, past rejections notwithstanding, had never wavered in his admiration for McGuigan. 'Above all else, the thing that has always made him stand out is his dedication. And dedication, for me, is ninety-five per cent of what professional boxing is all about. Talent is only part of the requirement; a lot of fighters can have talent, but too many of them don't have enough dedication. And none of them has as much as Barry has.

'I'm a strong believer in the principle that what you put into anything you do has a direct bearing on what you get out of it and, as far as Barry McGuigan was concerned, winning the world title was, I think, no more than he deserved. He's got tremendous ability and he's an exciting fighter who always gives full value for money. And that, of course, is precisely why he is such a major attraction.'

The McGuigan–Warren intention at the time of their initial meeting at the Dunadry Inn was for Warren to attempt to buy out Eastwood's half-share in the promotion of McGuigan's next two fights – McGuigan, remember, had been granted fifty per cent of those rights in the court case settlement earlier in the month – or, failing this, for Warren and Eastwood to find some way, in spite of their by now long-running antipathy towards each other, of actually working together, one as manager and the other as promoter. Such a union was not quite as outlandish a thought as some might imagine: mortal managerial and promotional enemies have been known to cast aside their principles and work together when either the occasion or, more frequently, the pursuit of profit, required it.

But, not for the first time in the McGuigan story, plans went awry.

On 27 June, a year and four days after his son had lost his world title in such controversial circumstances in Las Vegas, Pat McGuigan died in St Vincent's Hospital in Dublin at the age of fifty-two. No more would 'Danny Boy' be sung in the ring moments before the opening bell of a Barry McGuigan fight. No more would the father who had been the fighter's inspiration, who had urged and encouraged him from his earliest amateur days, be on hand to share the highs and lows of the career he himself had done so much to set in motion. When Pat McGuigan died, more than a little of Barry McGuigan died with him.

*

My father had been my inspiration from the very beginning. He was the one who had made it all possible, who had provided the money for me to have my own gym and to become, in effect, a full-time boxer even in my amateur days. He was the one who for years drove me all over Ireland at all hours of the day and night for amateur tournaments and championships, up and down to Belfast and Dublin and other places, and even as far as Limerick. And he was the one who handed over the money for me to travel over the first time to London to spar with professionals in the Terry Lawless gym. Daddy was the one who, more than anybody else in the world, made it possible for me to become a fighter. I owe him a lot, and it's a debt I will never forget. I can't even watch my old fights on video any more, because my father is there at the beginning of every one of them.

He died a horrible death. He had an operation on 4 May [the day before the court case, and a crucial factor in the decision by McGuigan to accept the settlement terms offered by Eastwood], when a large tumour was removed. The doctors told us a couple of weeks later that it was lymphoma, but that they hoped it would not recur too soon. If it did come back, they were going to give him a course of chemotherapy.

But he never did get better – fluid leaked out through the wound and he just got weaker and weaker. He never had a bite to eat for the ten weeks he was in hospital in Dublin. Jesus, I hate that road to Dublin ... every time I drove down it to see him it meant another upset, something else gone wrong.

Eventually he had a second operation. He looked great, and seemed to be improving. I went away that weekend to do the Royal version of 'It's a Knockout' and he was in great form when I left him. But he was only out of intensive care for one day when his heart started giving out on him. It was going crazy – like 155 beats a minute. When I got back home they told me he was in intensive care again. I couldn't believe it, so I went straight up to Dublin to see him.

He was lying there on the bed, and I looked at him. He put his arms up to me and started crying. I didn't want to break down in front of him, but that is exactly what I did. I went to him, and I couldn't stop crying. He couldn't talk. We were all with him in the hospital for the last ten days, sleeping on the floor and sitting with him in turns. At the end, he put his arms around me – he was so weak he could hardly lift them – and then he went into a kind of coma. His eyes were still open, but he couldn't see. He could hear, though – that's the last sense to go – and we were whispering in his ear at the end.

*

Pat McGuigan was buried in Clones Cemetery after ten o'clock Mass in the town's Sacred Heart Church on Tuesday, 30 June 1987. His son's plans to fight again, formulated in the Dunadry Inn only a month previously, died with him.

Seven weeks after Pat McGuigan died, Eamonn McEvoy received a letter from Eastwood's solicitors, John Johnson and Son. 'Under Clause 4 (b) of the Agreement, the first contest is to take place prior to 5 November 1987. Our client is in a position to arrange contests involving the following opponents in the near future.' The letter went on to list the potential opponents as: Danilo Cabrera (Dominican Republic), Juan Laporte (USA), Jim McDonnell (England), Steve Cruz (USA), Bernard Taylor (USA) and Jackie Beard (USA).

McEvoy, after discussing the matter at some length with McGuigan, responded two weeks later by informing John Johnson and Son that: 'Our client feels he is not prepared to fight in the immediate future. He is not, of course, under any obligation to fight at all. If the position changes during the coming year he will inform your client.'

Two days later, on 4 September, it became abundantly clear that the agreement worked out between the two sides in the Belfast High Court four months earlier was in serious trouble. It was, in fact, about to break down completely.

Eastwood's solicitors, in answer to McEvoy's letter telling them that McGuigan was 'not prepared to fight in the immediate future', began by quoting in full Clause 4 of the settlement of the previous May, and then added: 'Although we would be reluctant to embark on further litigation, we would hope that your client will honour his contractual obligations, which will be of mutual benefit, without recourse to the courts.'

The letter concluded with the second list of potential opponents for McGuigan: Jean Marc Renard (Belgium), Dwight Pratchett (USA), Harold Knight (USA), Tyrone Downes (incorrectly listed as from Trinidad, instead of Barbados), Lenny Valdez (USA), Victor Callejas (Puerto Rico), Bernardo Checa (Panama), Rocky Fernandez (Panama), Julio Ruiz (Panama), Manuel Baptiste (Dominican Republic) and Alvaro Bohorgreg (Colombia).

But McGuigan was not ready to think about fighting again so soon after his father's death. Besides, he and his legal team felt that the High Court agreement did not impose any obligation on him to fight again, though it required him to accord to Eastwood the option to promote his first two contests if he did decide to resume boxing. This was a view, indeed, that Eastwood himself appeared to share, at least in the immediate aftermath of the avoidance of a full court action.

Talking to Jack Magowan of the *Belfast Telegraph* within a matter of hours of the settlement being reached and announced, Eastwood said: 'On paper I am still Barry's manager, but paper has a habit of going up in smoke. I hope he's serious about fighting again, and in a few good, meaningful contests. I wish him every success and will do all I can to guide him back along the right lines. It's entirely up to Barry, however. Whether he fights again or not can only be his decision.'

But the Eastwood stance seemed to have altered drastically in the space of less than three months. Now, Eastwood was insisting, McGuigan was legally obliged to fight again. Legal interpretations aside, Eastwood's insistence on McGuigan resuming fighting so soon after the death of his father struck the boxer and his legal team as distinctly callous.

At least one member of McGuigan's legal team was – and remains – of the opinion that had it not been for the death of Pat McGuigan, the singer's son and the Belfast bookmaker might well have worked together again, albeit in a more formalized and more impersonal fashion than before.

'That Barry wasn't focusing on boxing when his father died was understandable,' he said, 'but I'm not sure that Barney really understood it as clearly as most. I think that perhaps Eastwood felt Barry was just using Pat's death as an excuse or even a stalling tactic for not fighting again. That, of course, was not true, but I got the impression that that was how Barney looked at it and that, as a result, he felt he had to go ahead with the second action.

'Had Pat McGuigan not died when he did, or had Barney not reacted the way he did to Barry saying that he did not want to fight again, then I think there was a distinct possibility that, after allowing a bit of time for the dust to settle, they could have got back together again in at least some form of businesslike relationship.'

McGuigan himself agrees that his father's death was the real crossroads for his relationship with Eastwood. He, though, has a different reason altogether for holding that view.

*

There was no going back after my father died; that was the real point of no return. Barney made no attempt to contact either me or any of my family. Not so much as a telephone call to either me or my mother, or even a card and a few flowers for the grave. And that, remember, was only the month after the court settlement and was therefore at a time when we were supposed to be planning to work together again, yet he still couldn't be bothered making any sort of contact or gesture. That was the real end between the two of us, because after that there was just no way I could ever have worked with the man again.

*

Eamonn McEvoy, in a letter to John Johnson and Son on 10 September, laid out the McGuigan attitude to what they regarded as Eastwood's about-face on the settlement terms. After outlining his side's recollections of the settlement negotiations, McEvoy wrote:

The absurdity of your Client's present contention becomes even more obvious when you consider the position of the second contest referred to in Clause 4 (c). Is your Client really suggesting that our Client was committed to a second contest, 'for a world championship', which would depend entirely on our Client's performance in the first, something no one could possibly predict?

Any alleged doubt about what Clause 4 meant is removed when you consider the terms of the agreed press statements attached to the settlement. Why did they not simply state that the Plaintiff [McGuigan] had agreed to fight for the Defendant [Eastwood] once within six months and a second time within a further nine months? . . .

The interpretation which your Client now seeks to put on Clause 4 is untenable when you bear in mind the eventualities not provided for in the Agreement. For example, what was intended to happen if our Client was unable through disability or indeed excess weight to fight? Moreover, our Client's agreement to the opponent is fundamental to the Clause, yet no machinery is laid down to cover the eventuality that he cannot agree the opponent or an opponent agreeable to him refuses to fight him. It is an elementary rule of contract law that no commitment can ever be complete and binding until all the essential terms are agreed. The Clause does not provide for the terms on which any such fight should take place, eg, the purse to be paid to the other boxer, the venue, the expenses and the weight, most of which could affect the feasibility of the fight and the profits, and in respect of which our Client would have to be consulted before he could be said to have commited himself to fight.

There can be no doubt that our Client was not committed to fight. If necessary, the Agreement can be rectified to reflect the true accord between the parties. Alternatively, if your contention is correct, which we, of course, completely reject, there never was consensus between the parties and our Client would be entitled to and will sue again.

Over five weeks would pass before, on 19 October, McEvoy received a response from Eastwood's solicitors. It was not encouraging for those who said they disliked seeing McGuigan and Eastwood ensnared in legal disputes.

After rejecting McEvoy's letter of 10 September as simply setting out 'your view of the terms of the settlement', John Johnson and Son went on to accuse McGuigan of being 'intent on sitting out the time clauses in the Agreement and then acting as a free agent in respect of future contests'. Consequently, the letter concluded, Eastwood was left with no alternative but to issue proceedings 'for the proper determination of his rights under the settlement and the assessement of damages in lieu of your client's refusal to perform the Agreement'.

The summons, again issued through the Chancery Division of the High Court of Justice in Northern Ireland and this time accorded docket number 1893, was short and to the point:
1. That it may be determined on the true construction of the terms of the Agreement between the Plaintiff [Eastwood] and the Defendant [McGuigan] dated 5 May 1987, whether the Defendant is under a contractual obligation to the Plaintiff to participate in two boxing contests.
2. A declaration that the Defendant is under a contractual obligation to participate in two boxing contests and that the Plaintiff has the option to promote these contests.

Within two days, McEvoy had drafted and dispatched his reply to the summons and its accompanying letter. After remarking that 'we note your client has seen fit to issue proceedings before showing us the courtesy of a reply to our letter [of 10 September]', McGuigan's solicitor continued:

We note that you have not responded in any meaningful sense to the facts and contentions set out in our letter of the 10th ult.... We totally reject the suggestion that the provision of Clause 4 in respect of the timing of the fights point to the conclusion that there was a binding agreement to fight. Bearing in mind your client's previous conduct it was important to safeguard our client's interest in the event of his deciding to fight. Otherwise he may have found himself frustrated by your client.

May we point out that up to now it has not been our client's intention to sit out the time clauses of the agreement and then act as a free agent in respect of further contests, though in our view he would clearly be entitled to do so.

After going on to quote the *Belfast Telegraph* article already cited, McEvoy's letter continues:

In the light of your client's decision to issue proceedings, we have no alternative but to issue cross-proceedings for rectification of the agreement (should this be necessary) and for further relief as shown on the copy Writ of Summons which we enclose by way of courtesy.

The McGuigan writ, lodged the day following McEvoy's letter to John Johnson and Son and issued as case number 1936, was rather lengthier than the Eastwood one. It sought:

1. A declaration that upon the true construction of an Agreement made in May 1987 between the Plaintiff [McGuigan] and the Defendant [Eastwood] in settlement of the Action in the Queen's Bench Division (Action No. 5404) and in the events which have happened, the option given to the Defendant to promote the Plaintiff's next two boxing contests was dependent on the Plaintiff deciding to box in such contests and did not impose any contractual obligation on the Plaintiff to take part in such boxing contests.
2. Alternatively, rectification of the said Agreement by adding to Clause 4 (a) thereof the words 'in the event of Barry McGuigan deciding to take part in such boxing contests' or words to the like effect.
3. Further or alternatively, a declaration that in the events which have happened the said Agreement is not binding on the Plaintiff and that the Plaintiff is at liberty to issue fresh proceedings claiming the relief sought in the aforesaid Action No. 5404.
4. Further, or in the alternative, a declaration that, upon the true construction of the said Agreement and in the events which have happened: (a) the Plaintiff will not be contractually bound, at any time after 5 November 1987, to permit the Defendant to promote any boxing contest in which the Plaintiff may participate; alternatively: (b) the Plaintiff will not be contractually bound, at any time after 5 August 1988, to permit the Defendant to promote any boxing contest in which the Plaintiff may participate; alternatively: (c) between 6 November 1987 and 5 August 1988, the Plaintiff's only contractual obligation will be to permit the Defendant to promote the Plaintiff's second such boxing contest if for a world championship subsequent to 5 May 1987; in any event: (d) the Plaintiff is not under any contractual obligation to participate in any boxing contest if the proposed opponent is not agreeable to the Plaintiff.
5. Further and other relief.
6. Costs.

McGuigan, for only the third time in the five and a half years since he turned professional, was facing a return bout. The first had been against Peter Eubanks at the Ulster Hall and the second against Gary Lucas in Enniskillen. The third would be against Barney Eastwood and would be staged in the same venue as their first battle: the High Court in Belfast.

Chapter Thirty-Five

'What is a world championship? I might have to be instructed on that.'
Mr Justice Murray, Belfast High Court, 1 March 1988

The second court case was very different from the first. It was, as one member of the former world champion's legal team stated, 'not really anything to do with McGuigan himself; it was between the respective senior counsel and concerned not McGuigan's original dispute with Eastwood, but counsels' contrasting interpretations of the agreement reached in settlement of that initial dispute'.* The chief witnesses, this time, would not be McGuigan and Eastwood themselves, but rather their respective barristers, Michael Lavery and Robert McCartney. The fighter and his estranged manager would largely fill spectator roles in High Court bout number two.

One thing had changed, though: McGuigan, nearly five months after his father's death, had at last begun to think again about resuming his ring career. Accordingly, on 23 November 1987, Eamonn McEvoy advised John Johnson and Son that McGuigan 'has been considering the matter and has decided that he would fight again if an opponent agreeable to him could be obtained ... our client is now prepared to fight Mario Miranda, who is rated in the first fifteen as set out in the original agreement, as soon as practicable'. Things, it seemed, were moving at last.

But not for long. Eastwood, who had completed one apparent about-face when contradicting his comments outside the court by seeking to insist that McGuigan fight again, now performed yet another reversal. (As recently as 10 August – just nine days before

---

*The Eastwood side contended that the previous years' agreement obliged McGuigan to have two further fights under the Eastwood promotional banner, while the McGuigan camp was of the opinion that the agreement was merely a 'dressing-up' exercise, designed to shelter Eastwood from being seen to have paid damages.

he began, through his solicitors, to insist that McGuigan resume boxing – Eastwood told the *Belfast Telegraph*: 'I've been convinced for a long time that McGuigan wants to retire; that he won't fight again. And nothing has happened to make me change my mind.') Within two days of being informed by McEvoy that McGuigan was indeed willing to fight again, John Johnson and Son responded that Eastwood 'has elected to seek damages for the existing breach rather than attempting to seek any enforcement of a contract for personal services which could not be obtained'. Thus, having got what he had publicly and legally been seeking (a McGuigan promise to fight again), Eastwood was now proposing to cash in his options in the High Court.

The reply from Eastwood's solicitors went on to allege that the nomination of Mario Miranda as McGuigan's opponent had not 'been made in good faith', in that as Julio Cesar Chavez had taken the WBC lightweight title from Edwin Rosario just two days before McEvoy forwarded Miranda's name, Miranda would now be fighting Australia's Lester Ellis for the WBC junior-lightweight crown previously held by Chavez. McEvoy promptly denied this two days later and went on to write: 'However, in the circumstances, and as a further indication of our client's good faith, we withdraw our client's offer to accept Miranda and instead nominate Gerron Porras as being an opponent agreeable to our client within the terms of the original agreement.'

Three weeks would pass before the Eastwood side responded by advising McEvoy that 'our client has not been able to complete his investigations into the availability of Porras'. Eastwood's solicitors then commented that McGuigan, by his appointment of Frank Warren as his manager – an arrangement made verbally at the Dunadry Inn get-together on 31 May 1987 – and by statements about his uncertain boxing future had 'undoubtedly prejudiced future promotions'.

McGuigan's 'public statements about his uncertain boxing future' had been made in the immediate aftermath of his father's death and as such were surely understandable. He had, further, already removed any lingering uncertainty about his intentions via McEvoy's letter to John Johnson and Son on 23 November, almost a month earlier. The implication that McGuigan 'by his appointment of Mr Frank Warren' had somehow contrived to prejudice his own fighting future intrigued McEvoy, and he raised this and other points in a 22 December letter to Eastwood's solicitors.

We note that it has taken you three weeks to respond to our letter of the 27th ult. We do not understand this delay, particularly bearing in mind your client's concern over alleged delays attributed to our client. Notwithstanding the passage of three weeks, our enquiries reveal that your client has not approached Porras' manager and we note the implication in your letter that your client has not carried out any investigations in relation to him. Quite frankly, we wonder to what 'enquiries' you refer in the first paragraph of your letter.

We put forward the name of Miranda in absolute good faith. He was available as a contestant when we put forward his name. It is incorrect to state that he was going to have a contest with Lester Ellis. No such contest has ever been arranged. In fact, the vacant title to which you refer is being contested by Azumah Nelson and Lester Ellis. We totally reject the suggestion that our client was acting in bad faith in putting forward Miranda. Such imputations of bad faith ill behove your client, who ... since the settlement has by his conduct and statements sought to undermine our client and diminish his public image. [The WBC super-featherweight title was eventually contested by Nelson and Mario Martinez, after injury forced Ellis to withdraw.]

You make the point that publicity for a fight prior to the 5th November, 1987 would have commenced in mid-July, 1987. This totally disregards the fact that it was not until the 19th August, 1987 that your client first raised the question of promoting a fight. If your client really believed he had a commitment to fight by our client, it is amazing that he did not take a single step to initiate the promotion between the 5th May, 1987 and the 19th August, 1987, bearing in mind the importance he now apparently attaches to a speedy return to the ring. The publicity value of our client has certainly not diminished since the settlement of the Action, and we reject the suggestion that the passage of time has been in any way detrimental to organising a fight at this time.

You ask for details of Porras. Apart from repeating the points made above about what your client has been doing over the last three weeks, we would point out that if your client wants to act as our client's promoter in the proposed contest it is for him to do the necessary promotional work, which necessitates the making of all necessary enquiries. We can confirm that Porres is available and no options are held on him by any third party.

On 8 January, over two weeks later but still without having received a reply to this letter, McEvoy again wrote to John Johnson and Son. After querying the lack of a response to his letter of 22 December, McGuigan's solicitor continued:

Seven weeks have all but expired since our client's offer to fight and your client has still not indicated his wish to take up the option to promote the fight... We therefore wish to advise you that unless within ten days we hear from you confirming that your client wishes to promote the contest offered, our client intends to make his own arrangements to fight and shall do so forthwith as it is clear your client has failed to exercise the option. As we have reiterated from the start, our client is not required by the terms of the Agreement to fight. He has, however, decided to do so and in the spirit of the Agreement we are offering to your client the option to promote the proposed fight.

This letter did receive an almost immediate response: an offer, on 12 January, to promote a McGuigan fight at the King's Hall on 16 April. The designated opponent, according to Eastwood, was Mario Miranda, the same fighter whose proposal by McEvoy and McGuigan on 23 November had been dismissed by the Eastwood side with an allegation of having been made in 'bad faith'. Also in the letter was a demand that McGuigan offer confirmation of his acceptance by Friday, 15.

Two days later that particular screw was tightened further when Eamonn McEvoy received a letter informing him that: 'We now confirm that terms can be agreed for a promotion involving Mario Miranda. Unfortunately, however, and in order to secure final agreement, Miranda requires an advance payment of $10,000 prior to Monday 18 January next'. The letter went on to insist that McGuigan confirm his agreement by four o'clock the following afternoon.

McEvoy, as he pointed out in a written reply that same day, found it 'indicative' of Eastwood's attitude 'that he takes over seven weeks to reply to the Plaintiff's offer to fight and then demands a reply within two days ... it is typical that he should at this late stage nominate an opponent who was withdrawn as long ago as 27 November 1987'.

McGuigan's solicitor then repeated that Gerron Porras was his client's nominee and, in a further letter the following day (the very day that Eastwood had set as the deadline for McGuigan to accept his proposal), went on to query Miranda's alleged demand for a $10,000 advance.

McEvoy ended his letter by repeating that Gerron Porras was McGuigan's choice of opponent. [The copy telex enclosed by McEvoy was from Miranda's manager to Frank Warren in relation to a proposed world title fight against Barry Michael. In its entirety it read: 'Terms of 10,000 dollars for Mario Miranda to box Barry Michaels [sic] for IBF junior-lightweight championship in England, October 29, plus 5 fares, hotel and food. Send contracts plus a tape of Barry Michael's bout.']

Back came the response from the Eastwood side that Gerron Porras was not acceptable on the basis that while he was ranked number eleven in the IBF ratings, he was not included in either the WBA or WBC lists.* Suddenly the IBF rankings did not count, although that objection had not been raised in John Johnson and Son's letter of 18 December, when, in fact, Eastwood's solicitors had actually asked Eamonn McEvoy to provide them with 'details as to his [Porras'] availability, purse and promotional options'.

Also in the latest correspondence from Eastwood's solicitors was a claim that 'our client has now offered Mr McGuigan a choice of eighteen opponents including Miranda and none have proved acceptable'. True ... but seventeen of those were offered in two lists submitted within nine weeks of the death of McGuigan's father and thus at a time when the former world champion was clearly not in a fit frame of mind even to consider fighting. The remaining name, Miranda, had been withdrawn at the behest of Eastwood's solicitors and replaced by Porras, a substitution to which the Eastwood side gave implied approval by seeking information from Eamonn McEvoy 'to enable our client to consider the matter further'.

Four days later, on 19 January, a copy of Miranda's apparent demand for a $10,000 advance was forwarded to McEvoy. Signed by Luis Spada of Panaprom SA fame, it stated: 'Att Mr Barney J Eastwood, We urgently request the remittance of dollars 10,000 (ten thousand dollars) as advance payment in order to close final arrangements fight Barry McGuigan *vs.* Mario Miranda.'

Upon receipt of the copy telex, McEvoy attempted to put it in what he saw as its proper perspective.

---

*The court agreement did not specify or exclude any organization's ratings, but merely referred to 'world ratings'.

'We have your letter of the 19th inst. enclosing copy telex from your client's friend and associate, Luis Spada. You will, of course, remember Mr Spada as the witness to the Promissory Note for $250,000 which our client signed in Palm Springs as a result of duress, threats and inducement from your client, ably assisted by Mr Spada. You will also recollect that the $1,000,000 secret profit which your client received for the Las Vegas fight was paid on your client's instructions to Panaprom SA, a Panamanian company controlled by Mr Spada and his wife. It is, therefore, not surprising that when in difficulty your client should again turn to Mr Spada who has, of course, no connection whatsoever with Miranda, whose manager, Mr W Martinez, we are informed, knows nothing of this supposed arrangement.

McGuigan and McEvoy subsequently offered the names of two other potential opponents, in addition to the still valid Gerron Porras: Felipe Orozco and Bruno Jacob. Eastwood countered with another list of three completely different names: Francisco Tomas Da Cruz, Hector Lopez and José Marmolejo. A day later he added in the name of McGuigan's world title conqueror, Steve Cruz. The following day McEvoy, on McGuigan's behalf, indicated acceptance of Francisco Tomas Da Cruz, but this plan too broke down when the McGuigan side declined to become contractually committed to the second of the two options. 'Until the first contest is over,' McEvoy had informed John Johnson and Son in mid-January, 'it is impossible to decide whether Mr McGuigan could or should or would wish or would be allowed to fight either for a world championship or at all.' All hope of McGuigan and Eastwood being able to avoid court case number two had evaporated.

In preparing for the case, Eastwood had turned in two sets of figures which McGuigan found particularly interesting: his estimates of the anticipated profits from each of the two McGuigan fights at the centre of this second dispute. For the first fight, the non-title one, the projected gross receipts came to £1,125,000 and total expenses amounted to £260,750, leaving an expected profit of £864,250. This profit, of course, would have to be split fifty-fifty with McGuigan, but still represented an impressive yield of £432,125 for Eastwood himself.

The gross receipts, it is worth noting, were expected to exceed, by quite considerable amounts, the figures for each of McGuigan's two world title fights in Ireland: Bernard Taylor in Belfast (by £186,886) and Danilo Cabrera in Dublin (by £82,185). The expenses, however, would evidently largely escape the ravages of inflation: 'Hotels, Travel and Entertaining', for instance, which had cost over £63,000 for each of the title fights, were apparently to be provided free, as there is no mention of them whatsover.

The pattern is repeated in the projections for the second bout, the proposed world title challenge by McGuigan. A profit of £956,100 was anticipated, after gross receipts of £1,830,000 – an impressive £304,369 greater than when McGuigan won the world title from Eusebio Pedroza before a 27,000 attendance in London – and aggregate expenses of £873,900. The growth in profit over the Pedroza bout would seemingly result from major economies as far as agents were concerned: they had cost all of £308,337.87 on the first occasion McGuigan had challenged for a world title, but were to be dispensed with altogether for his second championship challenge. Eastwood was to be highly rewarded for his obviously mammoth business acumen, and rightly so: his calculated combined profits from the first two fights in the McGuigan comeback would be a remarkable £910,175 – *after* the former world champion had taken his fifty per cent share.

On the basis of these figures Mickey Duff, a friend of the Eastwood family for thirty years, was apparently to be left completely out in the cold. The man who had worked so hard on Eastwood and McGuigan's behalf that he had to be paid at least half a million dollars from McGuigan's three world title defences evidently would not be needed any more. Eastwood, according to his own breakdown, had no intention of giving him a penny from the proceeds.

There was to be one last attempt at finding a mutually acceptable solution. When the case finally came up for opening on the morning of Tuesday 1 March 1988, it was an hour and a half late in starting before Mr Justice Murray as the respective Counsel – Paul Girvan, QC, and Nicholas Hanna for McGuigan, and John Gillen, QC, and David Ringland for Eastwood – held last-minute talks. At seven minutes past noon, however, the talks having proved barren, the hearing finally got under way.

Paul Girvan began by reading out the settlement terms of the original case of ten months earlier. Referring to the £650,000 paid by Eastwood to McGuigan, he told the court that £150,000 of this was for legal fees and that 'the remainder, half a million pounds, was dressed up as an option fee to promote two more fights and this was done at the behest of Mr Eastwood, who did not want to be seen to be paying damages as such'. (That it was very much a specialist case became evident less than half an hour into it, when Mr Justice Murray asked: 'What is a world championship? I might have to be instructed on that.') McGuigan's Senior Counsel went on to read all the other clauses in the May agreement, including that which specified that neither side would disclose the details of the settlement.

At 12.45, Mr Justice Murray suggested to Paul Girvan that he and John Gillen might 'get together and see if there are any joint thoughts' and a lunch recess was then called. It turned out to be a lengthy one: the two sides did not return to court in the afternoon, but instead informed Mr Justice Murray that the talks were continuing.

The following morning, after another delay of over an hour, the court was told that a settlement had finally been reached. Eamonn McEvoy, acting as a consequence of a telephone call to his Banbridge home late on the Tuesday night, had, for the sum of £200,000, purchased the Eastwood options on McGuigan's next two fights. McEvoy, to the surprise of no one, had done so on behalf of Frank Warren.

The final agreement had been drafted by McEvoy himself and handwritten on two sheets of A4 paper:

1. Eamonn McEvoy agrees to purchase for the sum of £200,000 such options rights as may exist under the provision of Clause 4 of the Agreement of 5 May 1987, such sum to be paid within five weeks from the date hereof, payable by banker's draft to John Johnson and Son.
2. On payment of the sum, Bernard J Eastwood and Barry McGuigan mutually release each other from all future obligations or rights as may exist under the said Agreement.
3. Bernard J Eastwood and Barry McGuigan hereby acknowledge that they will hereafter have no rights of any kind or nature against each other arising out of or in connection with their past relationship or the said Agreement of 5 May 1987, and in particular Bernard J Eastwood acknowledges that he has no rights of management or promotion over or in connection with Barry McGuigan.

4. No order as to costs.
5. The proceedings will be withdrawn by the parties.
6. These terms represent the entire Agreement between the parties.
7. In the event of any delay in the payment of the sum of £200,000, interest shall be payable at judgment rate of interest.

Three weeks short of seven years after it had begun with the signing of their British Boxing Board of Control contract, the union between McGuigan and Eastwood had ended for ever.

Chapter Thirty-Six

'I felt that Eastwood owned me, and that if he wanted to he could switch me off like a light.'

Barry McGuigan, 1991

I regret that it ended the way it did. I really liked Eastwood. I know we had our fights, but I really thought something of him. So many people can sit back and say 'I told you so', but I truly liked him. There are times when he is bitter as hell about me, and says things like, 'McGuigan was only an average fighter.' It hurts me that he can say that, because he knows that I was much more than that.

But there were a lot of things I liked about Barney. His sense of humour, for one thing: he was a great talker who had a marvellous fund of stories and a great way of telling them. He was very good company to be with and we had some really good times, especially on planes on the way to or from fights, when he'd keep up a stream of stories about all his different experiences of life.

He was a first class organizer; a brilliant one, in fact, the best I ever saw. If you wanted something done all you had to do was ask Barney and it was done, no matter what it was. And he was, in many ways, a very good manager – at least in the early days. He was good at building up my confidence. He told me right from the start that I could go the whole way to the top; he had faith in me and I had faith in him.

In my view Barney worked me too hard. I fought Clyde Ruan in December 1984, Laporte in February 1985, Gallouze in March, Pedroza at the beginning of June, Taylor in September, Cabrera in February 1986 and Cruz in June. I was doing so many things in between, and training my guts out. Because I knew I would have to go back into camp I'd be gorging myself, and my weight would go away up and then I'd have the struggle to bring it down again.

Apart from that, I'd gone ten rounds with Laporte, fifteen with

Pedroza, and even if Ruan only lasted four rounds I had still trained for fifteen. I trained like hell for Taylor, and the same for Cabrera. The Cruz fight went fifteen rounds too, and when you think of the amount of fights I crammed into those few months, you can see that I just worked too hard.

As soon as one fight was over Barney was arranging another one. I pleaded with him for a break, but he said, 'No, you've got to keep fighting.' I complained about it all the time, and told him I didn't want to fight yet, but he would say, 'This is the only date the TV people have got, and if we don't get it in now they won't take the next one.' Bullshit! TV would always have taken my fights.

OK, I know the Taylor fight was a compulsory defence, and there may have been a deadline to it, but there are always ways around deadlines. But Barney knew that a guy can only stay at peak for so long, and he was determined to make hay while the sun shone.

Sometimes I look back and ask myself where in hell did it all go wrong? The answer, I suppose, is that I realized towards the end of 1984 that I was just a product, a commodity. There was no particular single incident, no Road to Damascus that made me see what was happening. It was a gradual process. I was a bright lad, never an Einstein, but smart enough to see what was happening to me. I got involved in his family, and slowly I began to understand the way he had control of everybody. I thought, 'I'm just like all the rest of them.' What was the point of being world champion if I wasn't my own man?

Barney said once, 'I own every hair on McGuigan's head', and that really hurt me. He liked me, in his way, but it was the way you like a pet dog, where you'd stroke his head and say, 'Good boy, well done.' Barney used to keep German Shepherds, out at the back of his house. He had one called Jake, but then he got another that was much better-looking, and from then on it was the back seat for Jake. I felt at times that when I was used up I'd be thrown away too, and he'd get another one to replace me. That wasn't troubling me, though, it was too far in the future. What bothered me was mainly the fact that I couldn't do a thing without his permission, and I felt I was being exploited emotionally.

That's why I went through all that trauma. During the twenty-one months we were battling I went through every emotion possible. I didn't know what to think. It got to the point where I started wondering, 'Maybe I am to blame, maybe I am wrong.' He was coming out with so much rubbish about me, and I couldn't get through to any of those journalists to give them my side of the story. But then I decided to stay quiet until we got into court, and I'd tell my story there, but it never came to that.

Money was only one of my grievances; the lack of independence was much more important. It was one thing being Eastwood's fighter, but another being his property.

I felt that Eastwood owned me, and that if he wanted to, he could switch me off like a light. Many times I tried to do things on my own, and found that doors slammed shut in my face. In the end, that was why I had to leave Ireland. It was too small, and many of the important people I would need to deal with in TV and suchlike didn't want to know me, because they worked with Eastwood or were obligated to him. I felt I was in a cul-de-sac. Everywhere I went was closed to me, until in the end I had to get away.

Chapter Thirty-Seven

'No harm will come to him if he continues to fight opponents like [Nicky] Perez.'
Barney Eastwood's comment on Barry McGuigan's return to the ring in April 1988

The show, at last, was back on the road. Nearly two years after the loss of his title in Las Vegas, McGuigan was ready, willing and able to fight again. And free to do so.

Despite the lodgement of a formal boxer–manager contract between Warren and McGuigan with the Board of Control, the former world champion would, in effect, manage his own affairs, with Warren filling the role of resident promoter. The first fight in the comeback campaign was mapped out even before the announcement of the resolution of the second court case.

It would take place at the Alexandra Palace in North London on Wednesday 20 April 1988, and Lenny Valdez of Mexico, who had beaten Steve Cruz inside a round in 1984, was named as the opponent. He was soon replaced, though, by Nicky Perez, an eleven-year veteran who was the current holder of the North American title and who had once unsuccessfully challenged Wilfredo Gomez for the WBC super-bantamweight title.

*

When I signed with Warren he suggested that I be trained by either Jimmy Tibbs or Ernie Fossey. I went to work with Jimmy, and sparred with Mo Hussein. I liked Tibbs's attitude: he was very professional, a nice guy who was good to be with and who knew how to build your confidence. I thought he was the perfect man for me, and I started right away with him as my trainer.

I sparred with Mo and a couple of Americans at the Vauxhall Motors amateur club gymnasium in Luton, because it was handy enough for me when I was staying at Henlow Grange, which was only fifteen miles away. I'd have had to go into London otherwise, which would have been a murderous journey every day. Jimmy was very accommodating. He came up from London every day to work with me. George Pearce allowed us to use the gym in conjunction with the Vauxhall Motors club, and provided I was out by five o'clock every day – before the amateurs started training – we had no problems. There was never a penny changed hands. They were just nice, friendly, helpful people.

Dermot came over to help me get ready for the first fight, against Nicky Perez of America at Alexandra Palace. We'd had a look at who was available, because I didn't want to go in over my head to start with, so I thought he could give me a good workout. Only a month earlier he had fought Julio Cesar Chavez, and apparently had him in trouble with a right hand in the first before Chavez came back and stopped him in the third. I had watched him and read about him before anyway, and I knew he could give me a stern enough test.

It was made at nine stone four pounds, but he came in at nine-five and I was nine-four and a half. There was a great crowd, great atmosphere, and I was very nervous – not that there was anything unusual about that. Before every fight I was keyed up, switched on. I liked to have funny guys around me in the dressing-room, because it was such a tense time for me. I was wondering whether I still had it in me. You can be brilliant in sparring, but not be able to reproduce the form when it matters. I'd been dynamite in the gym, knocking sparring partners all over the place, but that didn't mean that the spark would still be there in the ring.

Anyway, I started slowly against Perez, walking after him and feeling him out. He had no power at all, although he was sharp, accurate, and a good counter-puncher.

I stayed on top of him; I knew I would get him, but my accuracy was not good at all. My timing was badly off, so I had to wear him down. I got a slight nick when we banged heads in the second round, but Ernie Fossey stopped the bleeding.

I nailed Perez a few times in the third and roughed him up a bit, and then in the fourth I hit him with a left hook to the body. He felt it a bit, so I switched it up to the head, turned it into a jab, and he went down. He got up, but he didn't want to know any more. It wasn't really a knock-out. I'd overpowered him to the point where he decided there was no sense in going on. He knew that if I didn't get him that round I would get him in the next, so the referee, Sid Nathan, stopped the fight.

I was back, and it felt good.

*

Barney Eastwood dismissed McGuigan's successful resumption of his career with the caustic comment that 'No harm will come to him if he continues to fight opponents like Perez'. What did he expect of McGuigan after almost two years out of the ring? When Eastwood was selecting McGuigan's opponent for his professional debut, he chose a man who had been beaten on forty-two previous occasions, Selvin Bell, and for his eighth fight the selected rival was Ian Murray, winner of only two of his previous thirty fights.

*

Perez hadn't answered any questions, as far as I was concerned. I felt that he hadn't tested me at all, and I needed someone better than that. We settled on Tomas Da Cruz, a Brazilian who was ranked number four by the WBC. Frank Warren and Tony Clarke, my commercial agent at the time, organized a deal with Luton Town FC to stage the show at Kenilworth Road on 25 June, two years and two days after I'd fought the other Cruz in Las Vegas. Tony was a good friend to me when I needed one most. He was a great support at the time of my father's death, and helped keep me going through the bad times.

There was a long build-up to the fight, and I had excellent sparring with Tony Pep, a lanky Canadian featherweight. Benji Marquez, an American who has fought in Britain quite a few times, worked with me too. Pep was a big help, but I didn't learn anything from Marquez. I also sparred a few rounds with Tony Ekubia, who won the Commonwealth light-welterweight title in 1989, but he wasn't much use to me either. Pep was perfect, though. He was fast, difficult to get to, and was much more in the American style. He had all the moves.

The fight was billed as an eliminator for Azumah Nelson's WBC super-featherweight title, and at the weigh-in Da Cruz complained that I hadn't made the weight. I had been two ounces inside the nine-four limit, but they wouldn't believe it so they raised hell. I had already gone back to my room at Henlow Grange, where the weigh-in was held, but I came back down and got on the scales again. It was like a replay of the Pedroza weigh-in row, and all my people were urging me not to weigh again, but I didn't mind.

As soon as the fight started I realized that Da Cruz was going to be a much better opponent than Perez. He had fought Chavez for the title in April 1987, and even though Chavez had completely overpowered him, he had shown a lot of guts. Da Cruz had knocked out Anthony English, a useful young Philadelphian, and was on a run of wins. He'd been beaten only twice in thirty-two fights, and was a good, lively performer.

He felt strong and durable, but I was much sharper than I had been the last time. My jabs were working well, and I felt that things were coming back to me. I took over from the second round, battering him with left hooks and right hands and, even though they weren't all clean punches, there was an awful lot of them. I hit him with a right in the second and his legs went, but I couldn't finish him. Against Chavez, Da Cruz didn't actually go down; he took a hammering but stayed on his feet, and it was much the same against me. I took a round longer than Chavez, but I dominated him all the way until Larry O'Connell said, 'He's had enough', half-way through the fourth round.

I was pleased with myself, satisfied with my performance. I felt that the speed was there, not quite to the same degree as before, but much better than in the Perez fight. My combination punches were improved; I was throwing right hands up through the middle, left hooks, left uppercuts; I had fought well on the inside, and avoided shots on the outside.

All in all, it was probably the high point of the come-back. The show had been a big success, drawing around 14,000 people, and I had fought well enough to push the doubts to the back of my mind.

*

More than a year and a half after his outburst against McGuigan in the *Express* (two days after he had been subpoenaed to attend the original High Court action), Mickey Duff yet again attacked him in print. This time his chosen vehicle was a first-person article in the *Today* newspaper on Wednesday 19 October 1988.

I've got no hesitation in saying that Barry McGuigan is the greatest fighter this country has ever produced [many in Ireland would blink at that] – but he's not a man I admire.

His behaviour since his come-back makes you wonder whether he really wants to win the world title again. I believe if he was really serious McGuigan could have a title fight right now, but so far he hasn't faced one serious contender.

Duff then went on to recall the title-winning fight with Eusebio Pedroza at Loftus Road and to praise McGuigan for 'an immaculate display of boxing', but continued:

[For me] as the matchmaker and promoter it was hugely satisfying, but it quickly all went very sour for me and for his manager Barney Eastwood. My admiration for McGuigan the boxer is enormous, but as a man I find it hard to say anything nice about him.

*

I've often been curious to know why Duff said the sort of things about me that he did. I never had any disagreement with Mickey, and I've certainly never done anything on him. In fact, I always had a very high regard for him in the boxing sense and felt that he was one of the best judges of fighters and fights in the whole business. Mickey made a fair bit of money out of me, and as far as I know he's never had any cause to dislike me or say unpleasant things about me. He had no basis for saying those things whatsoever.

I never had that many dealings with him. I don't remember ever sitting down with him and having what you could call a really serious conversation with him; he always just seemed to be around for my fights without me actually having a lot of direct contact with him. But we did have the odd chat, and I valued his opinion about different opponents or guys I might be fighting. But we never had more than a couple of sentences to say to each other at any one time.

Chapter Thirty-Eight

'That was the night when I finally had to admit to myself that things would never be the same again.'

Barry McGuigan, on a hard-earned win over Julio Miranda

Beating Da Cruz lifted me to number three in the WBC rankings, and now we started looking in earnest for a world title fight. Until the Da Cruz fight I had been uncertain, but now I felt that I could come all the way back to the top. It wouldn't be back to where I wanted to be, which was back to the pre-Las Vegas situation, but it would be near enough. I was making progress, sparring well, and felt ready to move on.

Frank Warren approached Nelson's people, but they made totally unreasonable financial propositions. We then tried for the IBF champion Tony Lopez, but he didn't want to leave his home town, Sacramento. That left the WBA champion, Brian Mitchell, but we didn't want him because he was a South African and I would have been labelled as racist if I'd fought him.

So we were snookered, and I had to take another fight. Frank came up with Julio Miranda of Argentina, a tough guy who had lost only once in thirty-four fights – and that was on a technical decision. He was the Argentine champion, unbeaten in his last nineteen fights and ranked fourteenth by the WBC.

The show was ill-fated from the start. Warren wanted to put it on in a giant tent at Mudchute Farm on the Isle of Dogs in East London, but objections from a local residents' group scuttled that and it finished up in a small arena at Pickett's Lock in North London, on 1 December.

Miranda was a typical Argentinian, a light puncher who took a great shot. He could fight inside well, and he wasn't a runner, and that was the kind of opponent I enjoyed, one who would punch with me and give me a good tussle. I had only watched one fight of his on video, but he seemed safe enough. But his manager was Tito

Lectoure, and if Lectoure is involved with any fighter then you can be sure that the guy can fight; he doesn't work with mugs.

It was a treading-water fight, a marking-time job. In those sort of fights you're inclined to become a bit complacent, and I think probably that's what happened to me. I took him lighter than I should have, and didn't give him enough respect for his durability. I knew that he could box a bit, and was a tough enough cookie, but I didn't give him enough credit for his ability to absorb punches.

The other thing was that he was really good at avoiding punches, and had lots of clever little moves. He was never going to be a world champion, but he would give anybody a good test.

I started the fight very over-anxious; I didn't use my jab or anything, just tried to set about him. Harry Enwright, a friend of mine, always calls the jab 'the bread and butter punch', but I wasn't using it. Every shot, I was trying to knock Miranda out, but he'd counter with fast, light combinations. I might miss two of them, but the third was clipping me, and it wasn't long before my face was lacerated.

I knocked him down at the start of the third, walked straight out and hit him a right, and down he went. He was stung more than hurt, but again I didn't stick the jab out or anything, only tried to nail him. But he was a tough guy, and he stood in there and we banged heads and he clipped me with these smart little punches, and all of a sudden there's blood flying out of me, blood everywhere. Half-way though the round the blood came down over my eyes like a curtain and I couldn't see a damn thing.

I was nicked above both eyes, and for the first time ever I had to wipe my eyes clean. It was like in the cartoons, where wee blinds come down over your eyes. I remember him coming rushing at me when he saw me trying to clear my eyes; it obviously gave him a spurt, and he tried to make more of a fight of it.

When I got back to the corner Ernie Fossey started working on the cuts, but they were both bad, really bad. They weren't that thick or deep; they were long, thin slices, and in the worst possible position, right above the eyes.

The cuts wiped out all the plans, destroyed whatever strategy I had. I couldn't walk in and try to bang him out, so I had to start using the jab. Jimmy Tibbs kept telling me to throw the jab and follow it immediately with the right, instead of hesitating or leaving the jab there. 'You did it once and knocked him down, so do it again,' he said.

So I had to change tactics. I didn't stop coming forward, but I wasn't advancing with the same urgency. I stayed back and popped his head back with the jab. He wasn't running away from me, but when he did move back I would stop punching and follow after him slowly, and then as soon as he'd settle again I'd open up on him. He came back and put up a good old effort, but out of the eight rounds it lasted I probably won seven. But he was so hard, so durable. Every time I nailed him with a good shot he took it; he could take a punch and a half.

I knew he wasn't going to go over easily, and that I'd have to start pacing myself. Late in the seventh I set him up with the jab, and then hit him with one of the best right hands I've ever thrown. It didn't hit him on the chin; it landed on the top of the head, but he shuddered to the floor – his legs shook as he went down. He was up at five, but he was completely gone. The bell rang before I could do a job on him, and Tito Lectoure jumped in to guide him to the corner. Another right hand put him in trouble at the start of the eighth, and I backed him against the ropes and banged the living daylights out of him before [referee] Larry O'Connell pulled him out of it.

Dermot was in the ring with me afterwards, saying, 'Well done, son', but quite honestly he was upset that it had taken me so long to do the job. I went back to the dressing-room in despair, very disappointed. I'd been cut, and had been forced to work really hard. I asked myself: 'Would it have taken you this long three years ago?' and I knew the answer.

That performance had undone all the confidence that the Da Cruz fight had given me. I thought I had made progress against Da Cruz, but against Miranda I was going back. *Boxing News* wrote that 'The Da Cruz performance had been eighty per cent of the old Barry, while we would rate this at seventy per cent, and that is not an encouraging progression.' But I knew that only too well.

It was the lowest I ever felt after a win. I had put on a great fight, a very entertaining performance. Eleven million people watched it, the biggest ITV audience of the year for a sporting event – and that was in an Olympic year, too. But that was the night when I finally had to admit to myself that things would never be the same again.

CHAPTER THIRTY-NINE

*'I went to the top of the mountain, and I honestly believe
I could have gone there again, but it wasn't to be, and
I've accepted that.'*

Barry McGuigan, 1991

When I thought about the Miranda fight, it was as if I had two heads, and one was saying to me, 'Ah, it was an off night', while the other was saying, 'Hang on a minute ... you don't *have* off-nights!' I remember Hugh McIlvanney writing in the *Observer* something on the lines of: 'We judge fighters from this part of the world on a certain level, but we judge McGuigan on a higher level. I hope that he will win a world title again, but on this performance I very much doubt it.'

Nobody had to tell me: I knew it myself. But we kept trying. We tried to get Lopez again, and couldn't, and we could have had Nelson over here and given him all the money, but for that sort of a ball-breaking fight I wanted paying. I reasoned that if I fought Lopez and won, then I could look for Nelson in a unification match and say, 'Hold on ... I'm a champion too, and you've got to pay me.'

But Lopez was fighting in Sacramento, and couldn't be tempted away from there, so I took another biding-time fight against Jim McDonnell. Barry Hearn had offered me a lot of money for the job and I didn't think McDonnell was anything special; a good mover, light puncher, with no power. I thought he was a safe opponent. With hindsight, I haven't changed that opinion. McDonnell has great legs; he runs like a rabbit, and even Azumah Nelson took eleven rounds to catch up with him. To be honest, though, I think Nelson probably took him too lightly.

The deal for the fight was negotiated by Michael Deeny, whose brother Donnell, who is now a QC, had been the junior barrister who acted for me against Eastwood.

Deeny, a chartered accountant, is also a big-time pop promoter, staging concerts for the likes of U2, Peter Gabriel, Sting and Bruce Springsteen in France and Spain. In the 1970s and early 1980s he managed Horslips, the first and best of the 'Celtic Rock' bands. So he knows the promotion business inside out.

What I liked about Michael was that he was very straight: in the pop world, you have to be. Ten years ago the pop business was like boxing, but it has gone through a complete clean-out. Agents work for ten or twelve per cent, and a lot of them work for less than that to become more competitive.

Frank Warren and I had done a two-fight deal plus a world title fight, and I had already had three fights with him, because for one reason or another – none of them his fault – he just couldn't tie down the world title shot. Warren and I got on very well. He's the sort of guy I like. It was great to do business with him, and I never had any complaint about our deals.

Hearn's offer was just too good to refuse: I got £250,000, Jim McDonnell got well paid, and Hearn and his partner Jack Trickett shared £70,000 – a good night's work. The difference between Hearn and some of the others is that he is prepared to take less and give the fighters more, and that is why he's getting so many fighters going to him.

I trained very hard for McDonnell, and my weight came down nearly to featherweight again. I sparred something like a hundred rounds. I worked with Joey Jacobs [British super-featherweight champion in 1990], Peter English [former ABA featherweight winner], Renard Ashton and Chubby Martin, who could run like McDonnell. I trained well, ran a lot, and got myself in great shape for the fight.

McDonnell had said he would be the aggressor, and I thought, 'Great – I hope he is.' I started much slower than normal. He fought in his usual style, coming in and out and away. I planned on my normal kind of fight too; just stay on top of him and get to him eventually. I was a better aggressive fighter than Nelson; he likes the centre of the ring, and much prefers opponents to come to him, but I could cut the ring down on them and stay on them. But I wasn't as quick as I would have been three or four years previously; then, I'd have been on top of McDonnell much quicker and he wouldn't have hit me with the punches he did. He caught me with two jabs, and then a long left hook with his hand open. Because he's not a natural puncher, he has to reach and make an effort when he throws a hook, so he hit me with the end of his glove. I felt it clip me. It wasn't a hard punch, but it was right on the bone above the eye. It felt like somebody nipping the skin of your arm; a sudden, sharp stab, and the next thing I knew the blood was flooding down.

It was only half a minute into the second round, but he didn't lose his cool. When I went back to the corner Ernie Fossey took one look at it and swore, but he did the best he could. The next round, I tried to stay on top of McDonnell. But he was cuter: he knew that I'd come out and go for him, so he stayed out of the way and the next thing Mickey Vann, the referee, came in and stopped the fight. It was just as simple as all that: the end of my career.

I never gave any referee verbals, but I looked at Vann and said, 'You're never going to stop this, are you?' There was no point in complaining; he had made his decision, and I couldn't reverse it. And Vann was right; it was a nasty cut, lying open.

I never got going in the fight, but I have no doubts that if I hadn't been cut I would have stopped McDonnell, slow starter or not. I would have got to him eventually.

But as soon as the fight ended, I knew that it wasn't there any more. I had taken four or five rounds too long to stop Julio Miranda, and all my hard work for McDonnell had been for nothing. Even if I had gone on, ground him down and stopped him in eight or nine rounds, I would still have been disappointed enough to quit. That would have made two hard fights in succession. There was no need for Miranda to have been a hard fight, and McDonnell wasn't – and still isn't – out of the ordinary. He's an average European fighter, quick and accurate and a nice lad, but he's not a puncher and was never a threat.

I'd had two terribly lack-lustre fights, I'd been cut three times, twice very badly. My reflexes weren't as good as they were before. My ability to slip punches, to see them coming a split second before they landed – that had all slowed a fraction, and I said to myself, 'I'm not going to do this any more.'

I remembered reading how Carlos Palomino [WBC welterweight champion in the 1970s] had talked about fighters being the last ones to know when it was time to go, but that he was determined to be the first to know when his time was up. I felt that those were my intentions exactly. I didn't want somebody having to tell me, 'Barry, you've gone on too long.'

I knew it myself, even though I could have gone on and said it was just another off night, and maybe even still fought for a world title. Maybe I could have made another million dollars fighting Nelson or Lopez, but what was the point? I was my own worst critic, and I always demanded perfection. I judged myself very harshly, and I said, 'No, you're not good enough any more, Barry – don't do it.'

In the end, it was an easy decision. Eamonn McEvoy had always been very concerned that my mental state should not be affected in the slightest degree by my boxing, so he suggested that I go to a clinical psychologist between every fight and get brain scans and tests done. I went to a specialist in Belfast, who would do an elaborate set of tests on me. I saw him three times, after each of the comeback fights, and there was never any change in the results. But Eamonn was always very concerned about me, and his priority was always to get me out of the game intact.

That night in Manchester, he put his arms around me. He didn't have to tell me what he was thinking, so I went out of the dressing-room and, sitting on a rubbish bin, outside a little room at the back of the G-Mex Centre in Manchester, I told the press and television I'd retired.

And that's how it ended.

But I count my lucky stars every day when I see people in the street who've never experienced what I have; I say, 'There but for the grace of God go I.'

I went to the top of the mountain, and I honestly believe I could have gone there again, but it wasn't to be, and I've accepted that.

Chapter Forty

'... I'll tell you this: boxing has been good, very good, to Barry McGuigan.'

Barry McGuigan, 1991

In reality, the boxing career of Barry McGuigan ended a round and a half earlier than when referee Mickey Vann signalled the end of his thirty-fifth professional fight. And one person in the G-Mex Centre that night knew it instantly, even before McGuigan himself did.

Ernie Fossey knew it within one second of the end of round two. As he scrambled between the ropes to meet McGuigan returning to his corner, Fossey got his first close-up look at the damage inflicted on McGuigan's right eye by the slashing left hook that McDonnell had delivered a mere thirty-nine seconds into the round. His instant assessment of the damage was brutally honest: 'Oh, fuckin' hell,' he said. The comment was made more to himself than to McGuigan, but the former world champion knew exactly what it meant. Ernie Fossey, rated by many as the best 'cuts man' in British boxing, was telling McGuigan that there was nothing he could do for him: the right eye was beyond immediate repair.

At the post-fight press conference in which he announced his retirement, McGuigan had been somewhat less than laudatory towards Vann. 'The referee did me no favours,' he said. 'I think Mr Vann was too quick in stopping it. I should have been allowed another round or two.' But two hours later, sitting on the side of his bed in Room 449 of the Midland Crowne Plaza Hotel, the ever-honest McGuigan made a public retraction.

*

I thought at the time that Vann had acted too quickly, and that the least he could have done would have been to give Ernie another round to work on it. And for a while afterwards, because the bleeding had stopped by the time I got back to the dressing-room, I was more convinced than ever that he should have allowed it to go a bit further.

But once my doctor [Dr Adrian McGoldrick, now Newbridge-based but formerly resident in Clones] had cleaned up the cut and started to put the stitches in it – I think it needed seven – I knew I had been wrong. It was a bad cut and I suppose I should have known that by Ernie's reaction. He's a pro and he was never going to make a panic judgement, but neither was he going to give me any bullshit about it not being serious. Ernie was right and so was the referee. Mickey Vann did the right thing in stopping the fight.

*

But Mickey Vann did not just stop a fight or even merely call time on a twenty-eight-year-old fighter's career. At twenty-seven minutes past nine on the night of Wednesday 31 May 1989, star-class referee Vann signalled the end of an era. As Hugh McIlvanney noted in an *Observer* tribute four days after the retirement announcement, 'McGuigan's career stands comparison for genuineness, excitement and brave deeds done under pressure, with that of any boxer from these islands in the modern era. If, amid all that is unreliable in boxing, you want to cling to a little sliver of certainty, just say that Barry McGuigan could fight. Say he could really fight.'

And Fred Burcombe, writing in the *News Of The World* that same Sunday, expressed similar sentiments in rather different language: 'He charged a lot, but you only get what you pay for and McGuigan was the best value. By far! No other fighter in this country, including Frank Bruno, could have enticed more than 8,000 people to pay an average of £50 per head to see a televised ten-round non-title contest.' (Burcombe could well have cited a figure almost twice as high: the 14,000 who watched McGuigan defeat Francisco Tomas Da Cruz in Luton.)

There is a body of opinion that maintains that the era terminated by Mickey Vann in a converted Manchester railway station had, in reality, actually ended almost three years earlier in the Caesars Palace hotel and casino complex in faraway Las Vegas. There is a degree of truth in this viewpoint. Given the traumatic nature of his defeat in the desert sun, the subsequent legal wrangle with Eastwood, the death of his father and the obvious physical impediments resulting from almost two years away from a sport in which continuity is everything, the second career of McGuigan was never likely to duplicate the first. He would, in short, always be striving to recapture the old magic in a climate and in circumstances, physical and otherwise, that rendered the dream all but impossible to fulfil.

The comeback was always going to be an uphill battle. But to suggest, as some have, that he should never have attempted to turn back the clock is not only grossly unfair to a fighter who was, after all, only just turned twenty-seven when he returned to the ring, but also indicates a total misunderstanding – if not ignorance – of what his split with Eastwood was all about. Las Vegas was an unfinished chapter in the McGuigan chronology, a point where for him to have stopped would have left his story incomplete. Had he not lost in the circumstances in which he did, there would never have been a comeback. There might not even have been the complete split with Eastwood that there subsequently was, although, regardless of the happenings in or out of the ring concerning the Las Vegas fight, the relationship between the two was already under severe strain and it is more than likely that some form of restructuring would have taken place in the summer of 1986.

Las Vegas was merely the last, albeit the biggest and most costly, entry in a catalogue of increasing unhappiness and frustration for McGuigan. Steve Cruz was an aside to the circumstances. It was not losing to him that proved the final straw for McGuigan, but the acceptance by Eastwood three months earlier of the fight itself – and, more explicitly, the controversial and complicated financial arrangements surrounding it.

'Barry was a normal young fellow from the country,' Father Brian D'Arcy said. 'But because he was so total in his dedication to his sport, he was well into his adult life before he started to fully mature emotionally. Most people are given a lifetime to grow up, he had to do it all in just three minutes, the three minutes of the fifteenth round. It was probably the worst possible scenario anyone could have had in their life.'

Given the traumatic nature of his title loss, a comeback was all but inevitable. It is easy to be wise after the event and coldly assert that McGuigan should never have tried to recapture the past, but there is little justice, or indeed consideration for what he had been through, in that stance. On two separate counts – the circumstances under which he lost his title and the undeniable fact that he had, in

American fight parlance, more than paid his 'dues' – McGuigan had earned the right to give it one more try. It was his dream, and after the nightmare of Nevada he felt entitled to pursue it.

*

I knew that I hadn't been beaten fair and square in Las Vegas and I don't mean in the ring. Steve Cruz is a nice guy and a very good boxer and I haven't, and never have had, any arguments with the decision in his favour. He was the better fighter over the full fifteen rounds on the night and he therefore deserved to take the title; not once have I ever said or suggested anything other than that. But I know, and an awful lot of other people know as well (including, I suspect, Cruz himself), that in any other set of circumstances and in any other ring in the world – and even in the same one an hour or two later – I would have kept my title. That was why the come-back was really always going to happen.

I knew in my heart and soul that I hadn't been beaten fairly in Las Vegas, not in the sense that I was given a fair chance to get ready for the fight, or a chance to have it held under conditions that gave me a fair chance of winning it.

But the couple of years I spent out of boxing were lost years. Between the legalities with Eastwood and the death of my father, my mind just wasn't on fighting. I thought I might be able to make up the lost time, but I learned that I just couldn't. I wondered, even before the McDonnell fight, about cuts. It wasn't the same injury that I'd had against Julio Miranda six months earlier, but I still can't help wondering if the time spent away from the ring softened up my skin and made it more susceptible to cuts.

*

The sad part of the Barry McGuigan story is not that he, like the vast majority of fighters before and after him, decided to set off on the almost inevitably unsuccessful comeback trail. The real tragedy is that he felt himself placed in a position whereby that decision was in itself inevitable. McGuigan, after Las Vegas, was always going to return to the ring; all that was uncertain was when, where and under what circumstances.

He had lost more than just a fight or even a world title in the Nevada sun. He lost trust and faith and confidence, and even his willingness to take people at face value – all the things that had helped make him such an exuberant media phenomenon. He was a professional fighter who could entice over 27,000 people to watch him ply his trade and who could, in the case of the Bernard Taylor fight in Belfast and the Danilo Cabrera one in Dublin, even entice them to pay three times the official admission price for the privilege. But the McGuigans of the pre- and post-Las Vegas eras are different people: he was forced, as Father Brian D'Arcy noted, 'to grow up in three minutes'. And in growing up he changed, as we all do.

Not, in the words of Yeats, 'changed utterly', but changed nonetheless. He learned, for instance, the reality of the subtle difference between an acquaintance and a friend during the almost two years of his legal disputes with Eastwood and his exile from boxing. He still makes new friends, but the process is slower now and more intricate than it once was. His relationship with Barney Eastwood was often cited as the perfect marriage between a boxer and his manager, but like many marriages it rarely – not never, but rarely – matched the general perception of it. And, to sustain the marriage analogy, when divorce came it carried with it several scars.

As a marriage, though, the McGuigan–Eastwood union did have its moments. Nobody, least of all McGuigan himself, has ever said or even implied that it was all bad. It was not. It was simply like so many real marriages: it had its normal quota of ups and downs and, even when the depths were reached, the two partners could usually find a path towards reconciliation. But then something serious happened; call it infidelity, call it whatever, and one partner knew that it was all over. The trust was gone. The marriage was dead.

Father D'Arcy shares McGuigan's opinion that Eastwood tended to resent the closeness of the fighter to his family: 'A boxer's best advisers are not necessarily members of his own family, so in a sense at least he was probably doing the right thing. But there has to be a proper balance between controlling their involvement and shutting them out altogether, which is what happened to Barry's family. The same applied to his friendships: Eastwood, certainly, was never insulting to me in any way, but he was never, ever, accommodating to me either.

'One of the problems was that the whole camp was rather unbalanced and disjointed, although there were some things they did very well. Eastwood, in fairness, did know how to whip up enthusiasm among an Irish audience, and he also knew how to generate interest in British boxing circles. You can't take that away from him.

'I think his problem, though, was that he didn't recognize that his talent was on the managerial and promotional side, outside the ropes and not inside them. He should never have been near a ring, and should never have attempted to set himself up as a boxing adviser or cornerman. Barry would have been much happier if the two elements had been kept completely separate. And then, of course, there was Las Vegas.'

To Paddy Byrne's way of thinking, the split may well have been inevitable: 'The bad feeling really only came out in the open when we were in the training camp in Palm Springs. I think maybe there had been a hint of it just before the Pedroza fight, but then they had always had their rows from time to time so it wasn't until Palm Springs that it became really obvious that something was wrong. It is hard to know exactly what the cause was, but things just weren't right. Here was the big chance, the Irishman who was going coast to coast across America, and things just hadn't gone right for him. Maybe he was just even more of a home boy than anybody realized, but they were both hotheads and, regardless of the Las Vegas fight and the money row concerning it, I think they just grew apart.'

Back in Room 449 of the Midland Crowne Plaza Hotel in Manchester, McGuigan was hosting a quiet and dignified retirement party for family and friends. He might have lost a fight, but clearly not his sense of humour. A journalist friend chanced to cross the room just as the main door to the suite was opened by McGuigan as he returned from the post-fight press conference. Punching his friend on the shoulder, the now retired headline-maker said: 'I've just put you out of business, haven't I?'

On the stroke of midnight he lifted the hotel telephone and dialled Jim McDonnell's room. His conqueror, naturally, was celebrating and could not be found, so McGuigan left a congratulatory message at reception for McDonnell and his manager, Barry Hearn.

Father D'Arcy, sitting with McGuigan on one of the two beds in the room, wondered if the former world champion might not have been a little hasty with his retirement announcement. 'You've made the right decision,' he said, 'but do you think you were wise in announcing it when you did? Things can often look very different in a day or two; should you not have slept on it before formally announcing it?'

'Father,' said McGuigan, 'you said Mass here in this very room at lunchtime and we prayed for what we always prayed for before a fight; not for victory but just that I and my opponent would both be all right, and that whatever happened after that would be God's will, didn't we?'

'Yes.'

'Well, God spoke loud and clear to me tonight.'

Shortly after his bedside conversation with McGuigan, Father D'Arcy left the former world champion's suite to make his way back to his own hotel. As he walked out into the heavy Manchester rain he met sportscaster Dickie Davies, on his way out of the G-Mex Centre, which was located directly behind the Midland Crowne Plaza.

'I've noticed you with Barry for a long number of years, Father,' said Davies. 'Do you think he really has retired?'

'Yes,' said the priest, 'he really has.'

Davies then invited Father D'Arcy to travel in his taxi. During the journey he asked if Father D'Arcy would like to join him for a Chinese meal, an invitation that was regretfully declined because the priest was due to return to Dublin at breakfast time and had to prepare a Radio Eireann broadcast before departing.

'Had you much influence with Barry?' Davies asked as the shared journey neared its end.

'No,' said Father D'Arcy, 'I am just a friend. Why?'

'I'd like you to give him a message,' replied Davies. 'I have met nice men in my life, but I don't think I have ever met a nicer man in sport than Barry McGuigan. I would like you to tell him that some time, because he may have no confidence tonight and I'd like him to know that, as a person, we will miss him greatly.'

*

Of course I'll miss boxing. It's been my whole life for the last sixteen years, morning, noon and night. I'll miss the general feeling of well-being that I've always had from getting down to my fighting weight. But I don't intend to give up training completely – I'll always be an out-and-out fitness fanatic. I've had a lot of good times and only a few bad ones. I've learned a lot, some of it the hard way, but I'll tell you this: boxing has been good, very good, to Barry McGuigan.

I miss it all terribly already, probably even more than I thought I would. But that doesn't mean that I miss it enough to come back, because that is something I will never, ever, do. I have accepted the fact that I will never be champion of the world again and I don't, nor did I ever, intend to become just another fighter. Sure, even now I could probably come back and win the British title and possibly even the European one, but they are not the same as the world title and that's the only one that ever really interested me. They are fine titles that any fighter would be proud to hold, but once you've been in a situation where you can wake up in the morning and say to yourself, 'I am the champion of the world', they can never have the same meaning for you that they once had.

There is another reason why I will never set foot in a boxing ring again: I have seen too much of the nasty side of the sport. I was unlucky in that I lost my world title in circumstances that will probably haunt me to the day I die. But – perhaps even because of that – I was also a lot luckier than most fighters in that, going as far as I did and getting involved in some of the things that I had no choice but to become involved in, I got insights into parts of the game that most fighters never see. They know those aspects of the sport exist, but they have no understanding of how they work or their true extent.

I am fed up with the way the game is being run, with the hypocrisy of professional boxing in Britain. But as long as boxing is the big-money sport that it is and is influenced by managers and promoters the way it is, nothing will change.

The British Boxing Board of Control contract is made out to suit the manager exclusively. To read the standard contract you would think that the manager owned the fighter when, in fact, it is the boxer who employs a manager to carry out certain functions and duties for him and to provide certain services, not the other way around. A fighter is not the property of a manager, like a racehorse or a greyhound or a performing flea. The fighter is the guy who puts in all the years and years of dedication and training. He misses out on a normal life and then he climbs into the ring and takes the punches and the pain, and the public humiliation when he loses.

The very least a fighter is entitled to is a fair say in how his career is handled. For openers, that means he must have a fair and balanced contract with his manager, something he certainly doesn't have at the moment. Sure, the managers will all shout that nothing like that could ever be allowed because fighters are thick fools who wouldn't know the first thing about management. Well, fighters are not thick fools, and they surely have a natural right at least to play a part in the planning of their own careers. Besides, as far as not knowing anything about managing their careers, they could hardly be any worse off; as it stands most of them know nothing about it because their managers won't tell them.

The manager/boxer contract should be for no more than twelve or, at an absolute maximum, eighteen months. And with no such thing as an automatic extension if you win a title. Right now it is little more than a slave contract. In what other job or profession do you have to sign a contract that says you are committed to working for a particular boss or company for what is effectively your entire working life? You sign a contract with a manager – a contract in which, remember, you are employing him to work on your behalf – and then, if you are good enough to win a title, he benefits by being rewarded with an automatic extension of that contract.

The fighter, no matter how unhappy he might be with a particular manager, has no way out. What can he do – go to the Board? Nine times out of ten the Board will rule in the manager's favour. If that happens his only other option is to go to court, and how many fighters can afford the huge legal fees that entails? Even if he wins at the Board, his relationship with his manager is no longer workable. It has to be a relationship built on trust and faith, and once you've lost that the relationship is over.

A manager can do what he likes with a fighter and there is not a thing the fighter can do about it. If he tackles the manager he can be left to sit and grow cobwebs and his career – and fighters, remember, have very short career spans – is frozen. Or else he is reported to the Board by the manager.

One thing that must, simply must, be done away with is this crazy situation where a manager can also be a promoter. The Board tried to abolish the practice in 1989, but all that happened was that a manager would get his son or a friend or a business associate to be the promoter of record and the whole charade continued exactly as before. The Board had to reinstate the rule at their 1990 AGM, but I'm sure that if the boxers had been organized enough to out-vote the managers and promoters the rule would have been abolished long ago.

There should never be any financial connection whatsoever, either directly or indirectly, between any manager and any promoter. Even a blind man can see that when you have the one person wearing two hats – or having somebody else wear one for him – then that is an obvious conflict of interest.

Part of the problem is the financial dependence of the Board on the revenue they get from promoters and managers: it doesn't want to rock a boat in which it itself is a passenger. It receives a percentage of the takings at each promotion, and while members of the Board probably suspect that the promoters are not showing them the right figures most, if not all, of the time, they are glad to be getting at least something. They know that if they shake the cage and annoy the promoters, then they will not get anything at all, which, of course, wouldn't please them very much.

Maybe some day I'd like to try to do something about it, because it is only somebody like me who would even have a chance of changing things. I don't mean that in any big-headed way, but only that there wouldn't be much point in a six- or eight-round prelim fighter trying to start any sort of campaign; how far would he get? Back in 1982 a good pro called Roger Guest tried to organize a Boxers' Union through *Boxing News*; he never got another fight after his article appeared.

I'm not sure if I'd ever become a manager, but I think that I would like to be an adviser to fighters. I've learned a lot during my eight years as a professional – much of it about things that a fighter wouldn't normally know – and I certainly think that there are lessons I could pass on. The most important lesson I could teach any young boxer is that if he has to be tough and wary inside the ring, he must be twice as tough and three times as wary outside it.

Epilogue

'I knew that I didn't make peace, but I knew that there was peace when I fought, that these boys were holding each other's hands and saying, "Come on, cheer this young kid on. He's fighting for us."'

Barry McGuigan, 1991

I never set out to become a symbol. I deliberately tried not to offend anybody, and I think Barney's attitude was that he had a lot of Protestant friends and he didn't want to offend them by me wearing green or fighting under the Tricolour. He was probably more concerned about it than I was. When I turned pro I was already going with Sandra, who was Protestant, so I had no interest in being aggressively Catholic. When Barney suggested that I wear neutral colours, I said, 'Great.' The whole peace thing slowly progressed, and I saw that people thought it was a good idea, so I went along with it.

But it meant something to me, too, that people came to support me and didn't care who or what I was. At the Pedroza fight, boys who grew up on different sides of Belfast and had never associated with one another linked their arms. Two sections of the Barry McGuigan Supporters' Club travelled together to the fight, one from the Falls and the other from the Shankill.

The whole thing took on its own impetus, like a snowball rolling down a hill. I was a sportsman, and it didn't make any difference to me who was who or what was what. I'm still the same: I hate extremism in any form, and when things like the Deal bombing happened only a few miles down the road from where we live now, I wanted to bow my head and weep. I'm afraid to open my mouth after things like that; it makes me embarrassed.

At the time, I knew that the people who were coming to see me weren't exclusively Catholics or Protestants. Obviously, we realized the appeal of the image of me as a peacemaker, but I don't want people to think that what I did and said back then about peace and unity was all lies and hypocrisy, because it wasn't. The bottom line was that I made a lot of friends from both sides during my fighting career, and I didn't hurt anybody's feelings.

When we went to America on the promotional tour in 1986, the peace angle was all people wanted to talk about. I was sick of it all by then, sick of saying the same things over and over again. I tried to get across to them that it was no big deal, but to them that was more important than me being a world boxing champion. I was tired of talking about it, but it still meant a lot to me. I thought I was really helping the people in the North. I wasn't stupid about it, or foolish: I knew they only came together on the nights when I was fighting, but at least it happened for those nights.

When I went up the Shankill they'd roll the red carpet out for me, and the same when I went up the Falls. I'd often go up the Shankill to pick up Davy Larmour for sparring, and it was great. I was welcome on both sides, and the boys on the street would cheer me.

I knew that I didn't make peace, but I knew that there was peace when I fought, that those boys were holding each other's hands and saying, 'Come on, cheer this young kid on. He's fighting for us.' I was representing them, and they wanted me to prove that not everything that comes out of Northern Ireland is bad. I would have loved to have been able to get down in amongst the crowds when I fought, and experience what it was like. Sometimes when I put on videos of my fights I don't watch the fight at all, just the reactions of the people at the ringside.

I know that I'll never again be able to excite people the way I excited them then, and that I'll never feel the same adrenalin again. That's a stage of my life that is gone, and past. But the reminiscing ... I don't even have to talk to people. I can just sit there, and smile to myself. I remember every moment, every punch.